Irish Heart, English Blood

The Making of Youghal

Irish Heart, English Blood

The Making of Youghal

Michael Twomey

Illustrated by Nathan Twomey

The History Press Ireland

For Katharine, Nathan, Max and Holly-Rose

First published 2014

The History Press Ireland
50 City Quay
Dublin 2
Ireland
www.thehistorypress.ie

© Michael Twomey, 2014
Illustrations © Nathan Twomey, 2014

The right of Michael Twomey to be identified as the Author
of this work has been asserted in accordance with the
Copyright, Designs and Patents Act 1988.

British Library Cataloguing in Publication Data.
A catalogue record for this book is available from the British Library.

ISBN 978 1 84588 822 0

Typesetting and origination by The History Press

Contents

Acknowledgements

Writing the early-modern history of Youghal was a difficult but hugely rewarding experience. It would not have been possible without the support of several people. I am very grateful for the education, inspiration and support I received from the history department at University College Cork, in particular from Prof. Jennifer O'Reilly, Dr Diarmuid Scully, Dr Hiram Morgan and Dr Andrew McCarthy. My research was enhanced with conversations with David Kelly whose knowledge and enthusiasm of, and for, the subject were invaluable and whose work on an Atlas of Youghal will have a far-reaching influence on future generations researching the history of the town. I received generous support and advice from writers, whose works were a constant reference point, my thanks to Prof. Nicholas Canny, Dr Micheál Ó Siochrú and Dr Peter Elmer for their willing correspondence. I am eternally grateful to Ronan Colgan of The History Press Ireland for his initial interest in the subject. Many thanks are due to my son, Nathan for enhancing the book with his arresting illustrations and to my close friends Louise and Conor Hegarty for their interest and for reading a draft of part of the book, affording it very helpful comments. My primary gratitude and debt is to my wife, Katharine whose perpetual encouragement seems to me an endless upward spiral of inspiration; the reading, conversations and support were the foundation, continuance and completion of the work.

Preface

The map of Youghal on the front of this book was drawn in the 1630s, having been commissioned by former President of Munster, Sir George Carew. The original drawing, with its precise lines and neat composition, is the construct of a propaganda-driven desire to suppress the fluid nature of reality. In effect, the map is a lie. Its very cleanliness betrays a murkier design. Yet, the DNA that makes up all propaganda contains a necessary strain of truth, no matter how fragile in this case, to make it believable. This illustration is an impression of the town of Youghal in the 1630s and there is much in the image that represents the reality of early modern Youghal; it was indeed, a walled seaport town. The purpose of creating this image was to promote the idea of Youghal's progress, its security and its wealth. It represents the success of Youghal's assimilation into English manners, culture and design. The image is boastful, the town's seemingly indestructible walls protecting those inside. It also invites those outside, such as merchants, adventurers in Ireland and England, as well as government officials, to muse over the great possibilities the town has to offer them. It was created at a time of high confidence in the belief that the English plantation programmes in Munster had yielded a sort of self-contained Eutopia, a minor jewel, but a jewel nonetheless, in the English Crown. This image has endured over other images and drawings of Youghal, drawings that are far less sterile. Like the story of Walter Raleigh planting the first potato in Ireland at his residence in the town, the image of this map has seeped into the public consciousness and solidified therein as historical fact.

The early modern history of Youghal from the mid-1500s to the mid-1600s is not as neat and clean as the map illustrates. Complex, never anything less than extraordinary, bloody and equally industrious, it is a history of survival, blind ambition and feats and failures from individual as well as national entities. It is also the history of the troubled relationship between Ireland and England. The ebb and flow of cultural assimilation, colonisation and resistance created a volcanic landscape of political and religious tension out of which the town grew to prominence. Populating this volatile and smouldering environment was a host of irrepressible characters and peoples whose stories reveal the unpredictable nature of the early modern period. *Irish Heart, English Blood* is an attempt to make sense of the social, political and religious tumult that erupted from these dynamics. For almost a century the town of Youghal acted as the theatre that housed the Ireland–England power play. Its history is imbued with shame and sadness, terror and triumph. I believe that in the years between the 1579 Munster rebellion and the witch trial of 1661, in the aftermath of the Restoration of Charles II, Youghal witnessed an unparalleled history that shaped its future for the next 300 years in a way that no history of the town had done before or has done since.

I have attempted to view this period of history through some of the main figures who played a significant role in the town's formation, such as Gerald Fitzgerald, Walter Raleigh, Edmund Spenser, Richard and Roger Boyle, Murrough O'Brien, Oliver Cromwell and others. All of these men's lives have been written about extensively elsewhere and while there are some narrative themes that are inevitably touched upon, the focus for this book is their direct involvement in, or effect on, the history of Youghal. Therefore, some general points of national or international historical interest are used only as frameworks to support the primary purpose of the book – to understand how Youghal was affected by the extraordinary events of the times and what role it played in them.

This is not the first history written about early modern Youghal. The most well-known document is Samuel Hayman's *The New Hand-book for Youghal*, which combines an ecclesiastical history of the religious buildings in and around Youghal with records taken from the *Annals of the Four Masters*. Hayman's content is valuable for research in these particular areas. The other significant and somewhat superior record is Richard Caulfield's *The Council Book of the Corporation of Youghal*. This monumental volume of Corporation records from 1610 to 1800 is complemented by the *Annals of Youghal*, including various letters and correspondences. Without Caulfield's Trojan work, this book would not have been possible, nor would many other works about Youghal. Caulfield's history comes closest to helping us understand the everyday life of the town. Details of the town's social and political workings provide the reader with an insight into the life of the early modern citizen, what the town might have been like in times of war and in times of peace. While Caulfield's collection of documents lacks a cohesive narrative to stitch them together, Hayman's history is full of romance, is unapologetically religious and desires to delight the reader as well as inform. Local modern writers, documentarians and historians relating the histories of Youghal have tended to draw more from the Hayman style of historiography with its emphasis on mixing facts with myths and legends. These works, from a plethora of journals, articles, pamphlets and so on, also rely on Caulfield. All of these works offer varying degrees of insight. And while they tend to include a cross-section of differing periods of history from ancient to medieval, modern and early modern they possess value in what might be termed 'fascinating history and fun facts in heritage stories' and have, to their great credit, driven a local history revival in recent years. This book attempts to bring together the social, religious and political history of the early modern period only and without the myths and legends, in some cases arguing against them.

Irish Heart, English Blood is the first book since Hayman and Caulfield to relate the history of Youghal's involvement as a significant player in the relations between Ireland and England in the early modern period. I have tried to write the narrative of the town's history in a way that has not been done before. To achieve this, and a better understanding of how Youghal came into being, I have relied mostly on Caulfield's collection of documents, Irish and British national archives as well as historians' writings on political explorations of the period and studies on the central historical characters. I have also relied on academic journals and articles on various topics from economics and religion to society at large.

For many years I had experienced an ignorance of the history of Youghal, though I grew up next to the town walls. Its history had been hidden to me and countless others for generations and had lapsed into nuggets of 'tales for tourists', many of which have clouded the facts about the town's past and have unfortunately endured as truth. I hope that *Irish Heart, English Blood* can afford an understanding of that history to people familiar with Youghal, to those beyond it and to those who are interested in the history of the relationship between Ireland and England. I hope, too, that the reader will see below, behind and beyond the ordered lines that create a false impression of Youghal, represented in the 1630s map as well as the false impression of history it has promoted.

Notes on the text

The prologue and epilogue chapters are there to offer the reader some context of the pre and post history of the early modern period into which the focus of the main chapters can be put. I have altered a number of spellings in some of the original quotes to make their reading more accessible. For some of the main figures that are prominent in the town's history I have chosen to reference them with their original names as opposed to their titles. So, for instance, Murrough O'Brien is referred to as O'Brien and not Lord Inchiquin.

Prologue

In 1761 Youghal harbour was returning revenues to the British Kingdom that put it only second to the cities of Dublin and Cork in economic prosperity. The bay and the harbour were littered with ships from around Europe and America. Harbour trade in Youghal linked England to Newfoundland. Imports were rich in variety and often exotic – from sugar-candy, oranges, ginger and spices to ready-made carriage doors, jewellery, iron and timber, all the products of affluence and industry. Exports included corn, beef, pork and butter. Employment was plentiful in wool manufacturing and pottery. A plethora of small businesses, shops, public houses, inns and services were expanding as was the town itself. Buildings such as the Clock Gate, Mall House and The Red House all grew out of the prosperity of the times. Such was the profitable nature of the society that the historically predominantly Protestant town allowed St Mary's Catholic Church to be built within its centre. The suburban sprawl decimated the restrictions of the old medieval walls, knocked for progress. By the end of the eighteenth century, Youghal was being likened to Margate and Brighton as the destination for the wealthy who gravitated to Youghal's long, yawning beach. It was a golden period. The town had reached a social and economic zenith. It was a period of growth not witnessed before or after. The town owed much of its stature to the dynamics of its early modern history, and for a century between the mid-1500s and 1600s it came heavily under the influence of the expanding English empire. Throughout this period its journey to prominence is a pathway laden with bloodied relics, shattered artefacts and torn articles strewn beside a religious, cultural and political tumult. Its history is a story of survival from invasions, wars, rebellions, sieges, natural and man-made disasters, constant change and suspicion.

The remains of Molana Abbey stand on the edge of the great river Blackwater a number of miles east of Youghal. It had been erected during the sixth century by Molanfide or 'Maelanfaith the prophet', the son of the King of Munster. The abbey would grow in stature, producing dozens of missionary monks with Rubin of Mac Connadh's *200 Years of Church Law* written there before his death in 725. The monasteries of Ardmore, Molana and Clashmore were then well established. The Gaelic–Celtic chieftains, who had crossed mainland Europe centuries earlier to settle the south coast, were no strangers to Christianity by this time. These farming and fishing communities, populating the banks and hills of the river, had been exposed to the teachings of Christ through Declan, a contemporary of Patrick in the mid-fifth century. Declan had built his monastery at Ardmore, a few miles from Youghal. He may also have built a small church in Youghal on the site of where St Mary's Collegiate Church stands today. Monks such as Palladius, Patrick and Declan were following the tradition of the apostolic mission: bringing the word of God to the ends of the earth. Just like the apostles, they intended on keeping their distance from the madding crowd while maximising their influence.

The monks, on a mission from the Holy See of Rome, would live humbly while teaching literacy, penitential law, and the gospels. They told the Celtic chieftains a life everlasting awaited them in paradise if they gave up their gods such as Lugh and Dagda for the one true God. They were told of the great altruist-hero Jesus and the sacrifice He had made on their behalf. Many of the Celts found the cultural and religious exchange highly attractive. They also recognised the role of the hero figure as a central theme to the narrative of their own culture. Christianity had made its 500-year journey from Jerusalem via Rome to the British Isles and Ireland.

While Christianity seeped into the culture of the Irish, Youghal's Gaelic tribe were vulnerable to attack from abroad, being exposed to the open sea. Just as the hunters and gatherers, Celts and Christians had come by sea from mainland Europe and Britain, so would new peoples. With the slow demise of the great Roman Empire ongoing since the mid-400s AD, the Dark Ages brought uncertainty for the farmers and fishermen, but Christianity remained the glue that held some societies together. By the end of the eighth century, Gaelic tribes, now mostly Christian, dominated Ireland's culture and remained invariably untouched while Europe was in a state of profound change. Migrating European tribes formed and reformed territories. Unknown to the Christian clan at Youghal, expansion and the hunt for new land drove the ambitious Vikings onto the sea toward mainland Europe and the islands of Britain and Ireland. Uncompromising and fiercely combative, the Norse tribes from Denmark and Norway sought routes south, east and west. In around 795 their hunger for conquest brought them to Ireland.

The first wave of Viking conquests and subsequent settlements in the eighth and early ninth centuries occurred along the traditional Celtic sea-trading routes of Youghal, Dublin, Cork, Wexford, Limerick and Waterford. Militarily superior to those that resided by the Blackwater riverbed, the Vikings took the settlement, assimilated and built the first outlines of what would later become the town of Youghal. The Danish Vikings had little respect for the Christian tradition, plundering Molana Abbey and Lismore in 813 and returning to Lismore in 820 for a second ransacking. However, after the plundering and killing and destruction of monasteries, some Vikings settled, intermarried, traded and, like the Celts before them, eventually converted to Christianity. While Viking longphorts were typically wooden with thatched roofs, churches were built of stone. The Youghal longphort had a boundary for protection, a main street and side streets that led to jetties on the water's edge for the use of fishing, trading and war vessels.

In the following decades a second wave of Vikings arrived in Ireland. The first generation, now called Irish-Viking or Hiberno-Norse, did not welcome the new conquests. The second generation of invaders fought their predecessors to gain superiority and to make the old generation subservient. This created internal feuding and in 869 a fleet of Vikings of the Desi clan from the Dungarvan area sailed into Youghal waters and attacked its fortress. The Desi clan was seeking revenge for the slaughtering of their people in 836. The battle must have been a bloody affair with the clan destroying some of the Youghal Viking fleet as well as torching the wood-and-thatch buildings and timber jetties. It is impossible to identify how successful the Youghal Viking longphort was in the years after its destruction but it can be presumed that reconstruction followed and the Hiberno-Norse society continued to trade and live in the area for at least another 300 years.

The existence of the Hiberno-Norse came under great threat during Brian Ború's efforts to become High King of Ireland. Though his limited successes at the Battle of Clontarf in 1014 brought him fame, banishment of the Vikings was virtually impossible following centuries of integration into Irish culture. Ironically, the new Vikings and the Hiberno-Norse would both be finally usurped, not by the Gaelic Chieftains, but by their own descendants' generations after their initial exploits on the high seas.

Despite relentless infighting and attacks from Gaelic-Irish rulers, Youghal remained a desirable location for settlers. Indeed, Youghal had made solid connections to Lismore, Dungarvan, Cork and Waterford, but its first incarnation as a 'town' was about to come to an end.

While Brian Ború had struggled to achieve authority over the Hiberno-Norse, similar struggles were being enacted in Britain where the Saxon culture also existed in an uneasy alliance with the Vikings, who had, just as in Ireland, assimilated into English life to become the Anglo-Norse. This particular branch of Viking traded with their brethren who had settled northern France – the Franco-Norse, better known as the Normans. The rise of the Normans would have a profound effect on Irish history and their influence in Youghal is still to be seen in the buildings they constructed there. Though the Viking blood running through the ancestral veins of the Normans had been somewhat tamed by Christianity, their military prowess and ideas of expansion remained. That prowess was now structured in a political hierarchy known as the feudal system.

The Normans were often the best practitioners of the feudal system though it already existed in other countries. The feudal system overarched Norman society with a Bible in one hand and the sword in the other. Their kings, as taught them by the Catholic Church, believed God had appointed them to be Christ's soldiers on earth. Their mission was to protect the Church while assisting in the conversion of pagans. The kings gave land to barons and lords as well as to the Church. In turn, they gave their loyalty and protection to the king. The peasants worked the land for the lords and paid a tithe (rent). They could never leave, not at least without the lord's good wishes. This arrangement offered security to the peasant farmers from plunderers, neighbour disputes and possible invasions. When the kings or lords died they were buried in the churches, ensuring a place in eternity and eternal commemoration on earth. The Church, with the nuance, skill and efficiency of an evolutionary gene, had adopted the old Viking hunger for fame and worked it into the Christian story. This mutually beneficial co-existence would propel the Church's influence over Europe while its kings and lords believed conquest was their divine right. This class system would be the basis from which both tragic history and prosperity came to Youghal.

1

Le Yoghel

The Norman Settlement and Construction of Youghal

In 1066, only fifty-two years after Brian Ború confronted the Irish Vikings, the Normans crossed the English Channel from France and defeated their Saxon cousins at the Battle of Hastings. The Normans would go on to dominate English culture and inevitably spread their considerably wide wings into Wales and eventually Ireland. While the Normans were establishing settled monarchies under the feudal system, Ireland remained an island of transient clans with varying degrees of influence, undermined by infighting and petty jealousies. Europeans such as the Anglo-Saxons and Normans had witnessed the ashes of the great Roman Empire; indeed, their ancestors fought the great legions toe to toe. They had been exposed to battle strategies, weaponry, construction, Roman law and social structure. The Irish chieftains and the Hiberno-Norse were removed from such powerful influences and had, technologically at least, fallen behind Europe's progress. While the Irish monks had brought Latin, literature and the concept of settling disputes through penance rather than revenge, this was an ecclesiastical development. They had also brought literacy to Britain in educating the northern English of Mercia and Northumberland.

Ireland's lack of political structure, military proficiency or a model of singular nationhood left it susceptible to invasion. However, it was not conquest or invasion that brought the Normans to Ireland initially. Under King Henry II and led by Richard de Clare (Strongbow) they were invited by Leinster's Diarmuid MacMurrough to assist in a political wrangle with his enemies, one of whom was Rory O'Connor. Prior to Strongbow's arrival, Rory O'Connor's son Turlough is recorded as taking a great army to the 'Youghal Road', possibly between Youghal and Lismore. O'Connor was trying to settle internal disputes with the McCarthys in the Kingdom of Desmond in south Munster following its creation in 1118. Such turmoil would prove an Achilles heel to the Irish upon the Normans' arrival and play a significant role in the development of medieval Youghal. Strongbow, as requested, assisted MacMurrough, married his daughter Aoife and became King of Leinster in 1171. It opened the door to the Anglo-Normans. King Henry II of England quickly recognised that Strongbow's rise to power might be a threat to his own and was concerned that the spoils gathered in Ireland should remain under the governance of the Kingdom of England. After all, there was tribute to be paid and land to be seized. Some Irish chieftains who resented Strongbow's influence supported the king's concerns about his ascendency to power in Leinster.

Like their Viking ancestors, the Normans settled on the established ports. The main areas to come under Norman influence were concentrated on the eastern and southern coasts initially. King Henry II would finance the expeditions, granting Irish lands to his lords, who would be successful in settling the new territories. The arrival of the Normans was hardly a wholesale military invasion and was driven by lords, barons and earls looking to take opportunities of gaining land in a technologically inferior country. Like the Vikings before them, the Normans found a country that was politically fractured, and so they had no cause to fear any national resistance. When Henry II's 400 ships landed at Crook, Waterford, on 18 October 1171, they found little objection to their arrival. Henry was met by Irish chiefs, including MacCormac MacCarthy, King of Cork and Desmond, of which Youghal was part. Also present was Malachy O'Phelan, Prince of the Decies, who would later fall foul of two of the most influential Norman Lords.

Battle of the Blackwater

Benevolent relations between the Irish and the Normans were blasted when knight of the realm, Raymund Le Gros, took Waterford from the Hiberno-Norse. This aggressive act marked a significant shift in the power play in Munster. The Desi or 'Deise' clan, now supporting its old enemies against a new common adversary, was dealt a further hammer blow in the winter of 1173. Raymund Le Gros and Strongbow, with their superior Norman forces, overran the county. They slaughtered the resisting Malachy O'Phelan, who stood in the way of their plundering treasures at Lismore. By February, the Norman raiders, travelling back to Dungarvan on the river Blackwater, under the command of Adam de Hereford, stalled in Youghal harbour to wait for favourable winds to continue with their booty along the coast. They were intercepted by thirty-two ships under the command of Gilbert, leader of the Cork Hiberno-Norse. A battle ensued. The Hiberno-Norse (Irish) fought with stones and axes while the Norman raiders fought with metal and bolts. It is thought that a Welsh adventurer took the responsibility of boarding Gilbert's ship, killing him with his sword. Victorious, the Normans continued on to Waterford. McCarthy, the King of Desmond, pursued the Norman fleet to Waterford but was also defeated. The repulsion of McCarthy and the securing of Waterford and the estuary of the river Blackwater allowed the Normans to establish a sound footing on the south coast and in the port of Youghal. It was the end of the Hiberno-Norse longphort and their culture and the beginning of the town of Youghal.

The new arrivals were as efficient in setting about acquiring land and establishing ownership as they were in taking it. Their building programme included castles, churches and walling in the towns. The feudal system ensured the political hierarchy would be shaped as it had been in Europe and Britain. The petty kingdoms, like that of Desmond in south Munster and, later, Ormond in east Munster would come under the control of the Norman lords. As was the practice across Europe, when a lord died he was buried in the church. Some of these churches, like St Mary's in Youghal, were rebuilt on the ancient Christian sites established by the monks. Being buried on these sacred grounds was a mark of the Norman lords' divinely appointed, historical lineage as Christian soldiers. They firmly believed their final resting place was the end of the ancestral line that went all the way back through the generations of princes and kings from the cold stones of Ireland to the hallowed halls of Rome and to the ancient sands of Jerusalem. Raymund Le Gros, who had played such a significant role in the Norman arrivals, was buried at Molana Abbey in 1185. Just before his death, he ordered the building of a preceptory (rest home) between Youghal and Glendine overlooking the bay. The house was for members of the Knights Templar, a branch of the crusaders, some of whom had travelled across Europe to the Middle East to defend Christianity and win back the city of Jerusalem from Islamic Turks.

A Norman Town

Youghal, as part of the Barony of Imokilly, came under the distribution of land ownership sanctioned by Henry II. One of the king's subjects, Lord Fitz-Stephen, was granted land that included the manor of Youghal. He gave it to his half-brother, Maurice Fitz-Gerald. In 1279, before a court in Cork, a final agreement was made between Maurice Fitz-Gerald and Thomas de Clare for the passing over of the town to Thomas' control.[1] So began the family dynasty that would build and later destroy Youghal. The arrival of the Fitzgeralds marked the end of Gaelic nobility's power in the area.

The Normans brought English traffickers, soldiers and other tradespeople in from Bristol to populate what was quickly becoming the outline of a European-fashioned town. The days would be filled with the sights and sounds of carpentry and masonry. By 1220 the new masters began building on the foundations of St Mary's Church. The Normans also quickly fortified the town by constructing a technically more robust wall on the outline of the old Viking longphort. The town would be enclosed with fortified gates at the south and north ends. The South Gate would become the most famous landmark of Youghal. It was the site of the imposing Trinity Castle and, centuries later to the present day, the site of the Clock Gate. The main street, with several narrow side streets, was constructed along the pathways cut out during the creation of the Viking longphort. The walls consisted of battlements and towers manned by soldiers and marked out the town from the countryside, creating a busy urban centre. Running high into the hill behind the town, a yawning stretch of steep, descending land filled the space between the imposing towers and the main street below. Dwellers of the town were mainly official, military, religious, trades and mercantile folk as well as labouring residents. The dwellings in Youghal were of typical Norman design. Houses and shops fronted a long rectangular plot of land behind, on which residents could grow fruit and vegetables. The houses and shops were built side by side, facing the main street, and had thatched roofs. Businesses such as blacksmiths, bakers, jewellers, inns, guesthouses and butchers operated out of the houses. Though paving was often built on shop or business fronts the streets were earth and mud and more often than not uneven underfoot. Human waste was dumped on the street and animals wandered freely, though fences were erected to corral cattle, pigs and horses. Curfew was normally called in late evening when the town gates were locked and fires were extinguished. Significant notices, such as the opening and closing of markets, deaths, mass and meetings were announced by a bell or drum.

The town had a self-contained economy and relied heavily on imports and exports, mostly by sea. A lighthouse was erected on a hill on the outskirts of the town at the mouth of the harbour. The St Anne's nuns were later housed there and given the task of keeping the light ever present for ships and mariners entering the bay.[2] Immediately outside the walls, peasant farmers lived in cramped wooden dwellings, toiling to make a life from market trade. Beyond, in the countryside, medieval villages consisted of clusters of animal pens and tiny houses. Some castles dominated these rural landscapes, like those at Mogeely, Killeagh and Barryscourt. The rural Norman lords collected rent from the farmers while families like the Fitzgeralds had the freedom of the use of houses in a number of towns across their lands.

The displaced Gaelic clans were resentful of their Norman masters, but as the decades passed the Normans became integrated into Irish life, often using a mix of Irish, English and French phrasing, wearing Irish traditional clothes and engaging in Irish traditions. Though this assimilation was a social and cultural inevitability, the class system they brought remained inflexible, causing bitterness for the Irish who found life outside the feudal system to be unforgiving. The McCarthy clan, once leaders of Desmond, now populated Kerry and the border of Cork. With great castles cutting into the naked Irish skyline, the Normans dominated large swathes of land, and Youghal, with its burgeoning port, was firmly in the control of the Fitzgerald dynasty. The neighbouring Norman dynasty of the Butlers, in the Kingdom of Ormond, whose land swept east of Waterford and north beyond Kilkenny and Tipperary, kept a close eye on Youghal's development.

Youghal established a network of trade from abroad but protecting imports was already a difficult task. The new prosperity meant Irish pirates found easy pickings along the southern coast. Youghal was trading with Gascony, as evidenced in the passage below, and its merchants were not best pleased to find their ships being pillaged. They also knew that the looters were destined for towns like Youghal to trade their ill-gotten gains.

> Wern Durran, Raymond Arrolan and Arnold de Rupe state that they had loaded a ship with wines at Bordeaux, but that certain Irish malefactors attacked their ship, boarded it, killed everyone in it, and carried off the ship and the goods found in it. They ask that orders might be sent to Waterford, Cork and Youghal, and elsewhere in Ireland and in the king's realm where the malefactors can be found, to arrest them, and to restore their goods to the petitioners with their damages, informing these towns that if they do not do this, the Seneschal of Gascony will take compensation from the goods and merchandise of those towns in Gascony.[3]

To improve legal structures in Youghal an inquisition, including a jury, was held in Inchiquin Castle, just outside the town in 1321. The agenda was to identify how much the land in the area and in 'Le Yoghel' was worth and who was the rightful next heir. From the beginning, the formal structure of land ownership, division, holding of deeds and setting rents would pass into law. Youghal would no longer be an agrarian backwater but a fully fledged town with legal structures.

The Fitzgerald Dynasty

For the next 400 years the Fitzgerald dynasty, taking the title 'Earls of Desmond', much to the chagrin of the McCarthys, continued to build infrastructure and solidify the political composition in Youghal. Over those four centuries the town would witness some of its darkest days while dissatisfaction and resentment remained amongst the native Irish who had witnessed a succession of superior opportunists reshape the kingdoms and change the landscape. Outside the walls of the town, those who owned the manors kept the native Irish as serfs, including the O'Cunnys, O'Kenachis and O'Molondonys. Not only did the serfs pay the lord but also the bishops in what were now the twin towers of governance: the Holy Roman Catholic Church and the Anglo-Norman lords. The monks, who had survived political and cultural strife as well as poverty and the weather, would come to lament the opulence in the houses of bishops. The bishops lived lives of privilege and were entitled to take sons and daughters for work, seize possessions at will, overwrite wills and collect rent. Thus the Catholic Church, with the finances of the Fitzgeralds, continued to grow in Youghal. On either side of the town two abbeys were built: in 1224 the Franciscan South Abbey was constructed and in 1268 the Dominican North Abbey dominated the land beyond the North Gate of the town.

Inside the walls, Youghal was a cosmopolitan centre of trade. Residents with names such as Reginald the Dane, Corgene, Jordan de Excetre, Silvester de Ercedekene and other European descendants showed its cosmopolitan nature. The first charter, undersigned by Edward I on 24 June 1275, reveals just how important Youghal was economically to the Crown and its development as a port. Money gathered from customs on goods such as timber, bark, salt, livestock, sheep, goat and rabbit skins, garlic, onions, soaps, wool, leather, wine, honey, cheese, butter, linen and canvas was to go to the repair of the town walls – a constant concern in terms of security.

The Black Death

No amount of security, money, military power or religious faith could prevent the traumatic demise of the town's population in one of Europe's greatest human tragedies in the summer of 1348. The Black

Death is thought to have originated in China where it spread to European merchant ships trading in the East. On their return to Italy the highly contagious infection had already afflicted the sailors. Fleas infected rats and then the sailors who infected each other. The contagion swept through Italy and across Europe with devastating effect and bewildering speed, reaching Youghal in late 1348, early 1349. The plague turned the skin black and was most evident by boils the size of golf balls, situated in the groin and armpits, filled with pus and blood. Flu-like symptoms were experienced at the onset with a fever developing at its height. Sufferers vomited blood and found breathing difficult. In some cases the plague killed the carrier in three days. Because the plague was also an airborne disease, the simple exercise of breathing became a fatal action. Conditions in a wintry Youghal could not have helped stem the onrush of the killer plague. Impoverished or non-existent sanitation created a death-inducing environment, particularly in crowded dwellings at close proximity to one another. A port town like Youghal created an ideal setting for the plague to flourish. In fact, the port towns of Cork, Waterford and Youghal, where it is likely the plague was brought into Ireland from England and the Continent, suffered more than the open, rural areas to the north and west.

Though exact numbers of fatalities cannot be quantified, it is estimated that 45 per cent of Youghal's population was wiped out, which is in line with the overall estimation of 25 million dead across Europe, in just five years. Unfortunately, there are no records of how the town of Youghal reacted to the swift appearance of the plague. It was typical across Europe for walled towns to close their gates to outsiders, some even charging a toll on entry. Suspicions ran high as to the cause of the plague from the wrath of God to the curse of leprosy, demonology to the almost inevitable blaming of the Jews. Infected corpses were often dumped just beyond the town walls as there was little room left in consecrated ground within the town boundary. Mass graves were dug and in some instances ships were filled with the dead and set alight. While this was a practice in Europe, it can reasonably be imagined at the port of Youghal. Desperate to find a cure but devoid of medical knowledge and expertise, people used anything from boiling water to vinegar in a vain effort to arrest the inevitable. The consequences of the plague manifested themselves in the mass confusion populating a near post-apocalyptic landscape. Serfs, who had until now been tied to the land, working for their lords, migrated freely to the towns in search of medicine, work and a place to live. They abandoned the care of crops, leaving some estates tenantless. Kinsalebeg, on the other side of Youghal harbour, is reported as being completely deserted. Without rent and food production, the lords' income dropped, and some struggled to pay their taxes to the Crown. For a period, the serfs, mostly the native Irish, were able to demand or negotiate better working conditions and pay. This led to competition before a limit was imposed at pre-plague rates.

The port of Youghal, like hundreds all over Ireland, Britain and Europe, witnessed a sharp decline in activity. Food shortage in the town was a direct consequence of slow trade and of a cessation of farming.

The breakdown of social structure undermined the feudal system as taxes and food prices steadily rose. Resentments grew between all facets of society. The native Irish chieftains, dislodged and disaffected by the arrival of their Anglo-Norman masters, took advantage of the relative breakdown in law and order with random acts of violence and robbery. Youghal appealed to the Crown for tax relief in an effort to protect the town from 'rebels'. Fortification of the walls and payment of soldiers was expensive. For many years after, the town was left vulnerable to attack, as was the Barony of Imokilly around it. As late as January 1374 King Edward III signed a charter stating that those governing the town under the Earl of Desmond: the Sovereign and several influential merchant families, would not have to pay subsidies for chasing rebels who were 'slaying lieges' in the countryside and who were a threat to the town. The Crown also took on the cost of replenishing the army.[4] The Fitzgeralds would, however, be compelled to pay towards the king's war efforts against France. Outbreaks of the plague would return intermittently throughout the following centuries but none with the rapier-like swiftness and devastation that cut down so many between 1348 and 1353.

The Anglo-Irish

Youghal slowly recovered from the paralysing pandemic and continued to trade. By the start of the fifteenth century the monarchy in England had changed hands twice. The Crown had concerns about keeping the successive Norman dynasties in Ireland, now almost 200 years old, in line with English law. They feared that the Normans were assimilating into Irish culture to the point that they would begin to strive for independence, which, inevitably, some did. Efforts to prevent assimilation were futile. Successive generations born in Ireland would spend time in England being educated and learning the etiquette of the court as well as the practices of war. Their home was Ireland but their politics was English. They would come to be known as the 'Old English' or the 'Anglo-Irish'. However, despite the Crown's concerns over Anglo-Irish lords' possible desires for independence, the powerful Youghal merchants, who effectively ran the town's affairs, had no designs for autonomy. Tied to England by the ropes of sea trade, the town's very existence depended on a strong and reliable relationship with Westminster. For the Crown, an economically viable port town like Youghal guaranteed a revenue stream that filled the royal coffers. The downside to Youghal's reputation as an urban centre of some note and its relative wealth was that it became a target for the disenfranchised, namely the poorer Irish clans. On 12 May 1404 Henry IV wrote that 'The town of Youghal is on all sides surrounded by rebels, who daily destroy the town, and same is partly burned, so that our subjects dare not go outside the said town without a strong guard.' The king may have protested too much, or at least exaggerated. He referred to the pillagers as rebels, but these agitators had no national design or even identity outside their clanship. They were pirates of the land, forced into roguery by Norman landlords, and full of hunger and envy.

The efforts made to protect the profitable port town, repairing its walls and overseeing its political structure, shows the importance of Youghal to England. Despite continuing spats between the Gaelic Irish and the Anglo-Irish the town continued to prosper into the fifteenth century, and the establishment of a College for Seminarians in 1464 was a significant symbol of such growth. However, more serious developments between successive Earls of Desmond and their neighbours the Ormonds ensured trouble was a constant in Munster and at Youghal's gates. The Fitzgeralds would also have a less than positive relationship with the Crown. With the borders of their lands propping each other up, the Fitzgeralds of the Desmond dynasty and the Butlers of Ormond were in constant dispute over land ownership and expansion from the very first days of Norman settlement in Munster. Another tumultuous event in central Europe would change the political and religious dynamics across the Continent in the first quarter of the 1500s, an event that would lead to hundreds of years of violence and death in Ireland. It would also polarise the opposition between the Fitzgeralds and the Butlers, and by the end of the 1500s Youghal would lie in ruins.

2

From my Heart I am Sorry for that Folly

The Fitzgeralds, the Butlers and the Sacking of Youghal

A few hundred miles south of Youghal Christopher Columbus had undertaken his adventure west across the Atlantic, believing India and its gold could be found by a quicker and safer route. When he arrived at San Salvador in October 1492 the New World was opened up to the expanding empires and seafaring kingdoms of Portugal, Spain, England, the Netherlands and France. These nations would inevitably go to war with one another for the spoils. The slave trade would bring Africans to the Caribbean and later to South America where they would work plantations for their white European masters. The Europeans brought disease, Catholicism, laws, weaponry, land, language, division and the feudal system to the New World. The natives, in awe of the explorers, were no match for gunpowder, horses, armour and the Bible. The Catholic Church expanded as cathedral spires spiked the sky across European horizons; swirling baroque designs celebrating their lavishness. It was an age of arrogance. The pursuit of gold, spices, silks, slaves and land created a drive of exploration on a scale not witnessed before. A rising tide of knowledge and interest in literature, art, science and discovery of a new world swept through the wealthier states in Europe throughout the 1400s. The explosion of confidence in achieving the impossible drove Leonardo Da Vinci to dream of machines centuries ahead of their time, while cartographers busied themselves reconstructing maps. The world itself began to expand beyond the previously narrow confines of mainland Europe and the Middle East.

There would be no such expansion in Ireland; it simply did not have the technology, finances or desire. Neither had England the desire yet to finance Ireland. While the romance of the Renaissance occupied European merchants and princes, life in Munster was often harsh. The province would fall foul of natural disaster in the late 1400s and throughout the 1500s with famine and flu epidemics (English Sweat) claiming the lives of the fragile.[5] Heavy and continual rainfall, added to extended droughts, made agricultural life vulnerable to the vagaries of the weather. Such extremes also created health problems for those in the urban centres. Towns like Youghal struggled to keep disease at bay in what was a hotbed of poor and claustrophobic sanitary conditions. Large numbers of cattle died due to disease and the effect on trade in Youghal was considerable.

Despite a sluggish economy, Base Town was added in the mid-1400s. Base Town was a square enclosure of fortified walls around the dwellings along Common Street (present-day South Main Street) stretching from the Trinity Castle (entrance to the main town) to present-day Mall Lane. The South Gate was erected for access. Base Town was built as a control centre for trade. International imports came through the Quay Gate (known today as Cromwell's Arch) and were carried directly up Quay Lane to Common Street. This meant customs officials could inspect goods, collect monies and divide the spoils before any of the merchandise entered the town centre. Many of the buildings in Base Town were warehouses for storing goods as well as offices and dwellings for those employed in the import and export trade. Merchants were required to lay their goods out for inspection by town officials, making Quay Lane an extraordinarily busy trade area. The new annex to the town would later become known as Irish Town due to its population being mostly Irish. Local trade, particularly in fishing, was imported through the Water Gate toward the centre of the town.[6] Local goods, imported from across the river, were unloaded here and brought up to Market Cross and sold on stalls or stored in the

Market House (junction at present-day North Main Street and O'Neill/ Crowley Street).

As successful as the Fitzgeralds were in running their part of Munster and Kildare, their achievements in the southern province, at least, were always tempered by antagonism towards their neighbours, the Butlers of Ormond. Youghal's burgeoning port had the Fitzgerald and Butler families vying for control over the trading of Spanish and Portuguese wines and over the town itself. Church property, in particular the first Youghal College of 1464 at the top of Church Lane, yielded a solid income, but monopolising the imports from foreign trade brought greater possibilities of wealth. The dispute would last well into the 1500s.[7] In one act of petulant defiance in 1527, James Fitzgerald entered the lands of the Butlers and stole a considerable number of their cattle. Underlining the complexity and fragility of the Desmond Lordship in this dispute was James' uncle, Thomas. In defending the interests of the Butlers against his own nephew, Thomas came into confrontation with James at Dungarvan. James took refuge in Youghal and rallied some support of his own. He also sought help from Spain in a vain attempt to pit the Spanish against the English Crown, thus hoping to break the Crown's growing influence over his affairs.

Petty quarrels about positions of power and influence between the Fitzgeralds and the Butlers and between the Fitzgeralds and the Crown were often a tiring and time-consuming process for England. Henry VIII had larger concerns to deal with, namely England's neighbour, France, as well as his marriage difficulties. Meanwhile, the lives of everyone in Christian Europe were about to change forever. The Catholic Church was to experience its greatest upheaval and challenge since its creation. The great schism in the Church would be the single most profound change to enter the political arena.

Building a New Religion

Martin Luther, a Catholic monk tired of the Church's corruptions, wrote ninety-five arguments against Catholic Church policy and doctrine in Germany in 1513. His protestations against abuses of power and faith circulated rapidly due to the invention of Gutenberg's printing press. Refusing to recant on his theses he was forced into hiding but found favour with those who sympathised with his assertion that the Holy Roman Catholic Church was more concerned with power and money than the teachings of Christ. This was as much a political schism as it was religious. As the Catholic Church experienced its first split, kings, princes, dukes, barons, earls and commoners had to decide which side they were on. The new Protestant religion found favour with some in power who saw an opportunity to escape the financial burden of supporting the Church and also saw the possibility of seizing Church land. For others the Catholic Church offered security and financial backing. It was a bloody divide with Protestants slaughtering Catholics and Catholics slaughtering Protestants across the Continent. The Protestants had splinter groups that followed an even stricter code to Luther's arguments. The Calvinists migrated to Switzerland and later to the Netherlands and Scotland. The Reformation would not yet affect Ireland and the Catholic–Protestant divide would drip into Irish politics over the middling decades of the 1500s. The English Reformation would further complicate the Crown's limited role in Ireland. Henry VIII, no supporter of Luther, fought long and hard with the Catholic Church and with Rome to achieve annulment of his marriage to Catherine of Aragon. A protracted and complex chain of events, with no little amount of executions and parliamentary acts, led Henry to break away from Rome and become head of the Church of England. The former 'Defender of the Faith' (a title awarded him by Pope Leo X following his book against Luther's ideas) had begun the English Reformation. By 1536 Henry's parliament removed the last legal authority of Rome in England when they passed the 'Act against the Pope's Authority'.

The Catholic lords in Ireland watched cautiously, as did the Church, with so much property and power at risk of confiscation. Only two years previously Henry was forced to deal with an uprising from the Kildare branch of the Fitzgeralds following (Silken) Thomas Fitzgerald's ill-fated attack on Dublin in 1534. In some quarters the insurgency was seen as a Catholic charge against Protestant England. Although Henry was no Protestant, he was anti-Pope. The Fitzgeralds were becoming increasingly sceptical about England's designs on taking more control over Irish affairs, and the Catholic tag attached to Fitzgerald's outburst may have been a currency of convenience rather than having real value. Henry VIII was aware that ideas of a 'Catholic uprising' being attached to disputes with the Anglo-Irish lords, such as Silken Thomas, could lead to England having to confront Catholic Spain, with the Spanish looking to defend their religious brothers and sisters in Ireland.

The Fitzgeralds' dissatisfaction with Crown policy was based on their belief that the old Norman families should have, to a point, autonomy in the running of Desmond affairs. They had other issues too. The feudal system only worked when all the parties were feeling the mutual benefits of the system, but the Fitzgeralds were experiencing problems with tenants refusing to pay rent and so the lords frequently resorted to bullying and violence to extract their dues. The Earldom of Desmond was itself a brittle political and social landscape. Throughout the decades the earls continued the practice of 'coyne and livery'. This meant that the lords and their vassals could, at will, expect free board and lodgings throughout the earldom. Superior action by the lords created tension and resentment amongst their tenants. Displays of power and arrogance revealed how the Fitzgeralds viewed their position in Ireland – their lands belonged to them and would be run accordingly. While they had become 'Irish', adopting the culture, clothes and some language, their Englishness separated them from the Gaelic Irish who viewed the Fitzgeralds with cautious, weary and resentful resignation. The Fitzgeralds also found themselves adrift ideologically (and increasingly religiously) from the English Crown and its designs for Ireland, which centred on control of financial affairs, business ventures and law. The Earldom of Desmond was in effect a mini independent state, neither loved nor hated by the Gaelic Irish families on one side and the coming power and growing influence of England on the other.

Youghal was a perfect example of how commercial interests were often caught between subservience to the local lord and loyalty to the Crown. The powerful families of the town put security of trade above all else. 'Silken' Thomas' action was more about his own self-interests rather than a religious crusade. It was recognised as such in Youghal and only a few months after Thomas' attempted coup of Dublin in 1534 the mayor, William Walsh, and his council in Youghal communicated in a letter to Lord Chancellor Audeley that the citizens of Youghal were the 'true subjects' of the king and were 'against his enemies' and sought assistance to protect the town. The letter was a clear rejection by Youghal of the idea that it could possibly support Thomas Fitzgerald's idea of an insurrection, faith driven or not. Thomas was a regular resident at Youghal and the practice of coyne and livery there was clearly disliked. The town's desire to disassociate itself from him was driven by merchants eager to protect their business interests. It was a strategy that would be repeated throughout the town's history, and through each and every national crisis the town would look to the power base at London. Despite Thomas' violent action, the wheels of governing Ireland and controlling the old Norman dynasties began to turn slowly and a little more heavily. Henry VIII had to be persuaded at first to adopt more influence in Ireland. He knew such a move would bring a massive financial burden upon the Crown. When Henry finally did claim Ireland as his kingdom in 1542 it began a chain of events that would end in the organised planting of the English in Ireland.

The Plantation Programme

Religious confusion reigned in England after Henry VIII's death in 1547. When the Catholic queen, Mary I took the throne it only served to suspend for a time the coming tide of religious division in Ireland. Her Catholicism did not alter England's determination to push ahead with colonisation of designated areas of Ireland. While her position on the throne brought restoration of the mass, there would be no return to a Catholic status quo. Showing some of her father's ambiguity, in a show of financial concern over spiritual integrity, Mary signed off on former religious properties being sold to merchants while earning the unfortunate name 'Bloody Mary', having put 300 Protestants to the sword. In Youghal, the Earl of Desmond and the local Dominican prior failed to secure funds for the friary at St Mary's to be restored.[8] In 1556 the English plantation programme of Ireland began in earnest.

The plan was simple if not presumptuous in design. Planters would create a town or village in the English manner. They would arm themselves to protect the plantation and new settlers with families would live and work on the land. The Irish would be moved into areas beyond the plantation where no mixing of Irish and English would take place. A trouble-free plantation, operating under the conditions of the Crown, would yield financial reward without having to extract rent from reluctant or rebellious natives. The land populated by the Gaelic Irish families of the O'Moores and the O'Connors was identified for plantation. This land was divided into counties: Queen's County (Laois) and King's County (Offaly). Forts were built at Maryborough (Portlaoise) and Philipstown (Daingean). Forts housed army officers and old English officers. However, the civilising of Ireland through the plantation model brought bloody retaliation from the Irish, who often had to retreat into woodlands. Frequent and violent attacks were made on the planters.

Youghal remained unaffected. Being an urban centre of trade, it was, to a large degree, already an Anglo town. The day-to-day running of business was controlled by the wealthy mercantile families who lived along King's Street in tall town houses such as the still existing Tynte's Castle. The most powerful and influential were the Annyas, Blewetts, Goughs, Ronaynes, Uniakes, Walshes and others. The merchants also took seats on the local council with the mayor at its head, though despite the annual elections it was hardly what would be recognised as a democracy. Such was Youghal's cosmopolitan make-up that William Annyas, the grandson of a Portuguese merchant, became the first ever Jewish mayor in Ireland when he headed the council in Youghal in 1553. The council received the Crown's charters through the office of Deputy of Ireland, the Crown's government in Ireland situated at Dublin Castle. This was, however, Fitzgerald territory and little was decided without their influence.

The arrival of new English settlers did not worry the Fitzgeralds at first and they leased land south of Cork City to planters, knowing that this might generate a steady income. The peasant Irish, who dwelled in small wooden huts in rough rural terrain, would be the most vulnerable in plantation campaigns. However, the continuing guerilla warfare between the Irish and the settlers meant financial reward did not return to parliament with as much ease as had been hoped. Indeed, protecting the plantations proved more costly than they were worth.

Unlike the Vikings and the Normans, the planters were separatists not assimilators. Officially, adoption or adaptation of Irish culture into English life was frowned upon and openly discouraged.

The Fitzgeralds may have underestimated the depth of England's cultural and religious policy for Ireland. Their continued obsession with the Butlers meant animosities erupted into open and bloody conflict between the houses in a battle at Affane, County Waterford in 1565. The 14th Earl of Desmond, Gerald Fitzgerald, who had a house in Youghal and was well known to Queen Elizabeth I since childhood, was susceptible to outbursts of violent action and had a penchant for irritating the government. He had been summoned on numerous occasions to account for his unpredictable and volatile behaviour prior to Affane. From 1562 to 1564 the Crown held him for his conduct before eventually returning him to his earldom, unchanged by English persuasion and mild restraint.[9] Throughout 1565 the houses of Desmond and Ormond presented legal papers to Dublin in an effort to win the right to possess the prize wines of Youghal and Kinsale. Queen Elizabeth ordered that the dispute be settled by a third party, and while awaiting an outcome, she would control the imports.[10] Gerald took almost 400 foot soldiers and close to 100 horsemen, a mix of Gaelic Irish and Old English, into Butler territory later that year. Gerald was, perhaps, frustrated by Elizabeth's decision over the prize wines and was also looking to exact rent owed him from tenants on Butler's lands. Cattle were slaughtered and houses set alight. A pitched battle between the two old Norman dynasties resulted in Butler humiliating Fitzgerald. It was a victory that would set seeds for the destruction of Youghal and the death of thousands in Munster in the coming decades.

Elizabeth saw the private battle between the magnates as a symbol of Fitzgerald's continued belief that he was not answerable to the Crown and could rectify disputes in his own fashion. The greatest worry in London though was the effrontery to the Crown by both houses in raising their own armies and carrying their own ensigns while being neither financed nor sanctioned by the government. It was at best the consequence of a typical Fitzgerald tantrum. At worst it was a snub to royal authority. Both Fitzgerald and Butler were summoned to London to appear before the queen and answer for their actions. Fitzgerald emerged with the less fortunate fate: detention under the pleasure of Her Majesty. Past indiscretions, resistance to Crown policy and the fact that Butler was a cousin of the queen stood against him. The Butler house of Ormond was also behind the push for the reformation of the Church in Ireland, declaring its conversion to the Protestant faith. Gerald Fitzgerald would later return to Munster, landing in Youghal port. Fitzgerald's action at Affane may have persuaded the queen that political stability in Munster was a necessity with so many port economies to protect. A president of Munster, acting for her interests and policing the great opposing houses of Desmond and Ormond, would be instated.

First Desmond Rebellion

By 1567 English political and religious control of parts of Ireland was intensifying. Agents of the queen, given positions of influence, were the model of the new English courtier – soldier, gentleman, poet and politician. These educated elite had exaggerated notions of their worth as civilisers. Their worldview was Anglocentric and they believed that God had bestowed on them the right to exact retribution on the bloodthirsty and uncouth Irish. Gentlemen soldiers of the court would write and discuss the finer points of poetry and history while plotting the ethnic cleansing of vast swathes of countryside. Added to their allusions of intellectual and physical grandeur was the hardening of their religious position. The Gaelic Irish simply ignored Protestantism for now. The Anglo-Irish, in particular some of the Fitzgerald family, increasingly identified their problems with English rule as a religious-centred dispute (perhaps to gain support from the Gaelic Irish). It was these factions that were cited as the main stumbling blocks to making Ireland a compliant component of the Kingdom of England both in government through the offices of Dublin Castle and in religion through the Church of Ireland.

Munster, and by extension Youghal, suffered from the internal feuding. The Crown set in motion a system to ensure safety in the province and to secure the financial wellbeing and coastal riches of

Waterford, Youghal, Cork and Kinsale. Provincial council in the shape of a President of Munster overlooking and administering colonial ventures would be the realisation of this policy.[11] The Lord Deputy of Ireland, Sir Henry Sidney, travelled to Munster from Dublin with the mission to survey its situation under the feuding Earls of Desmond and Ormond. His role was to demilitarise private armies being raised by the feuding factions in the province. Once he rode his horse across the rich soil of Munster, he found its surface was made heavy underfoot by corruption, violence, poverty and social anarchy. He reported his findings to the queen:

> … such horrible and lamentable spectacles there are to behold, such as the burning of villages, ruin of churches, … yea, the view of the bones and the skulls of the dead subjects who, partly by murder, partly by famine, have died in the fields as in truth, any Christian hardly with dry eyes could behold … Surely there was never people that lived in more misery than they do.[12]

No doubt Sidney let his displeasure be known to the reinstated Gerald Fitzgerald, who met Sidney at Carrick and travelled with him to Youghal during a wet and cold late January. Sidney had a guard watch Fitzgerald while they were together and played judge and jury in conversation with him, telling Gerald that Thomas Butler had also been justly questioned about the state of Munster and their continuing feud, but 'rather shewed favour than severitie'.[13] Having ended his Munster journey at Killmallock, Sidney claimed to have spoken with Fitzgerald's allies and Gaelic clans, one named Condon, who would attack Youghal over a decade later. He warned them that any rebellious action against the Crown on behalf of themselves or Gerald Fitzgerald would be crushed. He also informed them that he was aware that Fitzgerald had plans to escape his attentions. The untrusted earl was brought in front of his peers. Sidney claims he humiliated Gerald by arresting him and putting him on his knees before those Gerald claimed to lead. Fitzgerald was ordered to pay £20,000 to the Crown for his rebellious contempt of English law and for his family's actions against the house of Ormond.[14] Despite Sidney's assertion that all the clans were subservient, armed allies of Fitzgerald, though small in number, did appear between Limerick and Killmallock in a show of defiance. Exasperated by Fitzgerald's refusal to accept English policy, the queen ordered he be taken to the Tower of London where his brother, John, later joined him. He did not return to Ireland until 1573. The Crown would ultimately regret allowing Gerald to return.

Sidney's apocalyptic view of Munster may have been exaggerated to persuade the queen to quicken the process of putting an end to the hostilities of the Anglo-Irish earls and replace the feudal system with provincial presidents. The presidents would control matters of law and religion. Sidney placed Sir Warham St Leger as President of Munster, adding two assistants, Robert Cusack and Nicholas White to the office. These men were appointed to counsel Fitzgerald and Butler respectively. To some extent this showed that Elizabeth was not trying to replace the earls but attempting to bring them under the social and political workings of government. And, throughout the successive presidencies, what Elizabeth wanted and what actually transpired were often two different outcomes. The president would be expected to work formally and informally alongside the Earls.[15] To Sidney's disappointment, he stated that for all he had done for the Butlers of Ormond, including extracting £20,894 12s 8d from the Earl of Desmond in compensation, Butler moaned to queen Elizabeth about Sidney and continued his accusations against the house of Desmond. The Butlers would reluctantly accept and acknowledge the Presidency of Munster. Meanwhile, in Gerald Fitzgerald's absence, rebellious outbursts would continue.

While Gerald Fitzgerald sat in the Tower of London he appointed his cousin James Fitzmaurice Fitzgerald as Captain-General of Desmond. James was well known for his attention to Catholicism and was acquainted with two Jesuit priests, William Good and Edmund Daniel. Their school had been shut down in Limerick but they eventually reopened it in Youghal, thus ensuring Catholic education in the town under the watch of the Fitzgeralds.[16] Daniel was, however, as part of periodic persecutions of Catholics in Youghal, later arrested, tortured, hanged and quartered for conspiracy against the government. A second Jesuit school would open in 1577 under the care of Frs Roachford and Lea. 'Black Tom' Butler, Earl of Ormond, who had declared his allegiance to the Church of England, continued to pressure the queen for favour in the running of Munster, and his persistence paid dividends. Just over a year later, in 1568, the previously disputed prize wines of Youghal and Kinsale, now under the administration of the presidency, were awarded to Butler by Queen Elizabeth. Worse for the Fitzgeralds was the surrender of their Youghal home and the chief rent of the town to Her Majesty's exchequer. Later in the same year a petition was signed by a number of English 'adventurers', including Sir Warham St Leger and Sir Humphry Gilbert (half-brother of Sir Walter Raleigh), to lobby Queen Elizabeth with a plantation programme for west Cork, mostly the coastline. They wanted the land to be populated by new English planters. By 1569 a second version of the proposal sought to broaden the scope of powers to planters. They wanted the right to control imports and exports from the proposed plantation as well as the power to confiscate lands from a number of Gaelic-Irish clans, including the McCarthy Mórs in the west Cork–Kerry region.[17] The proposal was approved.

With reports circulating that the Crown had plans to populate Munster with English planters, and the hardening of a reformation policy for the Church, hostilities between the Fitzgeralds and the Crown were quickly becoming a religious insurgence, in name at least, between Catholic rebels and imperialist Protestants. The distinction meant that Spain would take an interest, as would Rome. In his role as Captain-General of Desmond in the absence of Gerald, James set about creating an assembly of influential Catholic leaders (Gaelic-Irish and Anglo-Irish) in an attempt to rally against the government's plans. The assembly would write to Philip II of Spain offering him the Kingdom of Ireland with the Pope's approval.[18] Meanwhile, John Perrot, the newly appointed President of Munster but not seated in the province as yet, further strengthened Thomas Butler's powers, much to the annoyance of the Fitzgeralds, by appointing him General of Munster. 'Black Tom' was given the role in the confidence that he would nullify any threat from James. However, riled by Crown policy, the now self-styled Catholic crusader struck Kerrycurihy Castle, south of Cork City, the site of the first planters in Munster, in June 1569. Youghal and Kinsale were on alert and were to be part of the route of rebellious action. Many of those who had fled Kerrycurihy found refuge behind the walls of Youghal, knowing the town's previous declaration of loyalty to the Crown. The rebels pursued them, putting the town under an intensive siege.[19] James put out word that he would attack any of those who had refused his call to arms, whether they were Gaelic Irish or Anglo-Irish. He amassed an estimated force of 4,500. By July he was at Kilkenny, the heart of the Fitzgerald's oldest adversary, the Butlers of Ormond. It was perhaps inevitable that the rebellion would navigate to Ormond given the players involved. However, unlike previous outbursts of violence, the 1569 rebellion was a direct attack on the Crown's authority in Munster rather than a private dispute. With the Butlers proclaiming their loyalty to the Crown and to the Protestant Reformation of Ireland, the previous animosity between the two houses was now identifiable by a distinctly sectarian hue.

Terror and Retribution

James F. Fitzgerald failed to make headway at Kilkenny. Sir Henry Sidney departed Dublin on a mission of retribution while 400 soldiers arrived at Cork. He recaptured lost castles, amongst them Castlemartyr. The arrival into the power play of Sir Humphry Gilbert saw a significant shift in favour of the Crown against the rebels. Gilbert, who had signed the petition for the plantation of Munster only a few months earlier, was an exemplar of the educated English warrior-gent. Atrocities were committed on both sides during the conflict but Gilbert's warfaring style was a vision of the world to come for the Irish. He swept through Munster like a military plague. Terrorism was a mark of his campaign. This description of his tactics written by a recorder during the campaign shows the severity of his nature:

> That the heads of all those (of what sort so ever they were) which were killed in the day, should be cut off from their bodies and brought to the place where he encamped at night, and should there be laid on the ground by each side of the way leading into his own tent so that none could come into his tent for any cause but commonly must

pass through a lane of heads which were used ad terrorem, the dead feeling nothing the more pains thereby; and yet did it bring great terror to the people when they saw the heads of their dead fathers, brothers, children, kinsfolk and friends, lie on the ground before their faces, as they came to speak with the said colonel.[20]

Gilbert had good reason to be so forceful, he was not just fighting for the Crown or England or Protestantism but clearing the land for his own economic gain. His tactics extended to killing those who housed or fed rebels, starvation being as deadly as the sword. Gilbert would be knighted for his efforts.

Throughout the rebellion, life in Youghal was extremely difficult. Uncertainty over security, lack of trade, the threat of prolonged siege and starvation contributed to a tense environment. The lack of movement in or out of the town during Fitzgerald's early campaign meant the fate of those within the walls was highly dependent on the outcome of the rebellion. Supporters of the Crown had much to be worried about. Catholics, on the other hand, had much to lose with a defeated Fitzgerald unable to prevent the plantation of Protestants and the influx of new residents to the town. Such was the weight of political and religious pressure that on 4 September 1571 the townsmen of Youghal held an emergency meeting and it was decided to write to the Privy Council requesting the release of Gerald from the Tower of London so he could 'return home'. As in the case of Silken Thomas, the council of Youghal was stating its preference for a return to the status quo of Crown control. They hoped and expected to see a contrite earl, having being released from the Tower of London, return to Munster and, in payment to the queen for her generosity, crush his rebellious upstart nephew and resume his position as head of Desmond.

Meanwhile, conditions in the town were deteriorating so rapidly that on 7 April Mayor Jasper Portengall sent Thomas Coppinger to Dublin to inform the lord deputy about the depth of their misery and to request immediate assistance. Coppinger, travelling by the King's Highway via Cork Hill, carried letters from town leaders but had to return on hearing that the lord deputy was sick. No little amount of fear had gripped the residents of the town with rebels encamped outside it and reports that their numbers had swollen to 800. Inside the walls, sickness, death and decay consumed any remaining optimism that the town could withstand either a siege or an all-out rebel assault. What is clear from the actions of officials in Youghal was the utter commitment to protecting the mercantile interests and putting commercial links to England above concerns about the plantation policy. Youghal, not for the first or last time, backed the bully with the bigger stick. They chose wisely as Fitzgerald's momentum began to wane.

Even at the decline of the rebellion on 27 November 1572, the government retained a high level of alertness. President of Munster, John Perrot, was given notice by Sir Henry Sidney that a ship from Marseille named the *Peter and Paul* and coming from Lisbon, Portugal, was to be detained at Youghal. A full inspection of the goods was to be carried out with all the cargo to be kept in Youghal until further notice. Added to this, 'We authorize your Lordship to imprison all such persons as shall detain said hulk, such persons convicted to remain in prison without bail.'[21] The capturing of the *Peter and Paul* was an act of piracy in the guise of martial law against suspect merchants who, in the eyes of the English, may have had weapons or soldiers or supplies on board to support the rebellion. However, having taken the ship to Cork, Perrot appropriated for himself jewels from the ship such as rubies, emeralds, sapphires, pearls and 'other Pearls of evil colour'.[22] Perrot would be taken to court for his loose interpretation of Sidney's direction but had enough corrupt influence in Dublin to avoid prosecution.

With the rebellion petering out, James F. Fitzgerald retreated toward the Kerry border, and Perrot chased him around the province, applying the same ruthless war methods as Gilbert. Appetite for rebellion was dying amongst many of those who had taken up arms for Fitzgerald's cause. Many who fought alongside him began to turn their attentions to the protection of their own homes and families. The seemingly inexhaustible pursuit to capture Fitzgerald finally ended with his surrender in 1573 at Killmallock, which he had previously burned. While the rebellion ran its course, Gerald Fitzgerald and his brother, John, negotiated their release from the Tower of London. They promised to give up their right to coyne and livery, support the Reformation and even assist in the quashing of James' revolt. They were taken to Dublin and held there while Perrot's plans for Munster were put into action, once peace was restored. Negotiations between Gerald and Crown officials over his long-desired return to Desmond were dependent on several conditions. The protracted discussions frustrated him to the point that he escaped Dublin and returned to Munster.

Second Desmond Rebellion

In just under six years Youghal would lay in ruins following a second insurrection, again by the persistent Fitzgeralds. In 1575 the defeated yet still surviving James F. Fitzgerald sailed to France in exile. New systems of set rents rather than coyne and livery were agreed between Gerald and the Presidency of Munster. Steady incomes paid to Gerald seemed to bring satisfaction to the house of Desmond but plenty of resentment to those under him. Most notably his brother, John, was increasingly marginalised by the queen's favoured rehabilitation of the earl. Gerald himself did not have to pay rent to the new Lord President of Munster, Sir William Drury. Indeed, a meeting between Drury and Desmond at the request of Sir Henry Sidney at Dublin in January 1578 ended in mutual respect. Gerald showed willingness to work in tandem with the new regime with promises of progression for Munster made.[23] Such was the positive atmosphere between Drury and the earl that Drury was invited to Youghal. There he was entertained by Gerald and his wife, the Countess of Desmond, at their residence the following October. The council of Youghal must have felt vindicated by its earlier pleas to have Gerald restored to his position as earl. Entertaining such a positive diplomatic visit in the town and the security that peace had brought to its commerce were all signs of an upturn in post-rebellion fortunes for Youghal. However, just when Gerald and Youghal thought it was safe to put their troubles behind them a number of factors conspired to make Gerald's new relationship with the presidency shatter into pieces. Without warning, the healing wounds between Gerald Fitzgerald and Queen Elizabeth would rip open to spill fresh Munster blood. Gerald's sudden and inexplicable destruction of Youghal would bring about viscious retribution and an end to 400 years of the increasingly fragile feudal system in the province.

Opportunists, with little care for those 400 years of social, political and religious culture, would see Fitzgerald's violent outburst as nothing more than corruption induced by a hunger for autonomy and alliance with the Irish. Even Elizabeth's more considered approach to her traditional acquaintances, allies and agitators alike, such as the earls of Desmond and Ormond, would be a policy ignored by the new wave of English. In their minds, the old Norman dynasties had, over four centuries, become more Irish than the Irish themselves. The new generation of coming English, hungry to take advantage of Munster's factionalism, carried a philosophy not estranged from ethnic cleansing. Over the next four years Munster and Youghal, in particular, would be laid to waste as the Anglo-Irish and the Gaelic Irish wrestled with the 'New English' to prevent Munster coming under Crown control.

What transpired in the winter of 1579 was not expected, certainly not by Gerald Fitzgerald, having found himself back home and settled on a personal tax-free arrangement with the President of Munster. Others were less satisfied with the new system. His brother, John, who had spent years in captivity with Gerald and was willing to help the Crown nullify the threat posed by James, now exiled on the Continent, did not receive the same privileges bestowed on the earl. It also would have irked the swordsmen who had fought in 1569–73 to see such favour bestowed on Gerald, who many regarded as the inferior of John. Seeing a bleak landscape of financial hardship as a subordinate to Gerald and the Crown, John cut his ties with the earl and became a renegade. Others, who had fought to preserve Gerald's position for over a decade, were now made redundant by his cosying up to Drury. They had stood by him against the Butlers and had worked to maintain the feudal traditions of tax collecting from tenants, sometimes by force. While all seemed progressive for Gerald, many under his stewardship viewed the situation with envy and resentment. That resentment was compounded by their unemployment as former soldiers of privately funded armies under the exiled James F. Fitzgerald and others. They would also face retribution from Drury and Henry Sidney for their part in the 1569 revolt. Another factor in drawing Gerald out of his relative comfort zone was the sudden return to Ireland of his aforementioned and rejuvenated nephew, James. Despite his defeat in 1573 and subsequent exile, he landed at Smerwick on the coast of Kerry on 17 July 1579 with sixty men in support. Two months later, in September, an estimated force of 600 Spanish and Italian soldiers under a papal banner arrived at the same destination. The papal trappings of the army, camped out at the small fort of Dún an Oír, alarmed Dublin and London. Not only did it represent an invasion by Spanish and Italian forces but it was also seen as a flagrant attempt to crush the English Reformation in Ireland and install a foreign Catholic monarchy.

The momentum of the second Desmond rebellion was slow at first. However, on 1 August in a tavern in Tralee the rebellion and the pressure on Gerald exploded when John Fitzgerald and his brother James assassinated two heads of Munster's military police, Henry Davells and Arthur Carter.[24] Gerald reacted quickly and promised Drury that he would help crush the rebellion but his words were more effective than his actions. He often followed and watched rebels without interfering or engaging in combat.[25] This inaction betrayed the dilemma he faced having taken the monumental step of allowing Drury effectively to take administrative control of Munster. When Drury fell sick and died, Gerald lost his only diplomatic ally. It would prove to be the first unhinging of Gerald's already loose armour. He was now politically adrift and neither side of the divide required his services. In Drury's place Nicholas Malby showed none of the patience for Gerald that Drury had. There would be no softly, softly approach to sorting Munster's instability. Malby mirrored the forthright militancy of Gilbert and Perrot. He sidelined the reticent and ineffectual Gerald to confront the rebels directly. Malby's actions radicalised tenants loyal to Gerald, driving them toward the rebel forces. Malby demanded Gerald relinquish all authority. When the earl refused he was proclaimed a rebel. He was, in effect, isolated and alienated. His path to rebellion had been forced upon him by Malby's directness, his family's determination and his own inability to dismount the political fence. However, insurrection was also a path that offered the possibility of regaining his seat as undoubted head of Desmond.

In an act of bewildering defiance or desperation, that only a few months previously would have seemed unthinkable, Gerald Fitzgerald attacked Youghal on 13 November 1579. Having plundered their way through the Barony of Imokilly, his forces camped before Youghal. They found the gates of the town locked, but its defences were poor. The town's vulnerability was a sign of its complacency under the stewardship of Gerald Fitzgerald. Finances were also lacking following a collapse of the economy from the previous Munster war. Fitzgerald's forces entered the town by knocking through weak sections of the walls without resistance. They raped, plundered and burned for five days. What booty could be found was sent to Strancally Castle. Gerald broke into the courthouse at Water Gate (at the bottom of present-day O'Neill/Crowley Street) and defaced the Queen's Arms, pulling it to the ground and stamping on it. The citizens of Youghal, and in particular the wealthy families who had written to advocate Gerald's release from the Tower of London only a few years previously, were now shocked into emergency action.

> The Geraldines seized upon all the riches they found in this town, excepting such gold and silver as the merchants and burgesses had sent away in ships before the town was taken. Many a poor and indignant person became rich and affluent by the spoils of this town. The Geraldines leveled the wall of the town, and broke its courts and castles and its buildings of stone and wood; so it was not habitable for some time afterwards.[26]

The destruction of Youghal was not just of its buildings. Resistance, however poor, took place and blood was shed on the streets and in the houses. Like a character in a Shakespearian tragedy, Gerald had found himself at the eye of the storm in his own personal Armageddon. The man who had served at the table of Henry VIII as a page, had been a captive of Elizabeth, had protected his earldom against the Butlers and had both befriended and fought the Gaelic Irish collapsed under pressure, a protagonist by default, his own downfall due to an inability to think and act decisively. Now, the town he had enjoyed and helped become so prominent was in flames around him.

In response to the sacking of Youghal, 'Black Tom' Butler sent a ship from Waterford under the command of a Captain White who entered with his men through the Quay Gate. Confronting the rebels on the street he was overrun by their larger number and killed. A number of his soldiers managed to run to the quayside, return to their ship and escape. The response from the English was swift. All properties belonging to Gerald were to be burned. Butler, on his way from Cashel to Youghal, was party to the indiscriminate murder of innocents thought to be associated with the Earl of Desmond.[27] On his journey he encountered

Patrick Coppinger, Youghal's mayor, who had escaped the sacking at its early stages or even before it began. Butler brought him back and found a town ravaged, still smouldering and devoid of men, women and children. It is thought that Butler did meet a friar in the town, whom he spared, because the friar claimed to be the man who had carried Henry Davell's body from Tralee to Waterford after his assassination by John Fitzgerald. Such mercy was not afforded to Coppinger, who was hung from his own door for his appalling defence of Youghal and for refusing the offer of reinforcements prior to Gerald's attack.[28]

Youghal continued to come under threat the following year as the rebellion dragged on. Patrick Coppinger's brother, Thomas, wrote to the Mayor of Waterford on 18 November 1580 to warn him that the 'traitors Eustace and John (Fitzgerald) Desmond' were camped at Aharlow, getting ready to make an assault on Youghal. He requested the aid of soldiers.[29] The memory of his hanging brother had taught him the lesson of diligence. Meanwhile, James F. Fitzgerald, though buoyed by the arrival of the Spanish and Italian troops at the Smerwick shore, would only find them rooted at their destination and unable to effect the slightest change to the rebellion. They came to support the Catholic rebellion against Protestant England and her heretical queen. They would be met, repelled and slaughtered by the English. It was the end of the Anglo-Norman-Irish dynasty of Desmond.

The End of the Fitzgerald Dynasty

Perhaps the destruction of Youghal was the manifestation of Gerald's frustration in trying, and failing, to keep hold of his traditional position of power in a world that was being torn apart on all sides. The bewildered earl found himself standing alone in a labyrinthine and hostile land. His mind and heart were vexed. He was torn between looking over his shoulder to the factions, who neither had the wherewithal nor the will to support him, and staring a queen in the eye who was devoid of sympathy or empathy. Her single-minded plantation agents were emerging on the horizon of a new vision for Munster, one that did not include power-sharing with the old Norman dynasty of the Earldom of Desmond. They were determined to change the old order, and so, Gerald, aware that his fire was dying, set his torch to Youghal. It was the most desperate of acts that propelled him into the wilderness.

Hiding out in the Kerry Mountains, Gerald had time to reflect on the sacking of Youghal and his regret was evident in the tone of a letter he wrote to Butler dated 5 June 1583. He expressed 'great grief' at how Elizabeth viewed him as an 'undutiful subject' and went on to describe his loyalty to her. In the most revealing passage, Gerald confessed to mistakes but remained defiant in his belief that he had been wronged. He hinted that his 'folly' was the result of a rage induced by the deviousness of others. It was a rage manifest not in spite but because of his loyalty to Elizabeth. He could not bear to be dishonoured by her.

> As I may not condemn myself of disloyalty to her Majesty, so cannot I excuse my faults, but must confess that I have incurred her Majesty's indignation; yet when the cause and means which were found and devised to make me commit folly shall be known to her Highness, I rest in an assured hope that her most gracious Majestie will both think of me as my heart deserveth, and also those that wrung me into undutifullness, as their cunning device deserveth. From my heart I am sorry for that folly.[30]

Gerald then asked to meet Butler to explain 'how tyrannously I was used'. How ironic for Gerald Fitzgerald that one of his last attempts as a figure of relevance in Munster was to parley with his oldest and fiercest adversary, who was afforded the luxury to snort at his pathetic plea. No meeting would take place. Gerald was killed on 11 November 1583 in Glenaginty, County Kerry, not in combat against Crown forces nor even 'Black Tom' Butler, but by the local clan, Moriarty. In an almost mocking symbol of his life-long struggle and torn loyalties, his head was sent to London to be spiked and his body was displayed in Cork. For the next twenty years Youghal would find itself the home of English adventurers determined to apply English culture and religion to Ireland. The town would be repopulated with new settlers and returning merchants as the bloody war for Munster came to a close.

3

The Mighty Hand of the Almightiest Power

Walter Raleigh's Adventurer Policies in Youghal

The Fitzgerald rule over Desmond, which had spanned almost 400 years, had come to a slow and painful end. The main protagonists, who all appear to have had varying motives for taking up arms against the Crown and its agents, would die. Not long after arriving at Smerwick, James F. Fitzgerald crossed the river Shannon and involved himself in a skirmish with a local clan, the Burkes. A number of James's men had attempted to steal horses from the clan. James died without glory, leaving a moderate and alienated papal force stranded on the Kerry coast whose fate would be equally unceremonious. In 1582, John Fitzgerald, who had in many ways instigated the rebellion by assassinating officers of the Crown in Tralee, was killed north of Cork City. His head was sent to Dublin Castle and his body was suspended from a high gibbet, by the heels, over the river Lee, on the north-gate bridge of Cork. It swung there for three years.[31]

Meanwhile, in Youghal, 'Black Tom' Butler tried to persuade residents to return to the ruined town following its destruction in the winter of 1579. Three hundred soldiers were stationed and a programme of rebuilding was financed. However, with the rebellion being fought in pockets throughout the province, individual rebel leaders, who had to raise their own small armies, continued to carry out sporadic attacks. Confidence that all was well in Youghal was blasted in early 1582 when it suffered another rebel assault. The Seneschal of Imokilly, John Fitzedmund Fitzgerald, along with long-serving rebel Patrick Condon, set upon Youghal with a reported 700 men 8–12 January. More burning took place and goods such as wine, corned beef, hides and corn were taken. However, with lessons learned from 1579, an early alarm alerted security in time to man the walls and towers. The new garrison forces successfully repelled the attempted sacking of the town. Condon would later be cited by town officials as a particularly persistent rebel for claiming he had: 'spoiled, burnt and ransacked the town, and murdered the people that they took, and killed divers others'. It was also reported that Condon had erected the 'Popes banner with [his] own guidon [army flag] in the top of the highest place in the town'. That place was either one of the towers of Trinity Castle, the main entrance to the south end of the town, or the towers on the hill behind the town. Whichever was the case, Condon waved his flags crying 'Condon Abú'.[32] Fear of further rebel action did not deter residents from returning to the urban centre, which, in contrast to smaller towns and villages, offered some military protection.

Walter Raleigh at Smerwick

Youghal's vulnerable state and the removal of its owners, the Fitzgerald dynasty, meant its land, property and profitable port were ripe for takeover. It is not clear whether Butler, long in control of the wine imports, had any designs on the town; if he had, they would be pushed aside. Certainly, for the merchants trickling back into the town to restart their businesses as early as 1580, the future was a blank canvas. Two figures whose reputations were written onto that canvas and whose names are synonymous with the history of Youghal are Walter Raleigh and Edmund Spenser. A portion of both men's time in Ireland would be spent in Youghal. Raleigh's involvement was the more significant; he would be granted lands and properties in the town and, for a time, occupy the seat of the deposed Fitzgerald family. Raleigh was the archetypal English knight of the period. A favourite of Elizabeth, he had fought wars against French and Spanish Catholics and would forge a reputation as an adventurer, soldier, gentleman, thinker and writer which endeared him to some historians as a 'hero' and 'universal genius'. The darker aspect to this complex and contradictory character is recorded in his Irish affairs. His involvement in a notorious bloodletting event would not only solidify his military standing but would afford him political, commercial, historical and social status in Youghal and Munster. Spenser, recognised as one of England's greatest poets, would also be present at one of Ireland's bloodiest encounters, but his reputation was built on a skill with words rather than the sword. Given what he would go on to write later, it could be argued that his pen was truly mightier than Raleigh's soldiery.

Raleigh, the future Mayor of Youghal, had cut his military teeth in France and Spain. The queen often conveniently ignored the actions of her knights and their acts of piracy. While officially frowned upon, piracy was accepted for the wealth it brought to the Crown exchequer. Piracy had more or less been sanctioned under Henry VIII but, for Raleigh, his anti-Catholic rhetoric was a tidy excuse for raiding French and Spanish ships. Indeed, his own father had financed piracy long before Walter became an active participant in its practice.[33] The unofficial policies of 'adventurer practices' often included trading slaves in the Caribbean with Spanish colonists. While Spain was England's great enemy such exchanges brought individual wealth to English officers as well as to the Crown. Ignoring the wilful habits of people like Raleigh would come back to haunt Elizabeth in a number of personal and ugly tussles with her agents.[34] The environment in Munster after the Desmond rebellions of 1569 and 1579 meant that, like the pirates, those who had helped crush the Fitzgeralds and the Irish clans would be rewarded for their services. However, some English agents adopted a self-appointed autonomy over their affairs, often ignoring official Crown policy to make personal and financial gains. Raleigh saw the fall of the house of Desmond as the perfect opportunity to seize lands and amass a fortune from trade, in particular at the port of Youghal.

Both Raleigh and Spenser were present on the day the Crown's forces descended on Smerwick in 1580 following the arrival of James F. Fitzgerald's small papal army on the Dingle peninsula. What transpired would swing the rebellion in English favour, but would also mark it in the consciousness of the Irish forever and draw condemnation from around Europe. Raleigh was one of three captains under the leadership of Lord Grey. Spenser's role, as Grey's secretary, meant the future poet was less involved. The estimated number of the papal army was somewhere between 600 and 700 Spanish and Italian soldiers. It was a modest number and hopelessly doomed to fail. The Crown viewed the rebellion with such seriousness that English troops in Ireland had swelled to 6,500 by October.

The arrival of a papal army, however small, alerted the Crown to the possibility of Spain using Ireland as a base from which to attack England. Such a threat drove the English on through war-torn Munster to the Kerry coast to intercept the arrivals at Smerwick. Hopelessly outnumbered, the Spanish and Italians retreated to the small earth fort of Dún an Oír; among their number was a group of Irish men and women.[35] Lord Grey advanced on the fort while warships, such as the *Revenge*, carrying in excess of 150 cannons, made escape by sea impossible. Following a stand-off, the surrender by Spanish officers was accepted. However, Grey ordered the killing of all inside the fort excepting the Spanish officers, who would make handsome rewards as bounty. The Irish men and women in the fort were taken and hanged. Raleigh and the other captains entered the fort with their soldiers and cut down those remaining. Their bodies were stripped naked and laid out on the beach. A report of the massacre was made to the queen's secretary, Sir Francis Walsingham. It read:

> The fortes were yielded, all the Irishmen and women hanged, and four hundred and upwards of Italians and others put to the sword … A friar and others kept in store to be executed after examination had of them … Next day was executed an Englishman who served Dr. Saunders, and one Plunckett, and an Irish Priest their arms and legs were broken and hanged upon a gallows.[36]

Plunkett and the priest were held down and had their arms and legs smashed by a Blacksmith's anvil. Their hanging, disfigured bodies drew disgust and fear from onlookers. The violence of the killings was such that its purpose of creating terror spread throughout Munster and beyond.

The massacre was widely condemned across Ireland and Europe. Conflicting reports of Lord Grey's reaction fluctuated between shedding tears to paralysed emotion. What is certain are Grey's own words of what transpired once the Catholic army accepted their fate and surrendered:

> I sent straight certain gentlemen in, to see their weapons and arms laid down and to guard the munitions and victual there left from spoil. Then put I in certain bands who straight away fell to execution. There were six hundred slain.[37]

Queen Elizabeth stated her satisfaction with Grey's works when she wrote:

> The mighty hand of the Almightiest power hath showed manifest the force of his strength … in which action I joy that you have been

chosen the instrument of His glory, which I give you no cause to forthink. Your loving sovereign, Elizabeth R.[38]

Raleigh, who perhaps in a moment of justification of his hatred toward the Catholic Spanish, would later write in 1591, 'Irreligiously they cover their greedy and ambitious pretences with that veil of piety.'[39]

Like Gilbert and Grey before him, Raleigh lived the contradiction of gentlemanly conduct improbably infused with an instinct for brutal violence. Smerwick, the Munster wars and the subsequent cleaning-up operations of remaining insurgents around the province solidified his burgeoning reputation with Elizabeth. Later in his career, reflecting on his military service while under the shadow of his impending death, Raleigh espoused the ideal that war should be fought openly and conducted with gentlemanly rules of engagement. He frowned upon guerilla tactics, adopted so often by the Irish, but his idealism was as hypocritical as his courtly aspirations. Throughout the Munster campaign from 1579 to 1583 the methods of soldiery adopted by Raleigh and his contemporaries included the hiring of assassins to dispose of rebels. These skilled operators, who often used poison, were to be paid or given land in return for their 'expertise'. The other method of 'ungentlemanly war conduct' was the most devastating: the killing of livestock and burning of land and crops to induce famine.[40] Raleigh's pretensions of the conduct of war were an expression of his notions of superiority. Killing rebels, no matter what the technique, was justified because the Irish were simply not on a level playing field. He was not alone in his thinking. Following the Smerwick massacre Grey boasted about his exploits, claiming to have killed 1,500 'men and gentlemen … not accounting those of a meaner sort' and others with a figure that was, by his own admission, 'innumerable'.[41] Edmund Spenser also observed, 'At this time, not the lowing of a cow, or the voice of a ploughman, could be heard from Dunqueen in Kerry to Cashel in Munster.'[42]

Raleigh, Spenser and Grey shared with their contemporaries a view that the Gaelic Irish had not, and could not, progress to civility. They also shared a violent methodology for the quashing of insurrection. However, their relationship reveals the complications that existed in the English campaign to colonise Munster and Ireland. Grey disliked Raleigh intensely.[43] 'I nether like his carriage nor company,' he remarked. Grey himself was recalled to London, perhaps for his persistent letters requesting funding, while his reputation was undermined by others such as Raleigh. His action at Smerwick was an embarrassment to some English officials, but the suggestion he was withdrawn from Ireland because of it does not sit comfortably with the queen's lavish praise for the exploit. What Grey's fate does reveal are the queen's contradictory actions in dealing with English officials in Ireland. Her sanctioning of the plantation programme was followed by an inability to take a more forceful role in its implementation. This meant that opportunists like Raleigh, who were operating almost as freelance developers, were allowed to take advantage of the collapse of any social structure following the decimation of Munster. The queen had effectively decided to view the plantation of Munster with the same blind eye she had cast so casually over high-sea piracy. This would directly result in Raleigh's attaining so much land in and around Youghal.

Famine

The rebellion dragged on for another three years after Smerwick. The rebels destroyed thirty-six English settlements. Meanwhile, Elizabeth, fighting simultaneous wars in Europe and other outbreaks in Ireland, reduced the size of the Crown's forces. Captains such as Raleigh found it increasingly wearing to be 'in the country and in the woods spent all this summer in continual action against the rebels'. One example saw Raleigh hunt renegade David Barry, who had been pardoned for previous involvement in the rebellion, to Ballinacurra. Barry and John Fitzedmund Fitzgerald ambushed Raleigh but failed to kill him.[44] These exploits only added to his reputation, but while his hand was clearly contracted to war, his eyes were firmly fixed on the acquisition of property. He tried in vain to secure the ownership of Barryscourt Castle in Carrigtohill, promising to fund it and 'defend it for Her Majesty'. Raleigh's frustrations were revealed when he attacked the reputation of 'Black Tom' Butler as being too lenient with rebels. Of Butler he said, the rebels would 'rather die a thousand deaths, enter into a million mischiefs and seek succour of all nations rather than they will ever be subdued by a Butler'.[45] Removing Butler would of course allow more room for Raleigh in negotiations for confiscated lands, particularly the Desmond estates and the town of Youghal. Elizabeth did exactly as Raleigh had hoped and Butler, for all his triumphs against the Fitzgeralds and the repopulating and securing of Youghal after its sacking, was relieved of his duty as General of Munster. However, with typical dithering Crown policy in Munster, he would be reappointed in early 1583. It seemed scant reward and harsh treatment for a loyalist who claimed to have killed 5,461 rebels in total, including fifteen prominent rebel leaders.[46]

The vast estates that Raleigh would eventually own were devastated by the rebellion. Spenser described Munster in both poetic and terrifying terms. In his article *A View of the Present State of Ireland* about how to bring civil English society and culture to the Irish, he drew an image of a land in the grips of an apocalypse. He described the Irish as zombie-like in feature, digging out the graves of their dead to feed on the carcasses, while others crawled on all fours like mange dogs to eat plants from the earth:

> Out of every corner of the woods and glens they came creeping forth upon their hands, for their legs could not bear them; they looked like anatomies of death, they spake like ghosts crying out of their graves; they did eat of the dead carrion, happy were they if they could find them, yea, and one after another seen after, insomuch as the very carcasses they spared not to scrape out of the graves, and if they found a plot of watercresses or shamrocks, there they flocked as to feast.[47]

This was the landscape around the Munster towns on which Raleigh would attempt to amass a fortune and plant English families. With the rebellion winding down, the 28-year-old returned to England in 1582. He was also focused on settling a plantation in a part of North America, eventually to be known as Virginia in honour of the virgin queen, Elizabeth. Meanwhile, in Munster, as the famine reached its zenith, Lord Pelham reported that suicides were common amongst those who could not survive the harshness of their conditions: 'The poor people ... offer themselves with their wives and children to be slain by the army

than to suffer the famine that now in extremity is beginning to pinch them.'[48] It is estimated that in the heaviest period of war, 30,000 had died from famine and related diseases. A report claimed that starvation was killing between twenty and seventy people a day in Cork city alone.[49] Youghal would see an influx of refugees towards the end of the century. For now, its rebuilding was still at an infancy stage. The plantation programme was still a number of years off and trade was badly affected, with little or no corn to export. Further to these problems, the straitjacket of martial law effectively stymied economic growth.

Confiscation of Desmond Land

By 1584 Munster had a new lord president, Sir John Norris, with Sir John Perrot appointed new Lord Deputy of Ireland. Plans for the repopulation of Munster with new English settlers were being drawn up in London. In September of that year a group of surveyors travelled for over three months throughout the confiscated lands of Desmond. Raleigh had already received an agreement about lands in Cork, including Youghal. The Desmond lands were estimated to cost £10,000. It would be two further years before the final draft for a plantation programme would be announced in London. Those undertaking the programme would be given land not in excess of 12,000 acres and had to agree to the transportation of ninety-one English families who would pay an annual rent of just over £66. Central to the plantation programme was the insistence by government of a separatist policy. Settlers had to be of English birth and the Gaelic Irish were to have no part in the plantation, or indeed, have any social interaction.[50] The quality and location of land available affected the pattern of settlement. Rich agricultural land that could yield profitable crops, therefore securing an income, was desirable, as was the availability of natural resources like timber and fish.[51] In this regard, Youghal and its environs made for a prime location. These factors would also influence prospective tenants who were making the move from English counties into unknown territory. Certainly, Raleigh's reputation as a protector of English interests and his war exploits made his plantation around a 'safe' and predominantly Protestant town like Youghal an attractive proposition for families starting a new life in Munster.

While plans, reports, advertising and agreements were being signed in England, Youghal's mayor, Patrick Brennott, and his council were busy rebalancing the books in an effort to get the town back on its economic feet. They wrote to the lord deputy to have a £4 'black rent', as they termed it, previously paid to the Earl of Desmond, cancelled. Perhaps expecting a boom to the economy brought on by Raleigh's prospective inheritance of the town's financial affairs and an increase in population by settlers, they asked that Youghal be given county status separate from Cork. They also made a request to use the land at Molana Abbey for a fixed rent.[52] Queen Elizabeth was 'contented' for

Youghal to become County Youghal but the manner of the boundary division with Cork would require further discussion. She also wanted to know how the council would use Molana Abbey to her advantage before granting it to them to rent. The council, rather cheekily, or over-optimistically, asked that goods taken from its members during the sacking of the town five years earlier be returned to them. The Crown simply replied that it was not possible due to the fact that such goods could not be found.[53] With the rebellion having cost close to £300,000 and innumerable of lives lost, the Youghal request may well have raised disdainfully mocking chuckles in the chambers of Westminster.

On 5 October 1586 the group of English surveyors commissioned to examine the confiscated lands of Desmond for plantation arrived in Youghal. Their meeting would most likely have taken place at the warden's house at Myrtle Grove or at the adjacent college in the orchard grounds. A committee consisting of English agents, including Valentine Browne, John Popham and Arthur Hyde sealed Raleigh's ownership of 12,000 acres. Among the party was Edmund Spenser as recorder of proceedings. The close friendship between Raleigh and Spenser had not yet developed. Spenser himself would later secure lands for his family at Kilcolman, County Cork. He was advised to build twenty-four houses for plantation families. Raleigh's possession of lands either side of the river Blackwater would finally be ratified five months later in March 1587. Such was Raleigh's influence that the committee stated that should he fail to attain all 12,000 acres, as contracted by plantation rules, everything should be done to secure his full quota. Raleigh would eventually own far more than his share, breaking all the seigniory rules.

The loose and fast attitudes in the land acquisitions of Munster led to some distasteful and unscrupulous manoeuvring amongst the various agents. The story of Arthur Hyde's problems is a perfect example of the chasm between plantation policy and plantation action. Hyde, who as a surveyor ensured the safe passage of land into Raleigh's hands, was awarded in turn with his own plot. However, he was forced to suffer a long and tiresome legal battle with the irrepressible rebel, Patrick Condon. Condon regularly terrorised Hyde and his family. In a rather ironic twist, for Hyde at least, Raleigh and a business associate would make a case for Condon in the courts. Raleigh's Machiavellian tendencies would come back to burn him though. In an equally comic turn of events, the persistent agitator, Condon, would later be central to attacks on Raleigh's land at Tallow.

The surveyors spent a number of days in Youghal discussing other deals with the property of 'traitor' Connor O'Mahoney, 'slain in rebellion', being part of the lands also given to undertakers. The committee expressed their dismay at the condition of the proposed plantation sites.[54] Having travelled the length and breadth of the plantation territory they observed to the lord treasurer and the English Council:

> We have stayed these eight days in meeting and bounding such lands as we hear Sir Walter Rawley is to have, which hath been exceedingly difficult and painful by reason that the lands having been long waste, and generally overgrown with deep grass, and in most places with heath, brambles, and furze, whereby, and by the extremity of rain and foul weather, we have been greatly hindered in our proceeding; and, for that we find all the gentlemen undertakers and their associates that came hither to be again departed into England, we surcease from further dealing therein until the spring.[55]

Despite its condition, English adventurers were confident that a rebuilding programme would yield a solid economy for the owners and a new start for the plantation families. Raleigh was rewarded for his war efforts in Munster with land 'within the counties of Waterford and Cork' amongst which were included, Inchiquin Castle, Killnatora, Ballynatray, Temple Michael, Tallow, lands adjoining Imokilly and most famously, a 'gift' of four houses and the wardenship of Our Lady's College in Youghal.[56] He would reside at the house now known as Myrtle Grove during his visits to the town. Raleigh's remit was straightforward in design and theory but more difficult than imagined in practice. The repopulation of the land with 'New English' would be carried out with tenants from the county of Devon and Somerset. English farmers would rework the rural areas while artisans, soldiers and tradesmen would rebuild and secure urban settlements like the 'decayed' village of Tallow and the port of Youghal.

The reality of emigration for the plantation families and for the undertakers did not match their hopes or imaginings. The new frontier that awaited them was rife with danger and uncertainty. Despite the separatist policy, the practicality of everyday life would inevitably force the English to interact with the Irish, whether through small trade, employment or relationships. English government officials had what might be termed rules of engagement or contractual laws for new tenants. Warnings were given to tenants that interaction with the Irish could undermine security and that they could come under the malign influence of rebels and thus be forced to help them. Tenants were told that soldiers who went out from Youghal into the countryside to collect taxes were often attacked, particularly those who ventured in small groups or without a commander. The implication was that tenants dwelling amongst rebels in the woods across the Barony of Imokilly would have their security compromised, as soldiers 'for safeguard of their lives' would act with impunity. The advice was simple and direct; if you live in the town, stay in the town.[57]

The English government's concerns about security in the rural landscape were matched by its efforts to restrict civil liberty, particularly in the interaction of people within the urban centre of Youghal. Security was tight. Residents were expected to announce their intention to leave the town and were obliged to gain permission to do so. The government also advised that tenants should arm themselves for protection of their properties, goods and neighbours but warned against taking any kind of vigilante action against rebels. They were required to report clandestine behaviour, including that suspected of each other. The climate positively reeked of post-war paranoia. It was an environment wherein Raleigh's new settlers, raw in their knowledge about potential enemies, would need to be educated and quickly. The settlers lived in constant threat of reprisals for occupying lands that had, for centuries, been home to dynastic families and Gaelic clans. Those groups, some of whom managed to successfully challenge confiscation of their lands in court, continued to live under the new arrangements while trying to evade paying full taxes. The practice of hiding what livestock they had, or placing livestock with others, was an attempt to avoid Her Majesty's sheriffs confiscating the animals for relief of the army. This outlawed habit was cited by the government as an 'ordinary custom' especially 'amongst the richer sort'. Further to this, many of the displaced Irish refused to assist in the cutting down of woods to clear the way for planters. The obstinacy of the Irish caused Raleigh enough distress to compel him to direct his grievance at the government, though he still had great support from the queen, who sent him a company of 'fresh horsemen'.[58]

Raleigh's Plantation Schemes

Walter Raleigh had a world vision, focused by pretensions of a seafaring English Empire overseeing a proliferation of colonies. His vision for Munster was no different to his vision for the 'New World' of North America, though the relationships between England and Ireland and England and America were vastly different. Raleigh would not set foot on American soil but sponsored voyages in his relentless search for fortune. In many ways he overstretched his financial capabilities to breaking point while his desire to be rich showed no strain in its elasticity. Business acumen may have suffered at the hands of creative desires, such as writing, while leadership of his plantations was anaemic due to absenteeism and financial ineptitude. His potential successes were also undermined by the difficulties planters faced. Readjusting to an openly hostile environment populated by a majority of disenfranchised and disaffected Irish was often impossible.

Raleigh may have had a reputation for soldiery and adventuring but the granting of so much land would serve to reveal his weakness as a property magnate and as a business operator. By 1587 Lismore Castle, though not part of his granted lands, was transferred to him and became his Irish seat. Youghal too, was important to Raleigh because when he needed to oversee plans for the exploration of the new world in America, mercantile connections between Youghal and Bristol were integral to his designs. Meanwhile, new Devon and Somerset families were arriving by sea in Youghal and Cork via Bristol.

The physical and ecological state of Munster following the '79 rebellion caused Raleigh plenty of discomfort. It took considerable time and effort to clear the land of overgrowth. However, as already mentioned, the clearing of the woods to make way for the new settlements would be the most consuming challenge he faced. Firstly, hostility continued between the new arrivals and the former residents. Secondly, Irish natives, though they were offered food and wages to help clear the trees, simply refused. It would be an oversimplistic assumption to suggest all the Irish were conscientious objectors. Many of them were starving and while their hearts may have been full of principle, their stomachs were crying out for relief. Non-compliance did not prevent an increasingly desperate Raleigh from using the threat of charging the Irish with treason, but they mostly ignored this. Looking for sympathy due to the hardships his plantation faced, Raleigh was forced to write to the government, but his complaints fell on deaf ears.[59] Even at the earliest stages of his programme he was under pressure. He had to make the plantation a success because England sought its own financial benefits from the venture. And whilst Raleigh struggled to secure his own rents and profits, the Crown showed little patience for his financial difficulties during the transitional period. The Dublin government also showed little respect for his reputation as the queen's favourite by dragging from his purse the trifling sums payable to England through distress warrants, evictions and costly legal processes.[60]

Whether it was the eagerness of Youghal's elite to have Raleigh at the head of the town's affairs or whether they were given no choice in the matter, Raleigh was recorded as Mayor of Youghal in 1588. However, his involvement was very limited and if he had any input in the town's affairs, it was delivered by proxy. The records show that William Magner was mayor in 1588 and 1589, though he is marked as 'Deputy to Raleigh'. It may be that Raleigh was officially mayor, but an absent one, who did not carry out any duties. It is the only occasion when a deputy is mentioned in the list of Youghal mayors between 1475 and 1800. Raleigh's absence from Youghal in 1588 was more than likely due to the Spanish Armada. The Armada had been defeated by England, and twenty-four ships, attempting a return to Spain, were forced to sail around the north of Ireland. The fleet eventually perished on the west coast. England feared a Spanish landing in Ireland and Raleigh, experienced in conflict with his old adversaries, was willing and able to confront them. However, he was frustrated by being given the less active role of policing areas of possible invasion.

Whether Raleigh was concerned or not about Youghal is impossible to know without active mayorship recorded on his part. While his and his tenants' arrivals in and around Youghal brought a much-needed boost to the local economy, following the 1579 destruction, little changed in the running of the town. Many of the wealthy families who had been officials in the town for a century and a half still held power and influence. The Coppingers, Portingals, Ronaynes, Blewetts and Walshes remained while John Merrick established a trading business on the main street that would, centuries later, become the archetypal department store. Some of the less affluent residents who had had property burned and businesses destroyed were replaced by new arrivals from England. Plantation added to the population of the town and its environs, but this may well have been offset by Irish emigration, especially to England and the Continent, as a result of the famine and natives being moved off the land.[61] For a period, employment was boosted as the landscape around Youghal changed greatly during Raleigh's time. He looked to timber as a business opportunity and he cleared the forests that had given the town its name. Employing over 150 labourers, the woods were cut down to make hogsheads, pipestaves and barrel boards for export to France and Spain. From there, the wines would be packed into the pipestaves and imported back into Youghal. However, the Privy Council made life awkward for Raleigh by putting constraints on the exports and he made a number of enemies in court.[62] By 1592 Raleigh was struggling financially and claimed that the then lord deputy at Dublin Castle, William Fitzwilliam, had 'invented' a rent of £400 to be paid to the queen. He wrote that 500 cattle were taken off his plantation by sheriffs as payment for the debt. Sympathy was thin on the ground but Raleigh complained bitterly that some of his Devon farmers 'are left with two or three [cattle] to relieve their wives and children; and in a strange country newly set down to build and plant'. Some settlers returned to England, preferring a low-risk farming lifestyle to promises of the future in Munster. His anger over the loss of tenants spiked him to remark, 'The doting Deputy hath dispeopled me.'[63]

The inability of Raleigh to make the plantations commercially effective and profitable also had an adverse effect on the economy of Youghal in regards to trading crops and cattle. With both his agricultural and industrial enterprises suffering, Raleigh found a slight reprieve in 1593 when the restrictions on the exports of timber caskets for wine were lifted, but with conditions. The reprieve would have also brought relief to the powerful merchants of Youghal who depended on exports and imports to maintain their status and privileges. Raleigh had complained that so much wood had been cut down it was beginning to rot while it sat on the land. He wanted it moved and he wanted to be paid. His labourers were also becoming restless.

Though England continued hostilities with Spain, and Raleigh was loath to pass up an opportunity to denounce that nation, the chance to profit from trade with the Spanish was not lost on him. Indeed, Spain demanded that ships arriving in its ports show proof of their Irish identity, such was the Spanish loathing for the English. No doubt Raleigh's ships coming out of Youghal passed themselves off as Irish, a common practice at the time. He was less assured in business than he was in war, compromising his previous attitudes towards Spain for the sake of profit.[64] Raleigh warned England that if the exports were halted from Youghal then other heavily wooded countries, like those in the Baltic region, would take advantage of the impasse. The Crown responded that it would take the exports but warned that Raleigh should not cut down woods on lands that belonged to the queen and had not yet been granted to new undertakers. They also told Raleigh, much to his chagrin, that other undertakers would be allowed to apply for licenses in the timber export business.

Matters deteriorated further for Raleigh as he broadened his horizons with sponsored ventures west to America. Between 1587 and 1602 he financed five expeditions to the new world to set up plantations there at a huge cost. Meanwhile, in Ireland, going into partnership in the timber export business with Edward Dodge and Veronio Martens, and later with the appropriately named Henry Pine, proved to be an error of judgement. With Raleigh's mind occupied by dreams of gold, like the ill-fated Columbus 100 years before him, and leaving his affairs in Munster to be run by a consortium, he was heading for financial ruin. In 1601 his business matters were discussed in court and it became obvious that his associate Henry Pine had 'gotten into his hands other sums of great value' by cheating Raleigh and the government. Pine was the equivalent of the modern-day insider trader and tax evader, living the good life in his castle in Mogeely. The result was that, with so much money owed, 'Sir Walter Raleigh is likely to be without recompense for his woods felled and consumed.'[65] The court ordered the immediate cessation of all exports of timber to the Continent and noted that 'in case he hath shipped any in the rivers of Youghal ... then to unload and sequestrate the same'.[66] It is impossible to know how the merchants of Youghal reacted to seeing Raleigh's ships unloaded on the quay, at least those that had not already sailed, but confidence was inevitably low. Locals could now see the physical manifestation of Raleigh's entrepreneurial collapse. One carpenter recorded, ten years later in 1611, that 7,500 trees cut down in a period of just two months were lying idle 'along the river of Youghal'.[67] He was also stung by an expensive outlay on the importation of miners from England in the vain hope of uncovering mineral resources. Munster was not the mythical land of 'El Dorado' and did not have a 'lost city of gold'. An insight into Raleigh's thinking is revealed by a passage from his account of the 1596 voyage, *The Discovery of Guiana*, when he remarked 'where there is store of gold, it is in effect needless to remember other commodities.'[68] Whether the erosion of Raleigh's business acumen was due to a romantic pursuit of a gold-laden city is impossible to conclude. However, his commercial affairs were overseen by an entrepreneurial spirit that had spread itself so thin it was transparently weak. Those 'other commodities', such as the wasted timber on the banks of the Blackwater river, appear to have interested him less than the golden beaches of Guyana.

Meanwhile, his plantation in America yielded little reward. Fifteen men who had been left on the sandy beaches of Roanoke Island, with provisions to last them for two years, all died. The Native Americans, cited as so welcoming by the Europeans, eventually found themselves, as the Gaelic Irish before them, fighting for survival. Like Munster, the full glory of the vision for Virginia would not be realised in Raleigh's lifetime.

4

Killer Poets
and Priestcraft

Edmund Spenser, Walter Raleigh, Dominic Collins and the Policy of Subordination

Raleigh's life wasn't all stress and he continued intellectual pursuits feverishly. His other significant residency in Youghal was during his second year as mayor in 1589, when he spent some time in the company of Edmund Spenser, the clerk to Lord Grey on the fateful campaign at Smerwick. Raleigh's friendship with Spenser blossomed at this time and Spenser made a visit to Youghal where, at Myrtle Grove, they no doubt discussed the state of Ireland. Spenser, admiring Raleigh as a poet, told him about his plans to write *The Faerie Queene* for Queen Elizabeth. As a clerk to the President of Munster, he had also recorded the handing over of lands to Raleigh at a sitting in Youghal with the commission of land surveyors in September 1586.[69]

Raleigh and Spenser shared the courtly visions of divine providence and civility that they believed fortune had bestowed upon them. Their literary talents gave them cause to boost each other's confidence and console each other in times of financial strain. They also shared a view of the Irish that was unforgiving in its snobbery. Raleigh visited Spenser at his estate in Kilcolman and they exchanged lavish praise, in period style, on one another through verse. Conventional Youghal wisdom, or popular history, has Spenser writing the final verses of

The Faerie Queene from a window at Myrtle Grove overlooking Youghal Bay. There is no evidence to support such claims. Both Raleigh's and Spenser's time in Youghal has been romanticised beyond recognition and reality. Spenser's connection to Youghal, regarding the writing of verse, was closer after he began a relationship with Elizabeth Boyle, a relation of Richard Boyle, who would later have Youghal as his home. However, presumptions have been made that Spenser courted Elizabeth in Youghal and that he immortalised her name with a line from his poem 'Amoretti': 'One day I wrote her name upon the strand'. The presumption is that the strand was in Youghal. This legend is disputed by claims the couple met in north Hampshire, home of Elizabeth Boyle and of distant relations to Spenser, where their courtship arose by accidental and geographical decree.[70]

Wherever Spenser's liaisons with Elizabeth Boyle took place it did not distract from his writing of *A View of the Present State of Ireland*. The tract was drafted and redrafted throughout his marriage to Elizabeth and its contents are in stark contrast to his standing as a romantic poet. It was circulated as a manuscript in the 1590s but only published as a part of his works, posthumously, in 1633. *A View of the Present State of Ireland* had three sections proposing methods for the civilising of Ireland. The first section argued that the Irish were, by nature, unable to adapt to English law. He argued it was 'vain to speak of planting of laws and plotting of policies till they [the Irish] be altogether subdued'.[71] The second and most notorious section outlined a policy advocating a militarised sweep of the country. He argued that burning the earth and slaughtering livestock could achieve control of the country. Such policies were not uncommon with others of the age. Spenser may have been impressed by the results of the famine in Munster a few years earlier in ending the Desmond rebellion and thought it a sufficient tactic for a national terrorist campaign. The final section envisaged a post-holocaust landscape whereby English manners, culture, law, religion, government and society could settle on the land. He also warned against complacency should the cleansing of the Irish be incomplete: 'If any relic of the old rebellion be found by him that either have not come in ... or ... do breakforth ... let them taste of the same cup in God's name, for it was due to them by their first guilt ... The killing, that is, must continue.'[72]

The concepts, beliefs and proposals in A *View of the Present State of Ireland* were not the workings of Spenser's imagination, they were contemporary methods of war and he was not alone in his thinking. Many of his peers reserved similar reflections in their view of Ireland and the Irish, Raleigh among them.

Nine Years' War

Raleigh's Irish fortunes were thrown into chaos when, as he and Spenser had warned, a new rebellion did 'breakforth' and the killing did indeed continue. By the time Raleigh was operating out of Lismore and Youghal and a relative peace had settled, tensions in Ulster were beginning to simmer. As in Munster, dynastic family factions in the north fought and manoeuvred with each other in attempts to win seats of power. Spenser's claim that it was impossible to put manners on the Irish seemed to bear fruit when the Earl of Tyrone, Hugh O'Neill, found himself at the centre of a political conundrum during the early years of the 1590s. He, like Gerald Fitzgerald before him in Munster, was caught between services he had given the Crown in helping settle local disputes and his resentment of the growing influence of the Crown over his autonomy. O'Neill's disputes in Ulster would eventually spread throughout the other provinces in what became known as the 'Nine Years' War' (1594–1603). The very gradual hardening of English policy in subjugating Ireland to Englishness meant Irish insurgency was sporadic, often chaotic and instigated for multiple reasons. Raleigh and Spenser would both be affected by the activity of rebels and by the time the war was over, their influence in Ireland had waned. The Nine Years' War would see Youghal once again on war alert with hardly breathing space for recovery from the '79 rebellion. The war would also throw up a Youghal martyr for Catholics but a 'devil' in the eyes of English officials. The traumatic event would split a family and a town and embody the complex relationship between religion and politics in the latter years of sixteenth-century Ireland.

Dominic Collins was born in Youghal into a wealthy Catholic family around 1566, at a time when Protestant influence was growing in the town. Dominic was a son of John Collins, who would be elected Mayor of Youghal by his business peers in 1575. He earned his education in either the first Jesuit school, which was established by William Good and Edmund Daniel in the 1560s or in the second school, which was opened in 1577 by Frs Roachford and Lea. Though persecution of Catholics was practised, celebration of mass was not altogether halted and the running of the town by the Fitzgeralds at that time meant Catholics still held positions of power. The fact that Youghal could have a Catholic mayor, and a Jewish one before Collins, in a time when England was pushing the Reformation of the Church, is evidence of the power of commerce, even over religion, in a merchant town like Youghal. However, the family fortunes were affected following the Desmond rebellion and the sacking of Youghal. Damage to property and a period of martial law meant the Collins family, like others, was forced to flee the town until it was secured for a return. At the age of 19 or 20, Dominic became one of the refugees who fled the country in 1586, the same year as the plantation surveyors arrived in Youghal. It is not known why Collins decided to leave Youghal. Given his education and family background he had every chance of obtaining a relatively successful life in Ireland. It may have been that a young Collins held hopes of a religious calling and foresaw difficulties in such a life with the increasing influence of a Protestant plantation around Youghal and the arrival of Raleigh. It is equally plausible that Collins simply fell out with his family. A number of family members are recorded as important figures in the town throughout the Nine Years' War and after. It might be argued elsewhere that the migration of young Jesuit scholars was common at this time and that Collins was part of that trend. However, he did not enter a religious order, college or school when he arrived on the Continent. Whatever the reason for his departure, the young man's fate would return him to Youghal in equally lonely circumstance.

Taking a ship from Youghal bound for France, Collins travelled to Nantes having landed at Les Sables d'Olonne. Throughout his early twenties he took a number of jobs working at inn houses to pay his way. His life then took a significant turn with entry into the cavalry. For almost a decade he moved through the ranks to captain and was well practised in the arts of war, having fought the Protestant Huguenots of Brittany as a member of the Catholic League. His burgeoning reputation was rewarded with the title 'Military Governor of Lepena'. By this time Collins was likely to have been aware of Hugh O'Neill's growing 'Catholic Confederacy' in Ireland, although O'Neill at this point refused to spread the war into other provinces.[73] By 1598 however, France had declared war on Spain, and Collins, sensing a more secure life in the Iberian sun, landed at San Sebastián later in the same year. His religious fervour turned to vocation once he met Fr Thomas White, a native of Clonmel. Collins required some gifts of persuasion, requesting entry to the holy order of the Society of Jesus a number of times before White agreed.

Now a seasoned campaigner in war and in his thirties, Collins cut the figure of the model Jesuit warrior after the fashion of its Spanish founder, Ignatius of Loyola. He was not long into his religious development when the proposition was put to him to leave Spain and support the Catholic Confederacy of O'Neill and O'Donnell that was gathering pace in his homeland. Dominic's motives for signing up to a proposed Spanish invasion may have been driven by his religious leanings. The war against Protestantism was a continual aspect to his life as a soldier and friar. Thoughts of his family in Youghal would surely have occupied the spaces between his thinking. Collins's decision to return to Ireland as a European soldier for the Catholic cause may also have been swayed by the actions of another Jesuit, James Archer, who was an activist in religious war both in Ireland and abroad. Archer was also a colleague of Fr Thomas White, though Collins did not have personal contact with Archer until the winter of 1601.[74]

While Collins grew from an emigrant worker to a religious man of firm reputation and conviction, spilled Ulster blood seeped slowly across the Irish landscape. The Crown wanted Ulster shired with an introduction of garrisons and sheriffs. Not for the first time a call for support from Phillip II of Spain was made by chiefs and bishops to aid the Catholic Irish resistance to Elizabeth's northern plantation and governing programme. While rebels Hugh Roe O'Donnell and Hugh Maguire began a campaign at Enniskillen in June 1594, Hugh O'Neill had gone to Dublin to barter with English officials for exclusive control over Ulster. However, a less-than-confident government, divided in their opinion of O'Neill and, suspicious of his motives, they could not finalise a clear policy with the earl. Queen Elizabeth also dithered, just as she had done with Fitzgerald, holding out hope that O'Neill would remain loyal. Frustrated by England's intransigence, O'Neill joined the rebellion.[75] By 1595 he fronted a northern Gaelic army, which unlike those of Munster in the winter of '79, were drilled efficiently, with veterans from both the English and Spanish armies in the ranks. More importantly, the weaponry had advanced from javelins, swords, axes and bows to muskets, which made up at least a third of the armoury.[76] The image of a Catholic Confederacy would ignite the imaginations of the dispossessed both in Ireland and abroad, most notably amongst the Catholic soldiers of Spain, such as Collins.

The economy in Ireland was paralysed by food shortages, rising food prices and the general costs of war. The veteran of the 1579 rebellion, 'Black Tom' Butler, Earl of Ormond, now head of military operations, made vain attempts to broker peace with O'Neill. However, O'Neill's reputation only grew after the Battle of Yellow Ford saw 830 of the English army killed.[77] By late 1598, buoyed by O'Neill's success, insurgents in Munster attacked plantations in Limerick and assaults spread through the counties. The O'Connors and the O'Moores, whose families had been dispossessed of land for plantations in 1556, attacked settlements in Leinster.[78] Youghal remained relatively safe but on constant alert. Its relative security was partly due to the influence of Butler, despite his uneasy relationship with the absent Raleigh. On 28 October Butler visited Youghal to make an inspection of the troops in the garrison. He found them ill equipped, but there was consolation in the amount of fresh beef in the town. Butler ordered it be preserved in barrels of salt and kept for soldiers so the town could be protected with a fit military presence. The army was large enough to have two Captains, Forde and Flower as well as Major Kingsmill. For now, Butler had a secure footing in Munster and Youghal was grateful for his presence as well as their shared loyalty to Elizabeth.

Both Raleigh's and Spenser's interests in Munster were being eroded by rebellious activity in the south. Whatever hopes Raleigh had of his Munster plantation yielding a golden period of Englishness and of personal fortune they were now fast diminishing. The rebels repossessed land at Kilcolman and Tallow, with Spenser's home burned to the ground. Meanwhile, news broke that James Fitzthomas, the late Gerald Fitzgerald's nephew, was proclaimed by O'Neill as the successor to the Earldom of Desmond. Such news must have brought back fearful memories for the residents of Youghal of the 1579 sacking of the town. With uprisings spreading throughout the provinces, the Crown responded by sending a force exceeding 17,000 men led by the Earl of Essex, Robert Devereaux, into Ireland. Much to Youghal's relief, half of this force would march south on Munster. Essex's campaign failed however. Raleigh attacked his reputation and character, warning Queen Elizabeth, as he had done with Butler, that Lord Essex was too lenient with the Irish.

By 1600, O'Neill was marching south. The Jesuit priest and activist, James Archer, carried a letter from O'Neill to Spain calling for its support against England. Queen Elizabeth now faced the very real danger of a Spanish invasion. Archer's letter was accepted by Spain while O'Neill's religious representative, Peter Lombard, tried to sell the concept of a Catholic crusade in Ireland to Pope Clement III in Rome. Much to the relief of Protestants and nervous Catholic merchants in Youghal, the rebellion, in Munster at least, was halted with the appointment of Sir George Carew as president of the province. Carew, a close friend of Raleigh, was well aware of the role of James Archer and also of Dominic Collins in the possible invasion of Ireland by Spain. Carew secured the safety of Munster during 1600. The new Lord Deputy of Ireland, Charles Blount Mountjoy, also marked out Youghal for high regard, due to its reputation and economic value. He wrote a letter to Carew urging that a company of the army under Lord Audeley be kept in the town because, '[it] being a place his Lordship desireth above any other, in regard of that commodity it affordeth of hearing out of England, and those parts where he hath most to do.'[79]

Meanwhile, O'Neill's confidence was reignited when news of Spanish ships arriving at the south coast reached him. Two Spanish squadrons had departed Belem on 3 September 1601 with Dominic Collins on board one of them. He sailed under Captain Zubiar. Archer sailed with the larger fleet under Don Juan D'Aquila, which landed at Kinsale twenty days later with 3,400 men. Zubiar's forces, having been separated from D'Aquila by a storm, joined up with Munster rebel O'Sullivan Beare at Castlehaven. Around the same time, O'Neill and O'Donnell joined forces in Munster having taken separate routes south to the province. The English were also camped with a force of 7,000 besieging Kinsale under the command of Mountjoy.

On Christmas Eve the Irish assault on the English camps was repelled and defeated. Coupled with the siege at Kinsale the rebellion was effectively running out of oxygen. The two events were a fatal blow to the pretensions of creating a Gaelic and Catholic Irish nation, or at least the imaginings of one. The Spanish squadrons were allowed to turn about and leave. Rebel leader O'Donnell, fleeing to Spain to find further assistance, died there. Meanwhile, O'Neill returned north, his national campaign shrinking back to concerns of the micro-rebellion of Ulster, where he would continue skirmishes for local interests. Mountjoy pursued him as the momentum of, and confidence in, the rebellion faded.

James Archer and Dominic Collins, cut loose from the departed Spanish forces, were now held up at O'Sullivan's castle at Dunboy throughout the winter of 1601. The following May, George Carew wrote about Archer and Collins as he continued his campaign against those left behind after the failed rebellion. He marked Archer as a 'priest that conjures the foul weather … if he remains in Dunboy I hope to conjure his head in a halter.' He then revealed his disdain for Collins while making an interesting fact about his connection to Youghal: 'He [Archer] hath a fellow devil to help him, one Dominic Collins, a friar, who in his youth was a scholar and brother to him that was this last year mayor of Youghal.'[80] The records show that the Mayor of Youghal in 1600 was Walter Collyne. The spelling of the name on the record may be wrong and it is very unlikely that Carew was mistaken given the powers of the mayors in the towns and their associations to figures such as the President of Munster in all matters. Also, the fact that mayorships were typically kept within wealthy merchant families such as the Collins family in Youghal made Walter's position inevitable following his father's title as mayor in 1575. If Walter was indeed Dominic's brother it makes for an intriguing familial division. As mayor, it would have been incumbent on Walter to do everything to protect Youghal against rebellion. He would be obliged to declare the town's allegiance to the Crown. Most intriguingly though, he would no doubt have been aware, as Carew was, that his brother, Dominic, who he had not seen since childhood, was besieged with rebels at Dunboy Castle.

In June 1602 Archer and O'Sullivan left Dunboy Castle to meet a Spanish vessel that was carrying powder, ammunition, food and gold further west to the Kerry coast.[81] O'Sullivan and Archer remained at Ardea, optimistically awaiting the next Spanish fleet. At Dunboy, Carew relentlessly pelted the castle wherein the seventy-seven remaining rebels hung on grimly. According to some later reports, namely from O'Sullivan, Collins offered himself up as an intermediary to save the besieged. The castle was eventually taken with Collins, McSwiney and Taylor surviving the mass execution of the remaining insurgents. Collins would spend the next four months in Cork Prison where he

was interrogated for information. Carew wrote that Collins was a
stubborn interviewee and hinted that offers were made in exchange
for intelligence.

> The fryer, in whom no penitence appeared for his detestable treasons,
> nor yet would endeavor to merit his life, either by discovering the
> Rebels' intention, (which was in his power) or by doing some service
> that might deserve favour.[82]

The nature of the 'service' to which Carew refers is unknown but
certainly Collins was kept alive for four months due to his connections
in Spain and the intelligence he had about James Archer and
O'Sullivan, who were still being hunted. O'Sullivan would later attest
that Collins was offered high positions within the Church of Ireland in
return for information. By late October 1602, while Collins languished
in appalling conditions at His Majesty's pleasure, the rebellion was all
but crushed. Ulster was left in much the same condition as Munster
twenty years previously. Thousands had died from famine. Spenser's
vision for war was realized with livestock being slaughtered and crops
destroyed. The plantation of Ulster that would follow differed from the
experience of settlers in Munster. The Crown had learned from past
mistakes. The plantation would be a success.

The End of the Road

The first three years of the new century would see the seeds of
economic and social recovery planted in Youghal and in other parts
of Munster. A number of the old players involved in the previous
tumultuous fifty years were either dying or were about to lift off from
the gravity of their mortal coils. In 1602 Raleigh's world vision and
his place in it were becoming increasingly myopic as his wealth
diminished. A man who had courted dreams of an English empire,
with his own hand and mind the signatures of its ideals, through
adventure, piracy and colonialism, was navigating his sinking ship
towards the rocks of personal and public humiliation. Raleigh's
sixteen-year association with his Munster lands came to an end when,

in December 1602, he sold the estate, then known as the Seignory of Inchiquin, to Richard Boyle for only £1,500, the purchase having been made on the insistence of Carew, Lord President of Munster, who also acted as broker.[83] Two months previously to Raleigh's financial collapse, Dominic Collins was taken from Cork Prison and was publicly hanged for treason at North Main Street, Youghal on 31 October. While Raleigh was perhaps relieved to see the back of Ireland and Youghal with exotic visions of foreign riches still fixed in his imagination, Collins's return home after sixteen or so years held no such allusions of glory on the horizon. What affect his return had on the Collins family is unknown. Nor indeed is it possible to cite what family members were present on the day of Dominic's execution. There is no record to state the presence of his mother or father or whether they were still alive. Walter Collins would surely have witnessed the hanging as an important public figure and former mayor from only two years before. Other Collins names possibly present were John and Patrick who would serve as bailiffs in Youghal in 1608 and 1610 respectively, as would Jasper Collins in 1633. If they were present then the dynamic between Dominic's execution and his family's position in the town serves as the epitome of social and religious tensions in Youghal and, by extension, Munster and Ireland at the time.

James Archer, Collins' Jesuit colleague, received an account of the execution on 19 January 1603. A man named Richard Haries sent the description in a letter. Haries stated that Collins spoke out in defence of the Catholic religion using a number of languages, including Irish, English and Spanish. A local fisherman was ordered to put the noose around Collins's neck and carry out the execution. Collins's body hung from the gallows for a number of hours before falling to the street when the rope snapped. The body was left naked after it was stripped of its clothing. Haries claimed that the body was removed under the cover of dark and buried,[84] but there is no account of where. It is unlikely that the local Catholics would have risked taking his body into the grounds of St Mary's Collegiate Church or carried it back up King's Street in open view of soldiers. The most likely outcome may have seen locals pay the north gatekeeper, being on the site of the erected gallows, to have the body ejected quickly and taken to the grounds of the decaying North Abbey.

On 24 March 1603, Queen Elizabeth died. She had wanted the conflict in Ireland to come to an end. The Irish wars of the preceding decades had cost the Crown exchequer more than the wars against Spain and the protection of Protestantism in the Low Countries and France. Six days after her death Hugh O'Neill, unaware of her passing, signed the treaty of Mellifont. Elizabeth took the Irish pretensions of the birth of a nation with her to the grave. Four months later, Walter Raleigh was arrested for conspiracy against the newly crowned King James I. He spent thirteen years in the Tower of London, much of the time writing A *History of the World*. After release in 1616 he took an ill-fated trip to Guyana, where his officers attacked a Spanish settlement a year later. It was the wrong action at the wrong time and he again fell foul of James I, who was trying to broker a peace with Spain. Raleigh was beheaded in 1618.

Both Raleigh's and Spenser's names have endured in Youghal folklore, so much so that the stories have overshadowed Collins's role in the events that shaped the town. When writing his *New Hand-book for Youghal* Samuel Hayman painted a picture of Raleigh and Spenser with a romance that swells the reputation of both men into prominent roles in Youghal's history. Describing their meetings at the house of Myrtle Grove, he states:

> In the gardens, the potato, originally brought from Virginia, was first planted in Ireland. Here also ... is a group of four aged yew-trees, which local tradition has ever associated with Raleigh's name. Beneath their shade he may often have sate, in his fixed musings on El Dorado which he was never to find; and here, perhaps, in more active moments, were composed some of those writings which remain to our own day, to prove him an almost universal genius. What needs it more to heighten the beauty of the ideal picture, than to image Spenser on a bright summer day his companion, while Raleigh lingers over the Faerie Queene, as yet in manuscript, and, with sudden start of joy, pronounces the fiat, that gave it forth to an admiring world?[85]

The misunderstood tale of Raleigh planting the first potato in the garden of Myrtle Grove should not be underestimated as an insignificant one because it protects and reinforces his reputation as a major player in Ireland's good fortune.[86] The potato became a staple diet of the Irish, assisting in population growth and boosting the economy. English writers who viewed Raleigh with sentimental awe were keen to promote the notion that he was a benevolent adventurer and benefactor to the Irish, singularly responsible for introducing such a vital product to a grateful nation. The real origin of the Irish potato is far less exciting. The potato had been brought to the south coast of Ireland by trading Spanish ships in the decades before Raleigh was granted his estate and his own ships sailed to Virginia. The Spanish had been travelling back and forth to the potato's place of origin, South America, for over one hundred years. There is serious doubt, given the breadth of Spanish trade along the south coast, that the first potato was even planted in Youghal. The writing of Raleigh into Youghal's history portrays a man with the foresight to add to the nation's worth rather than the fact that he only added to the nation's woes and was an apologist for creating a famine that killed an estimated 30,000 people during the Desmond rebellion.

Raleigh's exploits, in the time of his land ownership and position on the mayor's seat in Youghal, were in fact a catalogue of ill-judged business decisions. The killer-poet struggled to make the vision of a New England that was at the core of his superiority complex a reality. And while he did not directly order the destruction of the traditional Catholic sites in Youghal such as North Abbey, the Dominican Friary was allowed to fall into disrepair, as was Our Lady's College close to Raleigh's residence at Myrtle Grove. Both artefacts were reminders of the history of the despised Fitzgeralds. Contrary to Raleigh's apathy, Queen Elizabeth had ordered Our Lady's College of Youghal be maintained. In the culture of Renaissance thinking, which included reading ancient texts, and where education was a high priority to becoming a gentleman of the court, it would have been prudent for Raleigh to continue and even promote the college's reputation, for financial reasons if for nothing else. However, it had been a Catholic centre and for all the grandiose posturing of Raleigh's English intelligentsia the balance was weighed toward neglect because of bigotry. The government's policy was clearly stated: 'we must put a stop to priest-craft and superstition in Ireland: we must take the responsibility of educating the Irish in our own way.'[87]

Raleigh tried to plant an English rose on an Irish grave, but its roots could never grip a soil so damp with fresh blood. Spenser, too has frustrated historians, academics and lovers of literature because the image of arguably England's greatest poet advocating a scorched-earth policy, which called for ethnic cleansing through famine, is such a difficult one for them to reconcile. Certainly, the popular image of these two courtly gentlemen in Raleigh's garden in Youghal, in awe of each other's aspirations, under the trees, writing verse, that so warmed the heart of Samuel Hayman, is as tragic to the integrity of truth as it is befitting of myth. Had Hayman been present in this 'garden of earthly delights' he was as likely to hear something much darker than Raleigh's awe-filled sighs as he lingered over the drafts of *The Faerie Queene*. He might instead have seen Raleigh nod in agreement to Spenser's view that the Irish

> use all the beastly behaviour that may be, they oppress all men, they spoil as well the subject, as the enemy; they steal, they are cruel and bloody, full of revenge, and delighting in deadly execution, licentious, swearers and blasphemers, common ravishers of women, and murderers of children.

Raleigh's and Spenser's passing, the failed rebellions and the general peace that settled after offered Youghal an opportunity to fulfil its economic potential. For the next four decades the town would be the heartbeat of an Anglo-'tiger economy' with Ireland's first millionaire at the helm.

5

Rise of the
Nouveau Riche

Life in Youghal under Richard Boyle
and the New English

On the right-hand side of St Mary's Collegiate Church in Youghal, in the south transept, is a rather ostentatious tomb. It was built in 1620 and expanded in 1642–43. The tomb houses the body of Sir Richard Boyle, 1st Earl of Cork and several others. The tomb's vainglorious opulence betrays a brutal, even uncouth, lack of modesty. The monument is, in many ways, a representation of the man's vision of himself and an attempt to place his name, in this most historic site, in the company of noble lords also buried in the transept. It features statuettes of Boyle, his two wives and fifteen children. The monument demands the onlooker to imagine greatness and respect. The gate that surrounds it is joined at the centre by a set of arms, his mother's.[88]

Boyle is rarely referred to by historians as having any humility. That is not to say that characters doused in narcissism, while generally despised by contemporaries, are sometimes only loved by their mothers, for which they are eternally grateful. Boyle also has monuments in St Patrick's, Dublin, and two in Kent, England, but the Youghal monument is his eternal resting place. There is no doubt that Boyle loved the town. For four decades he was its master and his seat there was the capital of his Anglo-'tiger economy'.

He was a man without noble relations but his entrepreneurial spirit drove an unprecedented rise to fortune and power. For that success, he was often resented by his English peers as the epitome of the vulgar nouveau-riche who had prospered by ill-gotten gains. Youghal town and its population could not have cared after decades of war, famine, emigration, economic neglect and uncertainty. Unlike Raleigh, Boyle was not a soldier, nor did he have a world vision to distract him from the devil in the details when it came to business. And unlike Raleigh, he improved the life of Youghal's residents rather than use the town as a geographic springboard from which to explore the imaginings of lost cities. Indeed, Boyle understood, all too well, the value of property and land. While Raleigh had no centre, Boyle planted the English rose that Raleigh could not grow deep into the core of his mini-empire with roots so entangled in complex legalities it would take the English Crown decades of investigation to unravel them. For Boyle, business was business. When Raleigh returned to Munster in 1617, before his ill-fated voyage to Guyana, Boyle gave him supplies and money for the journey. It was an exchange that characterised the direction of both men's destinies.

Boyle's life is documented in detail elsewhere but it is noteworthy, in understanding his relationship with Youghal and his successes there, that his beginnings were humble. He had an unremarkable education and limited legal training. In 1590 he came to Ireland to seek employment as a clerk. He was exposed to legal documents centred on the escheating of land following the 1579–83 rebellion. He was astute and read the post-war chaos as a blank ledger onto which he could write his own fortune, keeping all documentation – patents, conveyances, leases and letters.[89] His first time in Ireland was a mixed blessing. While he busied himself concealing deeds and contracts, thereby acquiring land that should have gone to the Crown, the country was in turmoil throughout the Nine Years' War. Many of the estates he illegally acquired were overrun by rebel activity. His first wife died during childbirth and when the war was reaching its height in 1598 he took refuge in London. Boyle was being monitored by English officials obsessed with how the distribution of land to new undertakers and adventurers was being administered. He came under the spotlight and was accused of privately selling the queen's land for his own gain. Boyle managed to deflect the charges and returned to Munster in 1600, this time as a clerk of the court. While Raleigh's fortunes began to fade in tandem with Elizabeth's health and the Nine Years' War came to a close, Boyle's rise to prominence would usher in a new dawn for the town of Youghal.

Between 1600 and 1603, Boyle made a great ally in the President of Munster, George Carew, nemesis to Dominic Collins. Carew had also spent time in Youghal, either at Myrtle Grove or at Our Lady's College, as a friend of Raleigh.

Boyle worked relentlessly to secure the best land opportunities for Carew while ensuring Carew's influence was maintained through strong commercial connections. He reported regular intelligence about the sociopolitical dynamic in Munster to Carew, and in a relatively short space of time he had become indispensable in the running of Carew's affairs. In return, the grateful President of Munster secured a pardon for Boyle's past misdemeanours. This was achieved prior to Queen Elizabeth's death. Carew also brokered the deal between Raleigh and Boyle for Raleigh's estate and used his considerable connections to have Boyle knighted on 25 June 1603, Boyle's wedding day. The previously humble clerk was now a legitimate operator, a knight of the Crown and master of vast swaths of land in Munster. He secured Molana Abbey, the Church lands of Lismore and, what would later be the most contentious piece of property in his heaving portfolio, Our Lady's College of Youghal.

Boyle's sense of timing, or luck, could not have been better. His ability to seize an opportunity, leave personal animosities aside for the sake of business and promote a network of influential connections were the ideal attributes for an environment of post-war economics and coming peace. Elizabeth's death, the exhaustion brought to the Crown by multiple wars, the sheer weight of expense and a change in dynamic with the incoming King James I only added to Boyle's good fortune. The king lapsed into a laissez-faire policy toward Ireland, having broader concerns such as attempting to broker peace with Spain. All of these factors worked in favour of not just Boyle but his soon-to-be home of Youghal. His success enabled and promoted confidence in the continuing arrival of a significant number of English newcomers. He planted the town of Clonakilty, developed Bandon and started building projects that brought employment and prosperity to Youghal, Lismore, Dungarvan and Tallow. Industries such as linen-weaving, iron-smelting, timber trades and glass manufacture were established. Boyle effectively changed the economic, social and political landscape.[90]

Boyle's rise to fame and fortune was meteoric. From clerk to the Presidential Council of Munster and knighthood he was created Baron of Youghal on 6 September 1606 before being promoted to Irish Privy Counsellor on 15 February 1613. A seat in parliament for Lismore followed this success in 1614. He was then to become the 1st Earl of Cork and Viscount Dungarvan in October 1620, Lord Justice of Ireland in October 1629, Lord High Treasurer of Ireland almost two years to the day in 1631, and finally, an English Privy Counsellor in June 1640, by which time his elaborate tomb was well under expansion at St Mary's, Youghal. He would however, eventually, on his way up, be faced down for his property acquisitions by Crown officials. They found Boyle's business dealings to be as abhorrent as his character. The College of Youghal would be their main focus point of contention. However, for the next four decades both Boyle and Youghal grew together.

Controlling the Markets

Boyle inherited a town with huge potential in Youghal. The challenge presented to him was maximising that potential through official control. Youghal was at the centre of a landscape in constant growth and flux. The ebb and flow of social and political dynamics ranged, at their extremes, from a lawless frontier to obsessive government bureaucracy. Its position on the mouth of the Blackwater meant trade continued to bring economic security. Many inland routes were simply impassable due to the poor conditions of the roads and wet weather. Travelling long distances to trade goods on the highways brought its own obvious dangers but it was also made unattractive by a lack of inns or alehouses where travellers could find accommodation, food and drink. Therefore, trading by river and sea routes presented Youghal with the opportunities to maximise its business potential. Timber, linen and wool were the main exports at the beginning of the new century with commodities being sent to England, France, the Netherlands and the Mediterranean. The main imports included coal from South Wales, wine, iron and salt from Spain, which was used in Youghal for preserving meat, and more crucially the bounty of fish ever present on the quays, shops and main street.[91] During Boyle's early years at Youghal, town officials tried for a second time to have County Cork divided in two. A county of Youghal, they argued, would allow the town to be run more efficiently given the often haphazard infrastructure linking Youghal to Cork, as mentioned above, stating, 'that county, being about 100 miles long … sheriffs, and other ordinary officery ministers of justice … cannot be at hand to answer the services of the country.'[92] For now though, the council and Boyle had to concern themselves with the running of the town.

The main street itself became a commercial hub with shops beginning to emerge next to trades and businesses. They had ready-made consumers within the walled centre selling meat, bread, fish, spices, salt, sugar and tea. Such was the coast's abundance of herrings and cod that it attracted the attentions of ships from both Spain and France. Such visits were not always welcomed by officials in Youghal. Indeed, the corporation was obsessed with supervising trade, tariffs, rents and rates in order to control the economy and often set down stringent rules regarding times and locations of trade. Trading beyond the walls with 'foreign merchants' and bringing in the goods to sell in town was outlawed. Vigilant monitoring of trade meant all goods had to be presented to the Mayor of Youghal for inspection upon the quay walls, and the practice of going aboard vessels to privately barter, even for fish, was also outlawed.

The town had, almost by accident, gained a monopoly on the export of wool. Sheep farming had improved due to the plantations and the government sought ways to ensure the wool was exported to designated ports in England rather than in haphazard and private trading with Continental merchants. An offer was put to eight ports in Ireland to refurbish their old staple system of trade and taxation.

All except the port of Youghal declined and it thereby secured its monopoly. However, the consequence was an upsurge in wool smuggling and envy from competitors like the merchants of Cork. Securing the staple privileges was necessary to boost corporation accounts and strengthened Youghal's commercial connection to England. And while the elite of the town had first and richest pickings of imported goods, the increased traffic in trade also had a knock-on effect on all businesses in the town centre. Confining the trade to within the town walls helped the corporation's books and market days were closely policed. Hucksters were encouraged to set up stalls on the streets so that the 'poorer sort' could trade goods, but these were limited items and hucksters were forbidden to sell any commodities that were sold by merchants on market days such as fish, eggs, fruit, cheese and bread.

The measure of activity on market days presented problems other than just policing, as did the claustrophobic nature of the housing and narrow streets. Without plumbing or proper sanitation, infections and illness were common. Residents had little choice but to dump human waste outside their houses and businesses. Hogs, goats, cattle, pigs, cats, dogs, horses and fowl often roamed freely to the extent that the council lamented that the 'enclosed parks and pastures about the town are often by them spoiled and broken down.' Meanwhile, raw meat and fish were hung from poles outside shops. The stench permeating from this tightly bound, interactive social environment inevitably attracted rodents, seagulls and flies. Some social responsibilities were, however, made incumbent on residents and cleaning the streets was of paramount importance in the welfare of the town's citizens. A scavenger, or rubbish collector, was employed to offset the dangers of disease and the general stench 'to carry away the filth … on Wednesdays and Saturdays … to the scavenge [town dump]'.[93]

Perhaps the best example of the type of social claustrophobia experienced in Boyle's bustling urban centre was the construction changes demanded of dwellers following a near-disaster on the night of 6 December 1616 when a fire almost decimated the town centre. It was passed into law following the event that 'there shall be no thatched house hence forward erected in any place within the Town walls.'

Anyone with a timber or wattle chimney was told to 'pull it down and build another with stone.' The council placed two long ladders at the side of the Market House at the centre of town with '4 great iron hooks' and 'twelve leather buckets to be in readiness for quenching fires hanged up in the Town Hall'.[94]

A Militia Town

Despite a prolonged peace from 1603 to the mid-1620s, Youghal residents were encouraged to arm themselves. Though constables and bailiffs operated in watching and keeping the peace it was required of all residents to train in the art of using weapons. The council administered halberts (spears with battle axe attached) or black bills (spears with hooks) at a cost of five schillings. Residents were told to have the weapons ready for watching the walls and gates at night but were advised not to carry swords or pikes because they were 'not sufficient weapon in peaceable times'. This residency militia, as they might be called, were to have captains that would be provided with 'a good sword by his side, a culliver or musquet upon his shoulder, powder and bullets accordingly'. The social contract extended to residents carrying out militia-style training throughout the year:

> That every resident within the Town and liberties shall train and muster thrice a year for the good of the Town, May day and Easter Tuesday, from the age of 16 to 50, Aldermen and those of the Council excepted, to be ready to accompany the Mayor.[95]

Further to these measures, the Deputy of Ireland, Oliver St John, warned Boyle in an official letter in the summer of 1620 that the Youghal council was compromising the security of the town by renting a blockhouse for commercial use rather than stocking it with munitions for protection of the town. 'I pray you to call that Corporation together, and to let them know,' he wrote. The blockhouse referred to here may be the water fort at the head of the quay south of Quay Gate. Boyle's Youghal was a teeming mini-metropolis of early modern society and the measures seen here reveal the fragility of peace as viewed by officials, for which they had good reason. This was a town where Common Street, King's Street, the Trinity Castle, South Gate, North Gate, Water Gate and the Quay Gate were hives of activity, populated by locals and by traders of many nationalities, many carrying personal weapons such as muskets, calivers, (rifle) handguns, pistols, swords, rapiers and blades.

As a relatively wealthy urban centre and a location that offered employment, Youghal often attracted arrivals from rural settings looking to change their fortunes. Civil rights did not exist for strays and wanderers, while outsiders of a less than prosperous disposition were referred to as 'idle and lewd persons, being banished and as it were spued out of other good-governed towns'. These were expected to be presented before the Mayor and swear allegiance to His Majesty and the corporation.[96] Indeed, such was the level of human traffic in and out of Youghal that the council initiated a tax against people housing stray orphans. Though the town had several gates whereby people came and went, dilapidation of the walls allowed for covert trespass.

In the deputy's letter to Boyle there was a warning about the town walls. He advised Boyle that the town mayor should make sure all holes in the 'King's walls' be filled and if he failed to do so that he would be called before the Lord President of Munster to explain why not. Boyle responded and a programme of rebuilding took place, the best part of which remains today. However, he also allowed holes in the walls to become private gateways, particularly on the quay walls. It appears he was lenient in this regard with town officials, some of whom had gardens that ran from their houses on King's Street to the edge of the water. To the poor who lived in the stretches of land in the liberties beyond the walls, and across the river, the town may have appeared as a mini-metropolis, full of food and goods that caused them envy. Robberies were a regular occurrence with boats bringing thieves to the quayside in search of illegal access to gardens and houses through holes in the King's Wall. Thieves also gained entrance under the dark of night through holes in the walls along the hillside behind the town. It was passed by the council that because 'some of the inhabitants have been robbed, and ill-disposed persons pass in and out by night, Ordered, that said holes, shall before 25 July next be stopped up with lime and stone by those who use them'.

Crime and Punishment

How much notice Boyle actually took of directions from Dublin is difficult to evaluate, but the elite of the town certainly acted in a superior manner and set bylaws that were both self-serving and exclusive to class. Penalties for crimes were often related directly to whom the crime was committed against, as in the case of the abuse of girls and women. Of particular concern to the council of the day were 'young and silly virgin maids' who could be 'deflowered' by 'lewd and incontinent persons, not regarding God or goodness'. Of even higher importance, however, was the setting of fines. To deflower a mayor's daughter would carry a hefty £40 fine, whereas a groome's (horse groomer's) daughter carried the lesser charge of £5. The hierarchy of power was related directly to the severity of the fines and men of importance had their daughters protected according to their standing – 'an Alderman's daughter, 30li.; a Baylive's daughter, 20li. any Freeman's daughter, 10li'.[97]

General lawlessness in the town prompted the call for a jail to be erected inside the South Gate at the entrance to Base Town. There were other methods of public humiliation on the streets of Youghal with stocks and pillory cages, as well as public whippings, common sights to act as deterrents. As one would expect, alcohol played a significant role in the cause of many misdemeanours. Tradespeople in Youghal, the crucial cogs in the workings of its early modern society, were banned from running alehouses. Town officials were dismayed 'as is daily manifested' to see 'loose and idle people though having trades and mechanical mysteries themselves' spend their time 'keeping of lewd and incontinent tippling, alehouses and taphouses, to the great increase of idleness'. And so the law was passed that 'no tradesman ... shall keep any common inn ... or in his house sell any manner of wine, aquavite (strong alcohol), beer or ale.'[98] Drinking was certainly not outlawed but those who drank during church service were policed, apprehended and charged. The church warden and a constable were assigned to go through the town 'after the reading of the first lesson' to find anyone drinking and report it to the mayor. Alehouses and taverns were also inspected once every two weeks during service with fines handed out to both drinkers and proprietors, with the money going to the church.[99]

Piracy in the Bay

The apparently organised social chaos of early modern Youghal lent itself to the requirement of a strong political backbone and management. The placement of Boyle and others within this new and ever-expanding English venture opened colonial wounds, not just between the New English and the Anglo-Irish and Gaelic-Irish but between the New English adventurers and the Crown. Boyle's rise in fortune continued apace and was assisted by others who watched his success and desired to be a part of it. English officials in London and Dublin cast an envious eye. Boyle may have viewed their close attentions as a contradiction. It might have appeared to him that he was, in fact, living out the wishes of those who had gone before, like Raleigh and Spenser. They had envisaged a Munster that yielded a profitable economy for the Protestant ruling elite while bringing civility and cultural change. Boyle may well have thought that his good fortune had brought about such change. But nothing is ever so straightforward and Ireland, particularly the south and south-west, was a land occupied by speculators, adventurers and privateers. Many of these men had personal prestige in mind over England's desire to bring Ireland peacefully in line under King James I.

Whatever the concerns of officialdom, of which Boyle was to become a part of later in his career, new undertakers and planters from England viewed Ireland as a prosperous destination. During his political progress Boyle created the plantation town of Clonakilty. Writing to then Deputy of Ireland, Lord Chichester, he enthused, 'For that is a most convenient place for a town, where I have already made a plantation of some hundred English families.'[100] Many of those who had settled entered into private business ventures. While Youghal had strict codes of practice for trading, smaller towns and port villages, some in West Cork like Schull, Ballydehob and Baltimore, profited from dealing with roaming coastline pirates. Many of these were English with others hailing from the North African Barbary Coast. Pirates acted with impunity off the coast of Ireland and were often as not left alone by the English government, who appeared to encourage the black market. Some local English officials were former mariners with their own piratical backgrounds, which often disabled the arms of the judiciary and compromised criminal prosecutions through corrupt influence. Boyle showed some of his political skill in keeping Youghal safe from piracy while entering into business ventures with characters such as William Hull. Hull had a brief career of piracy in the Mediterranean before settling down in Leamcon, Schull. The two men agreed to go into partnership in fisheries but, for reasons unknown, Boyle withdrew his interest in 1618. In a typical Boylean act of business, the Baron of Youghal gave away his sister-in-law at St Mary's altar to Hull in January 1622. The two were now connected through family, and Hull acted as rent collector for Boyle in the far reaches of his Munster empire. Hull, in turn, benefitted from Boyle's patronage, which also legitimised Hull's character and standing in the social order.[101] While Boyle was quite relaxed in making connections with adventurers of ill-repute he did not want his beloved town of Youghal to succumb to the same vagaries as trading with pirates and wrote to Chichester insisting that he receive assistance in 'protecting' his plantations:

> The townsmen of Youghal have lately surprised at the mouth of the harbour one Angas, with 5 other pirates who were shipped in a new French bottom of 25 tuns, in which there were 4 and 5 tuns of Gascoyne Wines, whose taking Mr. Parsons can at large relate, and so beseeching your Lop. to enable these Corporations, with such addition of liberties as may encourage the English inhabitants to strengthen and enable my plantations.[102]

Despite his concerns, the anarchy on the waves meant it was almost inevitable that piracy would reach Youghal, and local sailor Hugh Baker recounted one extraordinary tale of notoriety in a Youghal court on 22 May 1623. Baker told the court that he had been taken out of his boat on 8 May while in the harbour of Youghal by the pirate John Nutt. The outlaw was sailing for England from Newfoundland to seek a pardon from the vice-admiral of Devon, Sir John Eliot, who was hunting Nutt at the time. Baker said he was kept on board for seven days before the pirates sailed for Dungarvan. Captain Nutt was an operator off the coast of Newfoundland in 1621 and was supported by colonial officials to protect their interests against the French and Spanish. Pirates like Nutt were well aware that being employed by figures of powerful influence could easily lead to a pardon while affording them an unwritten contract to plunder and pillage. It was this ambiguity that drew him to the waters along the south coast of Ireland in the summer of 1623 having previously received a pardon for attacking a French ship off mainland Canada. Whipping sailors like Baker out of the harbour was common practice and no doubt the hapless Youghal man was used for labour on board Nutt's ship.

The details in Baker's testimony may have been sharpened by exaggeration, excitement or good memory but it certainly encapsulates the high-sea corruption of the time. He informed the court that 'three hours after the said pyratt took a Barke of Morgan Phillips, of Podstowe, near the mouth of Dungarvan harbour.' Phillips gave chase in another ship only for Nutt to open fire three times until Phillips was forced to surrender. Nutt's company boarded the ship and during the five- to six-hour ordeal the pirate took £50 from Phillips while his first mate, Henrie Fallet, forcibly extracted 26 schillings from Phillips' pocket, presumably at gunpoint. Baker described how the pirates slaughtered a 'fat ox' on board before taking 'some 40 or 50 yards of fine canvas, 5 or 6 rugs, some linen and woolen Irish cloth and two suites of clothes, a gown and a cloak which Phillips wore'. He then, rather amusingly, added that Phillips wept, complaining that the cloak had cost him £20. A more sinister and unforgiving aspect of the piracy reported by Baker and which made a mockery of Nutt's pardon was the raping of women on board Phillips' ship. Baker said there were fourteen women on board, twelve of which were taken and 'ravished'. Nutt himself kept the wife of a man called Jones, a sadler from Cork, and raped her repeatedly for a week in his cabin before the outlaws departed for further piracy along the coast. His next entry of evidence reveals the depth of corruption at work throughout the opening decades of the century and also the width and breadth of the pirates' reach with their activities.

Nutt and his company then took a ship off Land's End that was bound for Kinsale. At its helm was a Captain Tucker. According to Baker the ship held over fifty passengers who were held at gunpoint. Nutt took '40 pieces' from Tucker while his crew collected 'plate, rings, jewels, and money, as much as came to £300 or £400'. Two men were then taken aboard Nutt's ship. Baker described Tucker's ship as a man-of-war, listing its weapons to the court in great detail. Baker's fate was then revealed. He said he heard the 'Captain' (presumably Nutt) in a quieter moment confess that he was willing to give £2,000 for his pardon. Baker expressed the belief that Nutt had such wealth due to the stories he heard on board from the crew of their dealings along the Barbary Coast, raiding Algerian and Moroccan pirates of gold. Baker finally revealed his means of escape and eventual return to Youghal. He told the court that he and one of the men taken from Tucker's ship cut loose a sea boat that was tied to Nutt's man-of-war while the

pirate and his company were drunk. They rowed silently and to their safety into the harbour of Kinsale before Baker eventually returned to Youghal.[103]

It is proper to assume that Baker enjoyed some infamy in Youghal after his piratical episode and that Boyle's concerns for protection of the town, the harbour and the bay were legitimate. Boyle's Munster, and particularly the coastline, was a vulnerable landscape open to corruption and speculation, the worst excesses of black market capitalism. The threat of piracy and visiting ships from enemies of the English state was ever present during Boyle's tenure as Youghal governor and for a long period after. Youghal and the southern coastline were effectively caught in the shifting tide of monumental change between the expanding empires of England, France, Holland and Spain, trafficking to the new world colonies of America. During this period of expansion English Puritans, disillusioned by perceived lapsed Protestantism under King James I, had sailed to what would become New England on the *Mayflower*. The French had established the colony of Quebec and the Dutch had begun trafficking North African slaves to 'New Amsterdam', later of course renamed 'New York' by English settlers on the island of Manhattan. The North Africans themselves added to the seafaring dynamic. The Barbary pirates scanned Irish and English waters for human and material commodities. The Muslim masters grabbed white slaves and populated Youghal waters in search of passengers travelling to England and the Continent. Eighteen years after Baker's account of Captain Nutt, Revd Devereux Spratt was aboard a ship called the *John Filmer* sailing from Youghal to England, probably to Bristol, in April 1641. Devereux and the other 120 passengers never made it to England. Almost all would spend several years as slaves in the Algiers. Spratt wrote: 'I took a boat to Youghal and then embarked on the vessel John Filmer … but before we had lost sight of land, we were captured by Algerine pirates, who put all the men in irons and stocks.' It is thought that Barbary pirates seized an estimated 35,000 slaves, with the most notorious event in Ireland seeing the sack of Baltimore in 1631 when the pirates effectively enslaved the village. In 1646 twelve natives of Youghal were rescued from the Algiers when an English-sponsored ship was sent with money and goods to the Barbary Coast in exchange for the slaves. The Youghal captives cost around £38 a head to buy their freedom. Meanwhile, Devereaux Spratt would eventually be set free by a Captain Wilde and he returned to the colder climes of Mitchelstown.

For all the possible dangers lurking along the horizon, around Capel Island and in the bay, Boyle was comfortable with the vices and vagaries of the commercial world on both land and sea as long as it oiled the wheels of progress and, of course, as long as it did not adversely affect the commerce of Youghal as a port. He could live with taxing his mind more than taxing his pocket while managing Youghal and his vast estates. In turn, the town and its officials, who had past history in putting commercial interests before any other concerns, had good reason to feel as equally comfortable as their governor. After all, they had not experienced twenty or so years of peace and prosperity such as those under the stewardship of the man who had seemed to appear from nowhere. During the years from 1603 to 1620 Boyle's governorship oversaw many of the elements that created early modern society in Youghal. His coming programmes for infrastructure, welfare and education would continue to modernise Youghal in stark contrast to the Raleigh years. The extent of its reputation as a little part of England was also coming to the fore. However, in the subsequent decades, despite his personal and political successes, Richard Boyle would have to withstand severe criticism and personal attack as England, through Dublin Castle, would try to rein in his phenomenal political and social rise and wrestle back some control over English adventurism.

6

God's Providence is Mine Inheritance

The English Town, Social Policy and the Battle for Our Lady's College

On 19 April 1625, dignitaries, commoners, officials and religious figures met at the Market Cross, Youghal. Having being called there by the banging of the public drum, they clapped and cheered and threw their hats in the air. 'Drums, bells, bonfires, and a hogshead of wine drunk at the Cross' signified the 'joy' of the residents that great news had broken. Sir Richard Boyle had dispatched a letter to the town official, that Charles I had been crowned King of France, Britain and Ireland. The officials in turn immediately informed the populace. The crowd cried 'God save the king' and hung the proclamation on a post at the Market Cross.[104] Evaluation of the joy and celebration amongst the entire population of Youghal is impossible to gauge but certainly the party atmosphere at the heart of the town signifies how Youghal was very much a royalist centre. Parts of Ireland had welcomed the recently departed James I with similar fanfare in 1603 and even the Irish poets wrote optimistically about how the new monarch would bring peace and prosperity to an injured and tired nation.[105] The poets, as if wearing the apparel of the druid prophets of the past, read the situation well and made predictions about a healing future that was indeed realised. Peace had brought economic prosperity and it was almost inevitable that the lighting of bonfires in Youghal was both an expression of loyalty to the Crown and a celebration of the good life, at least for those profiting from the new dawn heralded by Boyle. For the Catholics of the town there were also reasons to be cheerful with Charles marrying the Roman Catholic Henriette-Marie of France. While the marriage created deep mistrust amongst the Puritans of England, the Irish Catholic communities, and certainly those in Youghal, commoner and wealthy alike, may have viewed it as evidence of religious tolerance for the present and the foreseeable future.

Throughout the peace years, Youghal's reputation as a town to visit grew to the extent that it became a destination for the nobility. Sir Barnabas O'Brien wrote to Richard Boyle requesting that he meet O'Brien and his new bride Mary Sanquhar in Youghal. For O'Brien, Youghal made the ideal honeymoon environment because, he stated, his wife 'think she is in England'.[106] There was good reason for the newly wedded Lady O'Brien to think of Youghal as a little part of England. Boyle had created, in the grounds of the college, the archetypal English garden. The new, landscaped gardens were all the rage of courtly European fashion. The English poet Andrew Marvell, a contemporary of Boyle, proffered the analogy of the landscaped garden as a paradise on earth from which men could escape the ills of society. The ordered lawns, pleasing patterns and the carefully crafted floral symmetry were the symbols of civility: mankind's elevation from the baseness of earthly toil. Those who had tilled the heavy soils of war and politics could retire there to contemplate their successes. 'Society is all but rude / To this delicious solitude,' wrote Marvell in his poem 'The Garden'.

Boyle's college garden in Youghal encapsulates Marvell's 'delicious solitude' and also the prosperity of not just economics but Renaissance culture and thinking as seen through the eyes and policies of the English Protestant ethic. The garden, terraced into levels, reaches from the gates of Boyle's college house up the steep incline to the western side of the town walls. Weaving through the tiers is a pathway. Here, the aristocracy passed through decorated pergolas while musing about politics, science, music, magic, astronomy, art and God. From the top tier Boyle, and his contemporaries, held in their wandering eyes an all-encompassing view of his mini-empire, and beyond to the open sea populated by tall ships.

Much of this Englishness, for which Youghal was well recognised, was achieved during the Boyle period by oiling the wheels of a capitalist-driven colonial agenda rather than through a deliberate destruction of Irish culture. Boyle agreed with the principle that Ireland would need to be suppressed by force prior to the onset of civility. However, his confidence in Munster was manifest in his willingness to attract considerable numbers of artisans, weavers, fullers, tanners, coopers, fishermen, iron and timber workers, shipbuilders and merchants into the province.[107] This new prosperity in Youghal was not the green shoots of English culture growing through the ashes of a post-holocaust Irish landscape, as Gilbert, Perrot, Raleigh and Spenser and others had visualised it, but Englishness by commerce: an economic, cultural and philosophical colonisation. There was no outcry against a loss of Irish identity or culture from the Irish in the town, nor had there been. Gaelic, and indeed, Anglo-Irish grievances were based on a loss of autonomy over land, property, money and religion. The Irish welcomed the economic boom and it was strengthened by their inclusion, particularly through the wool and livestock trade in Youghal. Farmers, landlords, merchants, the council, Boyle and the Crown all gained.

To help the capitalist cogs turn more freely, Irish coins were phased out, though both Irish and English coins were used freely in Youghal without an established relation in value to each other. The standardising of an all-English currency improved business. By the mid-1600s Youghal coinage, some square, round and lozenge in shape, could be found in the markets, shops, businesses, quayside and offices. The coins had the initials Y T (Youghal Town) on one side with a ship (the arms of the town) or an engraving of an anchor on the other.[108] The written and verbal use of the English language was also becoming the dominant currency in communication in Youghal. While there were certainly cultural activities amongst the Gaelic population, such as language, poetry, storytelling and song, there was a deliberate attempt by the government to suppress the perceived incivility of Irish dress. This was evidenced by a new law given at Dublin Castle, ironically perhaps on 1 April 1624, which read:

> many instructions have been given, as well to the Lord President,
> the Justices of Assize, &c., for abolishing the use of Irish apparel and

reducing all men to wear and use a civil and comely attire according to the laws of this kingdom, yet, although they have endeavoured to take away the barbarous custom of wearing Mantles, Trouses, Skeines, and such uncivil apparel, we see the use of them rather increased than abated, to the disgrace of this kingdom amongst civil nations.[109]

The Irish were permitted to wear their 'barbarous' clothes as long as they wore them indoors. If caught wearing them on the streets of Youghal, their clothes could be forcibly removed and, 'before their faces', be 'cut to pieces'.[110]

Meanwhile, it marked Youghal's standing significantly that the town was visited three times by travelling theatre companies from England. The council often paid for the travelling companies' public performances. The Prince's Players visited Youghal and performed in the courthouse in February 1615. An unnamed company performed in 1619 with the King's Players following in 1625. Boyle was a patron to these arts and states in his diary that he paid a gratuity to the English dramatist, William Fennor. Boyle paid the 'King's Jester' with 'a hackney, with bridle and saddle'.[111] What performances took place is unknown but being under the patronage of King James I, and later Charles I, the companies were likely to perform the major theatrical pieces of the day such as Shakespearean plays. The King's Players were in Youghal as part of a kingdom-wide tour following theatre closures in London due to an outbreak of plague. Care for the courthouse (situated at the Water Gate at the bottom of present-day O'Neill/Crowley Street) in Youghal was of prominent concern to Boyle and, having been given the freedom of the town, William Durant was ordered to erect iron bars over the windows and to paint the building in 'Spanish white'. Durant was given the caretaker's job because 'those that then come in hither to see the said play do break and batter the glass there.'[112] Such rowdiness may have occurred on occasions when excess alcohol brought further intoxication to elements of an already overexcited audience. Certainly, events that broke the mundane of the everyday early-modern life brought gatherings of mixed class together. Social interaction at occasions such as theatre performances demanded protocols and etiquette. In one instance, officials were admonished for dressing inappropriately when stepping out with the mayor, wearing 'Cloaks instead of Gowns, which is unseemly'.[113]

For all its affluence there were plenty in Youghal's society that suffered. Moneylending was a practice frowned upon by the Crown, and the government made serious attempts to curb its growth. Many of the poor, exploited for rent, interest on loans, sales of goods and land contracts, were availing of lenders. The Lord Deputy St John cited the 'fretting canker of excessive usury' as a reason why many in Ireland, who had suffered during 'the troubles', were disadvantaged in better times by having to pay off interest they could ill afford.[114] Further relief came when the charging of five schillings for funerals and other services by the Church was also banned.

The town, though exact figures are unavailable, is thought to have doubled in population, which brought as much inequity as it did quality of life. There was no legislation from Dublin or London for the welfare of the poor or for administering poor relief. Problems of poverty were, more often than not, dealt with locally by the corporation, sometimes dealing in individual cases with relief given under discretionary measures in accordance to their merits. By 1621 it had been ordered by the council that an almshouse or hospital be 'built on the waste ground next the north side of the quay'. Lawrence Parsons had to give £10 toward the costs but was allowed to take the old hospital next to his house to rent. Parsons was living at Myrtle Grove at this time. This shows that a poorhouse, or hospital for the poor had already existed for many years in Youghal next to Myrtle Grove. The old hospital would later become stables. While the new almshouse was ordered by Boyle to be built in 1621, it was not until 1624 that it was completed and opened. Boyle, the mayor and the council agreed that money raised by a tax on corn collected on market days would be used to help the inhabitants of the hospital. A list of names nominated by the council such as labourer Maurice Fitzwilliam, fisherman John Hoblin and shoemaker Richard O'Murray were among the first residents. A number of poor widows were also elected. Widows were often 'kept' or looked after by appointed trustees: individuals who were paid for their duty of care. Widows of officials, on the other hand, received an annual sum from the corporation accounts. Phillis Annyas, who appealed directly to Boyle, for instance, was given 40 schillings a year for the duration of her natural life.

Public charity was another means of supporting the poor. A box, guarded by two overseers, with a lock and two keys was attached to a block outside the almshouse and locals were encouraged to put in what they thought fit. Money was also collected every Sunday when one of the overseers, joined by a man and a woman from the almshouse, went from door to door throughout the town, ringing a bell. People often contributed materials to the almshouse such as a pan for frying meat. Butchers were ordered to save 'the rump off every beef killed' and hand it in to the alms-people, or if they had no meat they paid a penny in lieu. Timber, coal, turf and salt were taken from boats at the quayside to provide relief. Being admitted into the almshouse depended on a number of criteria. Inhabitants had to be single, widowed or not caring for children and had to be born 'within the town and liberties'.[115] A 'leper' or 'Lazar' (short for Lazarus) house for the sick was kept outside the town walls on the north end of town and also depended on public charity for its upkeep.

The written and unwritten social contracts of supporting the poor may have been driven by a mix of personal patronage, taxes and religious conscience but there is evidence that charity also came from a desire to support ethnic communities. A Danish commander, Van Vaerdt, of a ship called *The Pearl* gave £100 to the Youghal council to help 'any of the King of Denmark's subjects' should they end up in Youghal 'in extreme poverty'.[116] Boyle must take some credit for improving both infrastructure and welfare in a society devoid of structured charitable policies. While he delighted in the portrayal of a persona with obvious grandeur and pomposity, he also displayed generosity toward Youghal, taking an active role in decision-making on issues of welfare and education.

The patent afforded Boyle by James I for the almshouse in 1613 had included a proposal for the building of a free school. It was three years before it was completed, with Boyle paying a Mr Langreddy for its construction. He also paid for its slating, painting, paving and the installation of windows. He wrote in April 1616, in what appears to be a diary entry after a sort of opening ceremony, 'My new school at Youghal

was dedicated to God and for learning.'[117] While free school meant no fees, those attending were male children and typically belonged to the mercantile and professional classes. Sons of nobles were sent to England to be educated, as was Boyle's son, Robert, whose later fame in chemistry was ably assisted by his father's fortune.[118] Some girls from wealthier families could afford to be tutored in their homes at a cost, but most learned practical skills. A sailor by the name of Thomas Sliee, for instance, placed his daughter Jane, aged 6, with Ann Essington for an apprenticeship of fourteen years in sewing and tailoring. Boyle refers also to 'petty scholars' in his reports on the education programme for

Youghal. Children of a young age were, presumably, tutored in the town by a schoolmaster before being '[made fit] for the free school here'.[119] This suggests the early modern education system in Youghal had three tiers: pre-school studies, free school or grammar school, which students entered at around 7 years of age, and finally, for the very wealthy, university abroad. Children spent long days in school from early morning until late evening, six days a week, with few holidays. The teacher at Boyle's free school in Youghal was a Mr Godwyn, who was paid £20 a year. It is not known if any Catholic children, particularly those of wealthy Catholic merchants, went to the free school in Youghal but certainly school life under the patronage of the Protestant elite would negate their presence, especially as religious instruction was the foundation stone of all education.

The Legal Battle for Our Lady's College

Once he was appointed lord justice in 1629 Boyle spent less time in Youghal, and while sitting in his Dublin seat he may have found himself thinking about his southern home. Protestant objections were raised in government about the growing numbers of Catholic masses, buildings and meetings across the country. Concerns were also expressed about increased entries into the priesthood. Catholic activity and practice had swelled in the relative air of conciliation during three decades of peace in Ireland. Youghal was, and had been, a Protestant centre but it also had its Catholic population and their inclusion in trading, construction, farming and shipping was a vital artery that carried lifeblood to the heart of Boyle's commerce. However, Boyle would have been well versed in the tone of disgust in the proclamation from the lord deputy, Lord Falkland, demanding a cessation to Catholic activity. Falkland wrote that Catholics were assembling 'in public places to celebrate their superstitious services in all parts of this Kingdom.' He admonished the building of 'oratories, colleges, masshouses and convents of friars, monks and nuns in the eye and open view of the state'. Owners of properties where Catholicism was being practised were ordered to 'break up' such meetings and celebrations.[120] The Catholic merchants, professionals and commoners

in Youghal had reason to be nervous and angry with this reminder of
the threshold that Protestant officialdom was willing to set. However,
if there was disgruntlement amongst the town's Catholic population,
it was silent. The return, if it may be classed as such, of public displays
of Catholicism was taken by some government officials in England as
a significant sign of the New English malaise in Ireland. Catholicism
had been associated with rebellion ever since the Nine Year's War and
before. The upsurge in Catholic activity was viewed as a consequence
of the rise of adventurers like Boyle who, some officials reasoned, cared
less for Church and State designs and more for personal ambition.[121]
For this suspected lapse in Reformation policy and his alleged illegal
acquisition of Church lands, Boyle would become the case study for
investigation into administrative corruption in Ireland.

Sir Francis Annesley, like Boyle, was one of the New English.
He resented Boyle's appointment as joint lord justice from 1629 to 1633.
Boyle had effectively worked his way up from speculator and minor
official to prominent government figure with a real power to determine
how Ireland would be run. Boyle represented a new breed of English
lord, operating with apparent autonomy in Ireland. They had risen
in rank beyond land ownership and began to permeate the offices of
law, government and the military. However, the real danger, according
to people like Annesley and others, was the arrogance these lords
displayed toward the lord deputies in Dublin by often going above their
heads directly to London, effectively acting like imperial agents hoping
to gain favour at the expense of the proper legal channels.[122] When
Thomas Wentworth was nominated for the position of sole governor,
Annesley hoped to influence him against Boyle. Annesley aimed
to reveal Boyle as a corrupt property developer and have Wentworth
investigate Boyle's unprecedented rise to power. Annesley pointed to
Boyle's acquisition of Church property that had been swallowed up
during his alleged falsifying of land patents during the 1590s and into
the new century. Annesley spared nothing in his criticism of Boyle.
He questioned his administrative actions, attacked his seemingly
grandiose vision of himself and blasted his manipulation of people,
especially what Annesley viewed as the Machiavellian use by Boyle
of his own family. Annesley suggested that Boyle married off family

members to secure property rights knowing that the marriages would later be dissolved to his advantage.

Boyle had fifteen children. His daughters were married into other noble families while the sons married English heiresses in what indeed appears to be a well-orchestrated plan to strengthen property rights and ownership in the great expanse of his private empire. Annesley accused Boyle of being factious, corrupt, vain and boastful and that Boyle's own children could not trust him.[123] Wentworth was sympathetic to Annesley's protestations and, as an Englishman, was disgusted by the land-grabbing lawlessness of the planters and officials. The greatest gripe, however, was how adventurers gained potential riches in the Irish Kingdom of England without the Crown or government of England receiving their entitled financial benefits from them. He called Ireland a 'kingdom abandoned for these late years to everyman that could please himself to purchase what best liked him for his money'.[124] Boyle, because of his prominence and wealth, became the focal point for investigation. He was the prime example of opportunism at the expense of England. Such was the energy of the campaign against Boyle that his alleged meanness and love of money, as well as accusations of being a serial liar, became legendary amongst those pursuing him legally. A less than flattering accusation was forwarded that he 'laughed and rubbed those filthy hands of his' after passing on land to his son and heir, Viscount Dungarvan. The reason for Boyle's apparent surreptitious glee was that the land was useless and that Boyle himself confessed it should never have been part of the inheritance.

The final insult, given the nature of the religious tensions of the time, was that Boyle was a hypocrite who amassed Church lands for profit while presenting himself on a regular basis as a humble figure before God's altar.[125] Boyle professed to be a deeply religious man who had done everything as God had wished it. He also professed to be a fierce loyalist and that all his actions were designed by a love of God, king and country. And though he kept all papers as matters of legal proof in disputes, defending his acquisitions in the framework of the court, he was never reluctant to thank God for making his fortune for him. While his adversaries could pursue him on legal grounds they found it infinitely more frustrating to argue against providence and Boyle's claims of how it had favoured him.[126] Nonetheless, for all his professed devoutness and loyalty, business was the core piston in Boyle's unstoppable engine. His proposal to have a monument to himself built in St Patrick's Cathedral was viewed as vainglorious and idolatrous. This very public display of the Boyle dynasty, a sort of personal propaganda with baroque pretensions, drew sarcasm from Wentworth, whose words betray a personal fixation with all things that Boyle represented and went beyond his official duties in an office darkened by animosity: 'The Earl hath made for himself already three tombs how think you if the Tomb makers at Charing Crosse [London] should inform against him, for taking upon him their trade, without serving his Apprenteship.'[127] Ultimately, Boyle and Wentworth's conflict would settle on Boyle's claim to the college and its grounds at Youghal.

Early in Boyle's career at Youghal, Sir James Fullarton had laid claim to the college, stating it had been included in a grant to him. Boyle settled a fee with Fullarton and applied to King James I for a new patent, which he was awarded. The college was thought to be worth an income of £800 a year. Wentworth knew the value of it to the Crown and considered Boyle's wardenship illegal even though Boyle would insist that those who worked there had their wages doubled and that the college had been neglected until his takeover. After years of accusations, rumour and attacks on his character, Boyle was called to court in 1635 in Dublin. He listened while the Crown prosecutor, Sir William Reeves, argued that Boyle had colluded with his cousin, also called Richard, Bishop of Cork, in drawing up false deeds to the college, which allowed Boyle illegally to collect its revenues. In turn, the court was told that Boyle's cousin and 'other fellows' did not even reside at the college. To add ire for officials they were informed that Boyle was the sole occupier. He was also accused of preventing elections and thereby new fellows from taking up positions at the college. He was derided for his paltry compensation to Fullarton and for colluding with the lord bishops of Cork and Waterford to ensure the sustainability of their cosy and illegal monopoly. The prosecutor lambasted the bishops' scheme of accepting payments from Boyle to buy their silence throughout three decades wherein he received numerous letters from injured parties demanding clarification over the contested deeds. Three years later, in 1636, Boyle settled out of court for £15,000. He was allowed to continue living at the college house but lost the grant and the college revenues. The compensation was an admission of guilt but one that helped him avoid public humiliation, or indeed imprisonment.

While he paid the compensation in instalments over the next two years, Boyle hoped to be re-granted the college. Outraged by the audacity of Boyle's persistence, Wentworth refused to entertain such a move and Our Lady's College became a bitter issue between the two men. Boyle's ability to see beyond personal animosity and even insult to his character would allow him to overcome the bitterness that polarised Wentworth's view. The court, the compensation and the loss of revenues were all business-orientated hiccups for Boyle, to be overcome by patience. The very weaknesses of character that Wentworth delighted in pointing out in Boyle, such as his blind ambition, were in fact the devices by which Wentworth would find himself immobilised in their battle for Youghal College. Boyle made assurances that his behaviour would be, hereafter, exemplary but he never took his eye off the prize. In a move that exemplified his astuteness, he reminded Wentworth of the family connection between them. Boyle had given his blessing to his son, also named Richard, to marry Elizabeth Clifford, a niece of Wentworth's, in 1634. The economic fate of both families was therefore intermeshed and interdependent, particularly on Boyle senior's fortunes. Any revenues lost to Boyle from the college would inevitably have a knock-on effect on his son, and subsequently, Wentworth's niece. The college was therefore an integral part of all their fortunes. By 1639 other factors were at play that influenced Wentworth's peace treaty with Boyle. Charles I was going to war with Scotland after it erupted in open revolt. Boyle's money was vital in supporting the Crown's forces and Wentworth was asked to accept Boyle's efforts to call a truce to their animosities.[128] Wentworth promised Boyle that he would see a re-grant of the college before he returned from urgent matters in London. By January 1640 the college was back in Boyle's hands.[129]

Wentworth's fall from grace was complete when he was executed in 1641 for misdemeanours against the laws of the Kingdom of England during the Scotland crisis. In an astonishing twist of fate, Boyle had been called to give evidence at Wentworth's trial. All of London expected Boyle to exact spiteful revenge. However, he astounded the court by acclaiming Wentworth and the government of Ireland, lavishing praise on his old adversary to the point that King Charles expressed his pleasant surprise and delight at the depth of Boyle's humanity.[130] Boyle had good reason for drawing the milk of human kindness from the dark recesses of his Christian well; he was protecting a government official who could undermine his reputation by revealing the murkier aspects of his rise to power, particularly in relation to Youghal. There was also the great uncertainty of who would become the next Lord Deputy of Ireland, and despite the animosity Boyle felt toward Wentworth, his nemesis was at the very least a devil he knew all too well. Following his evidence at court Boyle left London as a forgiving and God-fearing man with his reputation greatly enhanced and personal endorsements ringing in his ears. He would later write rather coldly and unforgivingly in his diary on hearing of Wentworth's execution, '[he] was beheaded on Tower Hill, as he well deserved.' Harmony was restored in the fortunes of the Earl of Cork's world, in his mind at least.

On 25 February 1642 Boyle sat down at his desk in his college house to write a distressing letter to the Earl of Warwick: 'Yesterday they [Irish rebels] took eight of my English tenants and hanged them and bound an English woman's hands behind her and buried her alive.' Boyle was describing events at west Cork. He added that he hoped God would bless his Majesty's forces and that he would soon be writing of 'killing of thousands', such was the white heat of revenge searing through him. He remarked to Warwick that he had kept '200 men here [in Youghal] for securing the town and harbour'.[131] Ireland was suddenly erupting into war after nearly forty years of peace. With the blast of muskets and clashing of swords Boyle's era was coming to a close. Youghal, and particularly its Catholic population, would plummet into paranoid chaos over the next decade. It would take the best part of a century to recover the same heights of economic prosperity that the

town had enjoyed throughout the Boyle years. The man who began as
a petty clerk to become 1st Earl of Cork would be dead and buried in
his decorative mausoleum two years into the war in 1643. For all his
corruption and ideas of grandeur, Boyle had achieved what Raleigh,
Grey, Gilbert, Spenser and Carew could not: he had created a part
of English society, manifest in culture, religion and politics through a
prolonged peace, in Youghal and other towns. His social policies were,
of course, imperfect but welfare and education were advanced to a
point, as was infrastructure.

In his final moments, Boyle may well have thought that God chose the timing of his passing appropriately. His business acumen would be a useless tool in the savagery of the war that was about to rip up the English gardens in Ireland. His motto, 'God's providence is mine inheritance', reveals the ambiguity of Boyle's persona, humble and egocentric in turn. He spent his entire life mapping connections and sewing the links together like a spider whose jewels would only became apparent after the fog of war had descended on his work. Yet, he professed that all of those works were by the hand of God. Perhaps, this conviction of having the greatest of connections in the highest of places allowed him to ignore the methods of his success and the celebration of his vanity.

7

The Wicked
and the Traitorous

Martial Law in Youghal as Peace is Broken

In 1628 King Charles I had ordered that towns of interest to the Crown required security improvements and Youghal was cited as needing a fort on the quayside. The town was perceived to be vulnerable to attack from the sea. The Youghal Corporation was asked by Richard Boyle and the Lord President of Munster, William St Leger, to pay for the building of a fort through local taxes on imports and exports. The council took it upon itself to write to the king and explain their views on the matter. It claimed that shifting sands and low tides negated attack from 'any great fleets'. It also suggested that six cannons be erected on the quay as sufficient cover, and while it was in full favour of a fort it could not afford to pay for the building of one. The council complained that the proposed taxation would drive away merchants and traders, leaving the town 'depopulated'. As a note of its loyalty to the Crown, should the king take offence to its reticence to pay from its own coffers, it reminded the king that Youghal had entertained the forces of James I when cities such as Cork and Waterford 'had denied them'. It was quick to add that Youghal harbour had a long history of receiving ships from England. Charles I received the council letter favourably and advised Boyle and the Lord President of Munster to find the money from their own offices to fund the fort project. The fort was designed to be 50 feet square with a parapet 6 feet thick and was to be built on the site of the old blockhouse at the edge of the south quay.

By 1641 the fort defence would not be enough to dispel fears of attack. As a Protestant stronghold and strategic port, Youghal would be a prime target throughout the rebellion that had first erupted without warning in Ulster on 22 October. The Catholic lord, Sir Phelim O'Neill, and other Irish lords planned to seize Dublin Castle but the coup was scuppered by English intelligence. Though the coup was well planned its failure meant that the insurgents became increasingly reliant on support from others who were willing to take up arms against Protestant Ulster planters. A few weeks later in Youghal town centre at the Market Cross, on 5 November, Mayor James Galwan read out a proclamation from the Lord President of Munster. It was a statement that tried to clarify who exactly was being blamed for the outbreak of war in Ulster. The Crown's government in Dublin had declared that 'Irish papists' were the protagonists for the treasonous conspiracy in the attempted October coup. However, they were now apologising for not making it clear as to which 'papists' they were referring to. Ireland was, they admitted, populated by Catholics who were loyal to the Crown and not rebellious, and 'that by the words Irish papists we intended only such of the old … Irish in the province of Ulster as have been actors in these treasons, and that we did not any way intend any of the old English of the pale, being well assured of their fidelity to the Crown.'[132] Lords and gentlemen in and around the Pale of Dublin feared that they would find themselves guilty by association through their faith and had written to Dublin Castle to distance themselves from the coup.

Catholics were already feeling a sense of dread following the call to halt growing Catholic activity under the deputyships of both Falkland and Wentworth. Whether the announcement, nailed to a post at the Market Cross, soothed Catholic tension in Youghal is impossible to evaluate. Youghal's population had swollen to almost 1,500 adults, a proportion of which were New English Protestants with another sizeable percentage taken up by the old Protestant mercantile and professional classes. The rest of the population was made up of both Anglo-Irish Catholics and the Catholic Gaelic-Irish. At the outbreak of rebellion, as yet confined to the north of Ireland, Youghal was considered by Protestants to be one of the financial jewels in the crown of England while Catholic rebels saw it as one of the jewels to be removed from that crown.

1641 Civil War

Historians dispute the reasons for the outbreak of hostilities in Ulster, pointing to a number of causes.[133] It has been suggested that the plantations were a cause of deep-seated enmity amongst the dispossessed, mainly the Gaelic-Irish and the Anglo-Irish families. It has also been argued that if these groups were angry about the success of the New English it would not have taken thirty years for their resentment to explode into open revolt. Yet, thirty years is but one generation of fostering ideologies based on prejudice, of drawing distinct lines of cultural and religious difference. Others argue it was the tightening of control of an increasingly Protestant parliament in Dublin and that the coup leaders, who had planned the attacks, were simply trying to force a reaction that would allow their grievances to be listened to or at least to find a bargaining position in the political arena.[134] The sudden violence certainly was a surprise to the Protestant population of the plantations. They found themselves being burned out of their homes with indiscriminate killings, causing outrage in His Majesty's chambers and government. The peace in Ireland was broken and, while Catholics and Protestants had socially interacted with relative respect in the preceding decades, it would be remiss to suggest that all Catholics were happy with the status quo. The government had made it clear that as long as Catholics toed the line and did not promote their religion, as they had done to the great offence of the State, then social interaction, particularly politics, trade and commerce, could continue apace.

The proclamation hanging on the post at Youghal shows how the English government had underestimated the demographic of animosity, hidden until now, throughout the island of Ireland. It may have believed that the conspirators were a band of violent Irish papists hell-bent on destruction in Ulster but Boyle's description of events in west Cork prove how quickly the lighted touch paper had spread its flames from north to south. It also shows how ready some Catholics were to take up arms and sacrifice whatever social and economic benefits had been won throughout the years of peace. Before the year was out, insurgency had spread like a virus throughout the counties, mostly manifest in robberies, burnings, scuffles, dispossession of goods and random violence. The proclamation of November 1641 with its apology to loyal Catholics in Dublin for the government's public relations gaffe would look increasingly antiquated as the unexpected violence in Ulster turned into national war. It is argued that the response by English forces to the Dublin coup was disproportionate. Charles Coote added fuel to the fire when he violently attacked the loyal Catholic gentry on the borders of the Pale. Such punitive measures led to some of the Anglo-Irish joining the rebellion. By November the hostilities morphed into a blueprint for a religious war when a planned meeting at the Hill of Crofty, near Trim in County Meath, brought together leaders of the Anglo-Irish gentry and Ulster Irish. They formed an accord under the banner of the Catholic faith from which to co-ordinate the insurgency. This move may have triggered the perception and then conception of a Catholic–Protestant war nationwide.

Meanwhile, the government continued to release proclamations. It tried to arrest the flight of rumour, such as the one which purported that Charles I had encouraged the rebels to rise against Scottish settlers in Ulster. The suggestion was that Charles was using the Catholics to his advantage against his own Puritan enemies in parliament. The Crown responded quickly: '… to vindicate the Crown and State from these calumnies, do hereby declare, that the reports spread by these wicked persons are most wicked and traitorous'. It even offered a sort of pre-emptive amnesty to insurgents, stating, 'So in mercy to those so deluded, we command them in his Majesty's name, to take a light to guide them from that darkness into which they were mislead, and to depart from them and submit themselves to his sacred Majesty.'[135] However, once the troubles broke out, stances were hardened and it was impossible to stop the stories of atrocities from spreading. Propaganda on both sides played a significant part in the 1641 war. Pamphlets describing the burning of children on open fire spits to smashing women's skulls against posts were printed and read in both Ireland and England. One extremely graphic description tells of Protestant settlers having their hands chopped off, their eyes gouged out, being stripped naked and left to wonder the countryside.[136] The most notorious event was the drowning of Protestants in the river Bann in November 1641. The victims were rounded up, stripped naked and forced into the freezing water at sword and gunpoint. A survivor estimated that at least 100 people died. By Christmas, violence had spread to several counties and seeped south. The close proximity of violence to Youghal by early 1642 changed the life of the residents dramatically. In his letter to the Earl of Warwick, Boyle tells how his second son, Kynalmeaky, commanded his 'new town of Bandon-bridge' and how he defeated 600 rebels outside the town walls, taking fourteen prisoners and hanging them under martial law at the town gate. Boyle reports that 104 were killed and his language shows the anger he felt that plantations, authority and the Crown should be attacked in this way: 'and now we have begun to blood ourselves upon them'.[137]

Martial Law

The attack at Bandon was not the only news received by Boyle that attempts to overrun his plantations and towns were being carried out. He received a letter in early January, only three months after the Ulster outbreak, warning him that rebels had designs on attacking Youghal. John Fitzgerald of Farnane, County Waterford, requested ammunition from Boyle to protect Dromana castle and its lands as the rebels had intended to 'infest' the waters and countryside between Youghal and Dromana.[138] Sir Richard Osborne also contacted Boyle on 25 January, complaining that he and others had been attacked at Knockmoan, also in Waterford. What is noteworthy is the speed and relative ease that rebels took castles and overran farms, particularly in isolated rural areas. It reveals England's protection of their interests in Ireland had been softened by peace and that the military-style training of locals in towns like Youghal was a piecemeal policy, wholly inadequate in the face of raging rebellion. Adventurers, officials and even government members had often taken it upon themselves in the years since 1603 to finance their own methods of protection, as evidenced in Youghal by the dispute over the payment of the quay fort. In an act of self-preservation, a skill almost unique to Boyle, he responded by building five circular turrets around his garden. From the moment he summoned soldiers to Youghal in the early months of 1642 the nature of life in the town changed dramatically. In a short period of time, concern moved from trade laws, bylaws and social moral behaviour to military security.

Munster President William St Leger, showing little confidence in the corporation, ordered Boyle to return from Dublin to Youghal and handed powers to him that effectively put the town under martial law from the beginning of 1642. In the creation of a distinctly alert atmosphere Boyle was to work with local officials to 'take command and government' of Youghal. This new military-styled governance was for 'exercising the men, drawing in other forces, appointing of officers, guards [and] watches.' The appointed martial law officers were also charged with keeping close surveillance of any possible mutinies, therefore creating an air of suspicion amongst the Catholic community. Catholics may however have retained some confidence given the social and commercial status of a number of families. Having never displayed any public grievance against Wentworth's policy of reining in Catholic practices and having remained totally loyal to King Charles, Youghal Catholics may well have thought the rebellious actions around the country foreign to their thinking and inconvenient to their commerce.

Meanwhile, Boyle wrote that he thought the town 'poor and weak' and had immediately brought in 100 soldiers and 60 horsemen. The worrying level of autonomy given to officials increased tension in Youghal. In an already politically claustrophobic atmosphere, officers were given freedom to punish by death suspected rebels or sympathisers. Boyle, feeling forlorn by age and the stories of atrocities, expressed worries about a possible uprising in Youghal by remarking that the Irish outnumbered the English 'three to one'. However, Boyle's estimation is not to be trusted. In a letter written much later, wherein he is extolling the loyalty of the town to the king, he says of Youghal's population: 'the greatest part inhabited by English Protestants.' It seems Boyle was wont to describe reality through the varying degrees of his fluctuating moods. Indeed, he had become increasingly pessimistic, stating he would die defending Youghal but was hardly up to the fight, being 'infirm'. Writing a letter to his friend George Goring he signed off, 'about midnight after a heavy and sorrowful Christmas'. He also remarked on the importance of protecting Youghal more so than Limerick, Cork, Kinsale or Waterford when he wrote, 'if this town should be lost, all the hope and retreat of the English in this province is gone.' His morose sense of dread and worst fears for Youghal's security were compounded by a natural disaster:

> A great part of the walls of Youghall being fallen down within these two nights which we are not able to repair … God bless us, for we are encompassed with an innumerable company of enemies, and have neither men, money, nor munitions. We are now at the last gasp; and therefore, if the state of England do not speedily supply us, we are all buried alive.[139]

Boyle's apparent panic when portions of the town walls collapsed, probably due to neglect and bad weather, can be excused. Intelligence about rebel movement, strength and location in the early stages of the rebellion was poor, though the earl certainly had a propensity for staring at the half-empty glass. William St Leger shared Boyle's doomsday prophecy for the safety of Munster when he told Boyle he could not guarantee the security of Cork. He informed his colleague that he would be coming to Youghal for refuge.

St Leger was not the only refugee to find his way to the garrisoned town; as weak as it was, it remained the safer option in an increasingly anarchic countryside. English and Irish Protestant strays migrated to Youghal to beg at the gates for entry. One such woman by the name of Rebecca Roberts, who had her cattle slaughtered, found that, upon entry to Youghal, she was threatened by imprisonment being unable to pay rent of any sort. Individuals often pleaded their cases to Boyle, requesting special orders of clearance to stay within the walls. Rebecca Roberts was afforded such limited luxury.[140] Meanwhile, the increasingly fatalistic Boyle recorded that Fethard, Cashel and Clonmel had all succumbed to the rebels who 'pillaged' and 'spoiled' the English Protestants.

As the year wore on a flurry of military movement was witnessed at Youghal's quayside with Captain Thomas Piggot arriving in the company of St Leger. Captain Piggot was ordered to remain with his men in Youghal until further notice. He was informed that Youghal council would 'furnish them with meat, lodging, fire, and candlelight, for which you are to pay ready money according his Majesty's rates'.

Despite reinforcements arriving in the town, Boyle's bleak prediction that they would all be 'buried alive' deserved attention and credence. They were not just the fatalistic ramblings of an ageing man. Civil war was about to flare up in England. King Charles's perceived absolutist-style monarchy was coming to an end with the rise of constitutionalists who were seeking to give more power to parliament. The parliamentarians' war against the Crown would be fought by Oliver Cromwell's roundheads. Boyle knew all too well that both arms and finances would be that much harder to obtain from England once hostilities there erupted.

With England on the verge of tearing itself apart, the lack of support to Ireland prompted a reaction from the new Governor of Youghal, Seargent-Major Matthew Appleyard. He ordered soldiers to drag

Youghal men from their beds, chairs and fireplaces if they did not attend
their watch-keeping duties on the towers, walls and gates at appointed
times. It is difficult to ascertain whether such reluctance by locals can
be read as apathy or defiance or perhaps even conscientious objection
by Catholics. However, ships led by Sir Charles Vavasour did arrive at
Youghal carrying troops. The next couple of months of 1642 saw a high
level of activity at the gates of Youghal. They creaked open and shut as
regular missions of search and destroy and search and rescue were carried
out. Boyle's son, Viscount Dungarvan, set off with Vavasour to rescue the
Countess of Ormond and her children and to secure them safe passage to
Dublin via the port of Youghal. On 31 March at one o'clock, the countess
and her children were sent to Dublin in *The Swan*.[140] Vavasour and
Appleyard then went on a mission through County Waterford, taking
Dungarvan Town before Vavasour encountered rebels on his way to
capturing Kilmacthomas. As the summer began to close, Boyle's sons
Viscount Dungarvan and Lord Broghill confronted confederate forces
at the Ardmore round tower. One hundred and seventeen rebels were
hung. Youghal, for the moment, seemed secure with the immediate
areas along the Blackwater such as Temple Michael, Strancally
and Lismore being held by the Boyles. The Earl of Cork's three sons
created a sort of triangular defence of their father's estates with Viscount
Dungarvan at Waterford, Lord Broghill at Lismore and Kynalmeaky at
Bandon. Correspondence between father and sons related mostly to the
war but Boyle was not reticent in expressing fears for extended family,
in particular women and children.

A Plea to the House of Commons

The Boyles lost an important ally in 1642. With the death of the
Lord President of Munster, Sir William St Leger, the dynamic changed
in the line of leadership. Murrough O'Brien, son-in-law of St Leger
with the title Lord Inchiquin, became military governor of Munster.
O'Brien was proactive in counteracting the rebels across the province
but he drew suspicion from the Boyles, who had no other choice than
to align themselves with him at this time. By 25 August the 76-year-old
Richard Boyle, unable to unshackle his mind from the chains of

misery, was compelled to sit at his desk and compose a lengthy letter to the speaker at the House of Commons in London. He opened his letter with a list consisting of the names of active rebels. Boyle asked the Commons to pass the names of

> ... Lords Viscounts Roche, Montgarret, Ikerrin, and Muskerry, and the Barons of Dunboyne and Castleconnell, with the son and heir of the Lord of Cahir, Theobald Purcell, Baron of Loghmoe, Richard Butler, of Killcash, Esq., brother to my very good Lord the Earl of Ormond, with all other the baronets, knights, esquires, gentlemen, freeholders, and popish priests, in number above eleven hundred, that either dwell, or have entered and done any rebellious act... [into] outlawry.[142]

Boyle revealed his surprise at the speed and spread of the rebellion into Munster when he added that he had 'eaten the most part of my bread in Ireland these four and fifty years, could not but apprehend that the infection and contagion was general, and would by degrees quickly creep into this province, as forthwith it did'. He told the house that '... the preservation of this important town and harbour of Yoghal was of principal consequence to be maintained and kept for the service of the Crown ...'

He then claimed to have paid out of his own pocket for 'the two foot companies, that guarded Youghal ... since the beginning of these troubles'. The ageing earl had one final swipe at his recently departed and now headless enemy, Thomas Wentworth, citing the former lord deputy as negligent in his care of Munster through the years of peace.

For all the fatalism that drained the ink from his quill, Boyle had just enough left over to scratch out a reminder to the House of his generosity, having sent £300 to England to pay for ammunition for his tenants. Had he not done so, he attested, he could not have guaranteed the safety of all his castles in Cork and Waterford. He thanked God for making Youghal safe and for also making it 'a receptacle, not only for shipping, but also for thousands of distressed Englishmen, which have been dispossessed and stripped by the rebels, and found succour and safety here'. He was at pains to stress his expenses having paid the soldiers 3*s* and 6*d* a week and asked that the parliament forward their wages for the coming period of November to March. He thanked the House of Commons for sending to his son at Bandon 'four hundred musquets with powder, match, and lead, fifty swords, two hundred belts, two drums, five new colours, and some other victuals and habiliments of war', and hoped the king or parliament might send 'money and clothes' for fear that the soldiers would mutiny. Boyle had good cause for concern as soldiers at Bandon openly expressed disquiet about a lack of pay. He went on to describe the poor condition of the English forces, expressly Charles Vavasour's company that had a few months earlier landed at Youghal. He recorded these soldiers as 'lessened, weakened, and made unserviceable by fluxes, small-pox, fevers, and with long marches, and lying upon the cold ground'. He warned that if support could not be given then the armies in the field would be forced to retreat to the walled towns of Bandon, Cork, Kinsale and Youghal while surrendering the harvests to the rebels.

Boyle was imagining full-bellied rebels setting siege to hunger-ravaged urban centres. The predicted doomsday for Munster was matched only by his own financial apocalypse when he added, 'I have been compelled to sell my plate and silver vessels to pay the soldiers. I have been a good constable to preserve this town and harbour, and the King's Peace in those parts. I have with a free heart and a liberal hand spent all that I have, and am able to do no more.' Finally, he concluded that ,'The one hundred and odd pounds which the House of Commons sent over by my son Dungarvan, to relieve this poor town, hath been faithfully distributed among the poor English Protestants, who in exchange do tender unto you their humblest thanks.'[143] The less than wealthy Anglo-Irish Catholics and the poorer Irish would not see any relief and their days, like those of Boyle himself, were numbered in Youghal.

A Change of Atmosphere

The timing of Boyle's less eloquent than desperate letter could not have been worse. He may not have been aware that three days prior to his plea to the House of Commons for money war had broken out between Cromwell's Puritan-led parliamentarians and King Charles's royalist forces. Within days of the commencement of the English Civil War, and most likely as his own letter was being read out at the House of Commons, Murrough O'Brien asked Boyle to give him all his soldiers at Youghal to make an assault on Irish rebels in west Cork. A battle ensued at Liscarrol at the end of August. Four of Boyle's sons were present as was Charles Vavasour. With an inferior force, O'Brien showed his taste for battle and bloodletting when, having defeated the confederate forces, he slaughtered what remained. In what proved to be a summer of great lament for Richard Boyle, his son Kynalmeaky was killed in action at Liscarrol with his body returned to Lismore. His son-in-law Barrymore would also die later from wounds inflicted at the battle. O'Brien, though defeating the Irish, was unable to press his advantage due to a lack of financial support from England. English troops were being withdrawn from parts of Ireland and sent to England in order to defend the king against Cromwell. The outbreak of the English Civil War had, to a degree, halted what might have been the conquering of Munster had a full-scale effort been afforded to O'Brien and the Boyles.

Undeterred by the defeat at Liscarrol, Catholic insurgents held a meeting at Kilkenny to create the Confederate Association. For O'Brien, the battle at Liscarrol would only be the beginning of his rise to both fame and notoriety. He would find an unflattering nickname attached to his reputation for setting crops, livestock and, in an infamous incident at Cashel, people alight. To the Irish he would be known as 'Murrough the Burner'. He would, in the following years of the war, re-enact the policies of terror from the traditions of Lord Grey and Humphrey Gilbert during their crushing of the 1579 Munster rebellion. His actions seemed the very embodiment of Spenser's words in *A View of the Present State of Ireland*. His suspicion of Catholics would also dismantle the Boylean world of Youghal. The scarred landscape of Munster had become slippery underfoot for those who occupied it. Castles and parcels of land changed hands between both sides in low-intensity skirmishes, with neighbours, familiar to and with each other, engaging in acts of aggression. Fortunes fluctuated like the early autumn temperatures with territorial advantage as precarious as the leaves on the trees. The 400 castles and estate houses in County Cork[144] were, as Boyle had contested in his letter, armed and provided for to a degree, but nobody was feeling secure. The only certainty for the English forces and Protestants was the welcome safety of the walled towns, in particular the ports of Youghal, Cork and Kinsale. There can be little doubt that during this period suspicions against Catholics intensified within the walls and closely guarded gates of Youghal. The influx of English soldiers, injured, hungry and grieving, could have done nothing to relax a nervous Catholic population.

The minting of coins, as discussed earlier, also shows that trade continued despite the threat and danger of war. No doubt trade became less about profit and more about provision with the very real possibility of sieges being realised against the port towns. Boyle had feared that the confederates would have access to corn and other food supplies in the rural areas while towns such as Youghal would depend on imports from England, a country now at war with itself. Also, judging by Boyle's accounts in his letter to the House of Commons, though caution should be taken against his evaluation of how bad things actually were, residents in Youghal were unlikely to be spending anything in the local economy. The knock-on effect was that shops and businesses were suffering a downturn in their fortunes.

The extent to which this negativity occupied the thoughts of officials is evident in a deposition given by Roger Greene of Ballyshambles. Greene would later testify to Minister Bisse, head of the commission into the events of the rebellion, that in October 1642 he and ten others from Youghal, including Garret Barry, Ann Merryville, Richard West, Ursula Gullyferr and Alexander Grase, were sent by Major Appleyard into County Waterford on the Youghal ferry boat to reap and tie some corn to bring back to town. Greene said they were caught by rebel soldiers, forty on horseback and sixty on foot, and taken to the confederate stronghold of Dungarvan. More worrying for the commission was the evidence Greene offered in which he described ships from both Spain and France supplying salt, powder, arms and ammunition to the rebels. He also testified that a shipment of '... three hundred musketts, sixteen barrels of powder, and five thousand weight of match' was being taken by a rebel activist from County Clare for transportation across Munster. He concluded that the rebels at Dungarvan cursed the Puritans for Ireland's problems.[145]

The presence of French ships off the coast was confirmed by an English navy captain, Thomas Powell, in his logbook.[146] Powell had been monitoring the southern coast, blocking trade throughout 1642, and recorded the capture of several French ships carrying goods such as wine and corn. Though these ships were merchant rather than military and their purpose commercial, their trading with ports with a strong rebel influence caused great concerns for security in Youghal. Further to this, the overnight disappearance of eleven residents, now prisoners of the rebels, could only have exaggerated the siege mentality of those living in the town. In an environment of high suspicion those making their way to Youghal as refugees hoped the town would protect them or offer an exit route to England.

Murrough O'Brien remained vigilant and suspicious. In the absence of a Munster presidential office he had assumed military government over Protestant interests and affected provincial laws through discussions with his war council. If he could not protect the port towns through an official title such as president, then he would exact control with his sword. In November, as the war entered a second winter, he ordered that no person was allowed to sell tobacco unless they had express permission through special license of the war council. His reasons for controlling the commodity were based on the notion that 'under pretext of selling Tobacco divers [many people] keep intelligence with the rebels to the prejudice of His Maj. Service.' In effect, O'Brien claimed there was no smoke without spying, adding that the frequency of subversive behaviour was 'notorious' across the province.[147] He then chastised the Youghal mayor, Thomas Stout for not forwarding £200 from the council coffers to support his army. O'Brien said the money had been promised and warned that a heavier levy would be imposed should he not receive the funding. The council, ever respectful to its superiors, replied that it had met and would extract the money from the inhabitants, excepting those who had come to town having being 'spoiled' by rebels. Ironically, the ever-subservient Catholics in Youghal would pay for the Protestant army that would kill those fighting in the name of their faith.

The contrast in the quality of life only a year before could not have been starker. Jasper Collins, almost certainly related to Dominic, executed forty years earlier, had his properties of ten thatched houses pulled to the ground by Major Appleyard because they were viewed as a potential fire hazard in a time of war. Collins, whose family had been so prominent in Youghal for at least a century, found himself petitioning O'Brien for permission to leave Youghal. He asked to be allowed to live under the generosity of his father-in-law on his land at Ballymaloe with his wife and children. Other prominent families also found themselves disturbed by the militarising of Youghal. Patrick Coppinger was moved to write a letter to Murrough O'Brien complaining that he was forced to live with his mother because his house was being used for army supplies. He was at pains to profess he was owed £10 in rent from the army whom he had supported financially when they first arrived in town.

Pressure on the town's resources became even heavier when, on 4 December, around 140 weaponless soldiers arrived at the South Gate seeking refuge. They had set out from Cork but were ambushed by rebels on the road. They were offered the chance to carry on to Youghal without their armaments. Though the town was short on supplies the soldiers were given barrelled butter and bread, salted beef and water to drink. A letter from O'Brien to Boyle describing the extremities of the army's condition shows the jaded pace at which the war was being fought throughout 1643:

> Our present condition falls out now to be more miserably desperate than ever, in regard we have no manner of help or relief amongst ourselves and the provisions we depended on out of England doth fail us, which will put us to a desperate extremity, here being nothing to deliver forth [in this store] on the next pay day.

O'Brien then asked Boyle for £300 to pay the troops in Youghal. If Boyle did not have the £300, O'Brien suggested he borrow it. Then, with no little amount of forlorn lassitude, he mused, 'To-morrow with a heavy heart I shall march forth to linger out a few days in the field, where I am not likely to continue so long as to enterprise anything of advantage.'[148]

O'Brien's words betray the lament of a man missing the perverse thrill of confrontation. The Catholic Confederates in Munster appeared equally listless. There would be no great battle, such as Liscarrol, to fight as the war entered a state of semi-paralysis. The stalemate was brought on by a lack on finances on both sides, as evidenced by O'Brien demanding money from Boyle and Boyle pleading with the House of Commons, having been ignored by the excessively pre-occupied parliament and king. Financing a war was extremely difficult. Threats of mutiny were very real amongst soldiers. The Catholic Confederates shared the same concerns, being dependent on financial support, coupled with food and shelter, from landowners whose territory they occupied. However, given the fragile and transient nature of land occupancy and sympathy to the cause, there would be no guarantees of a stream of income to satisfy war-weary fighters. For the English at least they had the port merchants to call upon.

In the meantime, Youghal officials received some harsh criticism for the 'abuses and neglects' of the town. The council was to give £100 a year from the beginning of the war in 1641 towards the restoration of damaged areas of the town walls and fortifications in and about the town. Almost two years later they had only trumped up a measly £50. They were lambasted with equal disdain for not having anywhere on the quay to mount a cannon. It was pointed out that foreign ships and pirates had delighted in easy passage for pillaging and robbing. The council had promised five years previously to mount a platform at the quay. The letter of complaint came from Chancellor Hooker, who concluded that the mayor and council 'have performed nothing' and the town 'is subject to great dangers and the inhabitants, your Majesty's loyal subjects, much grieved there at'.[149] One of the final acts Boyle carried out before his death was to respond to the government regarding the security of Youghal. He revisited the proposition of a 'royal fort' for the protection of the harbour. He argued, as the council had before him, that taxing the imports and exports would kill off the merchant business. He insisted that the shifting sand bar acted as a natural deterrent to a serious naval assault, making the waters too shallow. He forwarded the proposition that the council could pay for a smaller fort and platform out of their own funds and suggested that the building and maintenance of a royal fort would cripple the town financially. He asked that six more cannons be joined with the two sent by Queen Elizabeth over forty years earlier, to be placed along the quayside. Again, Boyle extolled the virtues of the 'Protestant English' in the town and the 'best of the natives comfortable in religion' (compliant Catholics).

The Solemn League and Covenant Oath

While Youghal Council counted its newly minted schillings and drew up plans for its not-so-royal harbour fort, mooted peace talks had begun as early as April, but a truce was still months away.[150] By June, relief from boredom had finally come for the terminally frustrated soldiers when they confronted the Confederate commander, James Touchet, Earl of Castlehaven, along the river Blackwater between Kilworth and Fermoy. The Youghal soldiers were called from their slumber and, exiting the North Gate, dragged themselves and ox-driven armoury to join an army in excess of 1,000 who were gathered along the route from Tallow to Cappoquin. Vavasour and Boyle's son, Francis, ventured into Condon country, taking the castle at Cloughleagh. It was reported that men, women and children were stripped and slaughtered in Vavasour's absence. Marching south from Kilkenny, Touchet and other prominent rebel commanders confronted Vavasour, defeated him and took him prisoner. It was a significant morale-boosting victory against O'Brien's Protestant Munster army. On hearing the news in Youghal, Boyle wrote, 'all the wagons and carriages, and seven colours taken, and worst of all, the Colonel, noble Sir Charles Vavasour, was a prisoner. God in his mercy turn his heavy hand from us.' An incensed O'Brien asked Boyle for money to attack the Confederates. Boyle obliged but, rather optimistically, put the cost of £1,000, a part of which O'Brien contributed, down to the king and parliament. Confederate commander Thomas Purcell attacked Boyle's home at Lismore Castle, much to his chagrin, though he was glad to record that the Irish failed to breach his property after a week of battery.

Meanwhile, Boyle's two sons, Broghill and Dungarvan, arrived back in Youghal from England and rode out to meet O'Brien at Tallow. They intended to confront the rebels but their urgency was unwarranted as the Confederate force failed to turn up.[150] On returning to Youghal, Broghill and Dungarvan informed their father that King Charles intended to call a truce with the Catholic Confederacy. The date for the cessation of violence was set for 15 September 1643.

The announcement of the truce was indeed made on the 15th, the very day that Richard Boyle would finally win eternal rest in his opulent tomb. His death was certain to have been mourned by the majority in Youghal. Boyle would not live to hear the truce being announced. Five days after his death and his body stiffened in the cold marble, the details of the truce were read out at the Market Cross, a version of it having been published in the town. It read:

> Whereas, after a long debate and treaty between, both sides it was this day, 15 Sep., at 12 of the clock, unanimously concluded that there shall be from this date, an absolute cessation of arms and acts of hostility in all parts within this kingdom for one whole year, to begin 15 Sept., at 12 of the clock.[152]

The cessation gave many people time to reassess their positions. Some hardline Protestants were against the truce, believing King Charles's motives were driven by a need to use royalist troops in Ireland for the civil war in England, and indeed, 4,000 royalist troops did depart Dublin for England in November.

For the residents of Youghal, Boyle's passing marked the end of an era. With no official President of Munster and the fortunes of the province still in flux, despite the cessation, the future was uncertain. In England the king's once absolutist powers were being diluted. Scottish Presbyterians and the Long Parliament entered discussions on how to bring peace to England, Scotland and Ireland. They created a Protestant oath called the Solemn League and Covenant. They believed that by making subjects of the three kingdoms take the oath it would bring peace under a single Church. By making the king take the oath a symbolic gesture had, with one movement of his quill, isolated those who had hoped for moderation and tolerance. One of the conditions in swearing to the Covenant was to promise 'That we shall, in like manner, without respect of persons, endeavour the extirpation [removal] of Popery, Prelacy, superstition, heresy, schism, profaneness, and whatsoever shall be found contrary to sound doctrine and the power of Godliness.' The Covenant was designed to bring all State affairs under the Church. In England, those still pushing for a separation of powers between parliament and king remained dissatisfied. In Ireland, those unwilling to raise their hands and swear to the Covenant would be isolated and extirpated. The Catholics in Youghal who had been so loyal to the king, who had resisted mutiny within the town, who had suffered financial loss and paid for his armies to kill their own, would surely have felt dismayed at the news of Charles's signature. Conversely, Youghal Protestants, though in a dilemma over the loyalty to king or parliament, would have been buoyed by the concept of providential power under a single Protestant Church for the three kingdoms.

For his part, Murrough O'Brien spotted an opportunity. The oath would be taken in Munster but O'Brien disliked the broad terms of it, preferring to try his hand at adapting his own version.[153] Above all else, his concerns remained focused on crushing the Catholic Confederacy and protecting Munster. Irked by the king's unwillingness to appoint him President of Munster and judging that parliament was increasing its control over England's affairs he began to express his favour of parliament. Also, his 'loyalty' to parliament could now become the means by which he could procure money for his army. O'Brien was, and would prove to be, extraordinarily flexible in even the most paralysing political circumstance. It would not be O'Brien's final twist or turn. Meanwhile, the ongoing truce was inconvenient to him as was the loss of soldiers drawn out of Youghal and other towns to return to England.

The truce would not last because it was not based on a desire for peace but on the need for the realignment of power and a re-energising of the troops. Protestant extremists, determined to adopt the 'extirpation of Catholicism' clause into action, were still hungry to dissipate the Confederate threat. By suppressing this menace they would make the Irish Catholics subservient under the guise of God's providence. The truce would also offer the Confederacy time to rethink strategies for the nullification of Protestant progress and designs, one of which was the protection of Youghal. Appetite for destruction was the most active bacterium in the bowels of both sides. Youghal was entering a period where divisions would be polarised at both ends of the dark tunnel of war, where light was growing faint. Residents would fall into a social nightmare from which they would take as many decades to wake up as they had enjoyed before the onslaught of a rebellion they neither wanted nor expected.

8

Ill-Affected Papists

The Expulsion of Catholics

The anarchic and unpredictable nature of what was to become known as the 'War of the Three Kingdoms' in Ireland, Scotland and England throughout the 1640s often created opportunities for men like Murrough O'Brien to operate with autonomy. So occupied were the powers that be with their own efforts to seize control, whether it was the parliament in London, the king, the Catholic Confederacy, the Dublin government, the Scottish army or even the commanders on the ground, that solutions were often more complicated than the war itself. For now, and for at least the next several years, Murrough O'Brien followed one singular discourse, the protection of Protestants in Munster. Whoever would finance that outcome would win his loyalty and his considerable soldiery. With the passing of Richard Boyle, O'Brien had assumed administrative and, more crucially, military control of Youghal. He would appoint Roger Boyle (Lord Broghill) Governor of Youghal in August 1644, but for now the town's destiny lay in his considerably restless hands. Earlier that year and with peace still holding, O'Brien travelled to Oxford with the intention of petitioning the king to serve him with the office of Lord President of Munster. Unfortunately for him, despite support from the Lord Deputy of Ireland, the Earl of Ormond, it was a wasted trip.

The king had already appointed the Earl of Portland to the position so coveted by O'Brien. This apparent snub would certainly have hurt a man of O'Brien's self-appraisal, particularly having had the influential support of Ormond. With a bruised, rather than deflated ego, he would continue to find support where necessary to keep the garrison of Youghal in faith of his designs and his soldiers loyal to his leadership. That, however, would take money.

Writing to Ormond, O'Brien claimed to be 'utterly destitute of means to sustain the soldiers of Youghal' and asked him to intervene by taking responsibility to contact the 'townsmen and to obtain their consent' for the payment of the army there until the end of Easter. O'Brien added that he would, by then, have had enough money out of Limerick to cover the costs. He told Ormond that he had expressed the same financial concerns to Sir Percy Smith at Cloyne and would seek Smith's help should Ormond meet any resistance from the townsmen of Youghal. O'Brien certainly lacked confidence here and it is noteworthy that he himself was reluctant to go cap in hand to Youghal for support. Whether this was due to the financial state of the town or whether it was because O'Brien was disliked, particularly after forty years of Boyle stewardship, is difficult to qualify. It is also difficult to know if the royalist town was aware of his growing tendency to lean toward parliament and away from the king. Either way, the town did forward the funds and Ormond sent a letter informing them that one of His Majesty's ships was on its way carrying 'corn and victuals'. This was followed by a proclamation from the king that a shipment of wheat, rye, oats, peas, bacon, barrel beef, butter, cheese and coals would be sent to Irish ports by English and Welsh merchants, who were not to be charged for the custom.[154]

Meanwhile, O'Brien became increasingly frustrated throughout the passing months of 1644. The king and Ormond continued to negotiate with the Catholic Confederacy, which appeared to O'Brien's vision to be the antitheses of why he had waged war across the province of Munster. His disenchantment with the policy of the Crown led him to declare outright for parliament. This afforded him military support through the parliamentarian navy that dominated the Irish Sea. The link between the strength of the navy and protecting the vital ports of Munster was, for O'Brien, irresistibly logical.

Papists Expelled from Youghal

It is difficult to gauge if the Catholics of Youghal had any warning of what was about to happen to them on 26 July 1644. There had been enough statements in official letters between people such as Boyle and O'Brien regarding their suspicions of a possible uprising within the town. The efforts made to control the trading of commodities such as tobacco, which was suspected to be a cover for swapping intelligence amongst Catholics inside the walls and rebels outside, was very much a public affair. However, there is no evidence to rely on that can reveal the feelings of Catholics in their everyday interaction with Protestants, many of whom were business and trade associates. After all, Catholics and Protestants in Youghal had enjoyed, in commerce at least, relatively positive relations throughout a prolonged peace between 1603 and 1641. The embargo on selling tobacco was a sign to the Catholic population of the town that they were not trusted by government and certainly not by Murrough O'Brien. Whether misgivings about Catholic intentions were shared amongst the general public in the town is not as clear. The treatment of Jasper Collins, whose Catholic family had held important offices in Youghal and had stayed silent when Dominic Collins was executed in 1602, and the tearing down of his ten thatched houses, may have been the type of action that kept other Catholic merchants awake at night. They certainly would have understood what it meant when Collins was forced into exile to Ballymaloe, where he and his family were exposed to the vagaries of war, along with the indignity of having to ask to leave. Yet, these signals could not have been read as an indication of what was about to come and it must have appeared inexplicable in a time of ceasefire while the King of England, to whom they had shown such loyalty, was in talks with the Catholic Confederation of Kilkenny.

Whatever their feelings, worries or predictions for the future, Youghal Catholics were told on the 26 July to leave their homes and everything they owned behind them. They were ordered to walk out of the town gates in the clothes they were wearing and never to come back. The expulsion of Catholics was also taking place at Cork and arrests were being made in Kinsale. Youghal Governor, Broghill, wrote to the Lord Deputy/Lieutenant, Earl of Ormond stating:

In obedience to the last part of your Lordship's letter, we have removed out of … Youghal all the Irish, as we conceive ourselves able to master. In Youghal we caused the goods of such persons, as were removed, to be restored, albeit they were warned to depart suddenly without their goods for quicker expedition.[155]

The actual notice, as written by Broghill, and announced, most likely at Market Cross, published and hung there on the fateful morning in July, gives a much more detailed insight into what Catholics were awoken to. It read:

These are to give notice that all persons as well men, women as children, of what estate age, and condition so ever they be of, who are papists and reside within Youghall, that they, within half an hour after publication hereof, depart there out and not presume to carry away with them any coin, plate or any goods, saving only the wearing apparel now on them, and hereof they fail not upon pain of death. At Youghal, 26 July, 1644. Broghill.[156]

As stated in the notice, papists, regardless of whether they were English or Irish, had thirty minutes to leave the town. The thirty-minute window was most likely to prevent hidings, possible resistance or the spreading of intelligence to rebels beyond the town. To get rid of the Catholics from the town at this speed would have required soldiers going into houses and aggressively ordering the ejection of the inhabitants. Those being removed were certain to try to grab personal possessions, food and clothes. They were clearly denied this, though in his letter to Ormond, Broghill said some goods were restored. Why this happened is difficult to identify clearly. Possibly there were some soldiers who found the exercise pricked their conscience, or the inevitable cries of the expelled created some level of pity. Another plausible reason is that the order was thought overly severe by those carrying it out, hence ignored in part. After all, many of those involved were known to each other while some may even have had close associations.

Given the time frame for the expulsion and the inevitable panic that would have ensued amongst the Catholics and their families,

the exercise was likely to have been chaotic and at times violent. It is
not known whether they were gathered in one area such as the Market
Cross or expelled at both the South and North Gates. If the expelled
refused to comply with the order they were to be killed on the spot.[157]
Adventurers in London, aware of the expulsions, were already bidding
for the properties.[158]

A number of questions about the expulsion will remain unanswered.
Where the Catholics would go was not a concern to Broghill, O'Brien
or Ormond but we can only assume that their first port of call was to
Confederate-held areas where they might find comfort and security.
Dungarvan would certainly have been an option but it was a long, long
walk. The first question on the lips of the exiles would have been why
it had happened at all. As already noted here, peace negotiations and
diplomatic bargaining had been in process between the Earl of Ormond,
under the direction of King Charles and the Catholic Confederacy.
There was little or no hostile activity in the immediate area. Catholics
in Youghal had toed the line, not just since the outbreak of the war but
for the previous forty years. They had willingly given money to support
O'Brien's soldiers, regardless of which side he was on. There are only
two possible reasons why the government decided to suddenly expel the
Catholics from Youghal. Firstly, it was suspicious or had intelligence that
a fifth column (mutiny within the town) was being created. Secondly,
a decision was made to use the first possibility as an excuse to expel a
large section of the population in order to relieve hunger amongst
Protestants and the army. When one remembers how Youghal merchant
Patrick Coppinger demanded rent from the government because the
army was using part of his house for munitions, it is easy to see how the
government might have viewed his request with a jaundiced eye at a time
of war. It is conceivable that Coppinger was joined by other Catholic
merchants and businesses expressing similar complaints. The expulsion
certainly came as a surprise and shows the double-handed nature of
Ormond's diplomacy. While appeasing Catholics in his discussions,
with promises of religious tolerance on behalf of the king, he worked
in tandem with Broghill and O'Brien to rid the south Munster ports of
'ill-affected papists'. Sixteen years later, in 1660, Broghill would tell the
government that the Confederates had agents inside the city of Cork and

justified the expulsion of the Catholics while exonerating O'Brien for his part in the decision. His reason for the removal of Catholics from Youghal was rather weak:

> Nor were the Popish inhabitants of Youghal free from the guilt, since in their daily meetings they constantly prayed for the advancement of that good design, then on foot, for the Catholic cause as they termed it And though their wickedness might well have authorised a sharper revenge, yet, all that was taken of them was to put them out of a capacity of repeating that evil.[159]

This gives a clear insight into Protestant leadership thinking in Munster. They firmly believed that Catholics meeting to pray in Youghal were in fact plotting an uprising. Broghill offers no real evidence other than sectarian paranoia. He had stated in his original letter to Ormond in 1644 that he was 'not ignorant' to what the 'adverse party' were 'publicly boasting' but no reference is made to Youghal Catholics and it appears a decision was taken from intelligence gathered out of Cork. Whatever their reasons they were acting out the first oath of the Presbyterian Solemn League and Covenant, 'That we shall … without respect of persons, endeavour the extirpation of Popery.'

The savage reputation of Murrough 'the burner' O'Brien has been solidified further by historians who cite him for carrying out the order of 26 July. However, it was Ormond who requested the expulsion. In Broghill's letter to the deputy three weeks later he wrote that both he and O'Brien had obediently carried out the order for the expulsion as requested in the last paragraph of Ormond's letter. None of this was of upper importance to the expelled Catholics whose families had lived in Youghal, some for as much as two centuries, and now found themselves outside its walls with an uncertain future. How far or wide the radius of expulsion measured beyond the town into the suburbs and liberties is impossible to know. It is reasonable to suggest that Catholics were cleared from the immediate vicinity in the south, such as the Road to Hell (present-day Friar Street), Knockaverry and the Claycastle marshlands, as well as to the north of the town at the road to Cork, King's Highway and to the roads to Dungarvan and Tallow at two mile bridge.

A Garrison Town

Fitzgerald's, Raleigh's and Boyle's Youghal was dead and quickly forgotten. Within twenty-four hours Broghill dispatched orders for the upkeep and maintenance of the now Protestant-only town and most of these were directed at soldiers.

> These are to give notice that no officer, soldier, or other person, garrisoned or resident within this Town, on pain of death, to break open the houses of any persons who have, in obedience to my proclamation left the Town, or any house belonging to the Irish or papist, or carry away any goods of what nature so ever. And if any shall be found faulty herein, in the least, I shall not fail by death to punish their outrage and contempt.[160]

Why Broghill would threaten to execute anybody for breaking into vacant houses and businesses previously belonging to Catholics would become clear at a later date, but he certainly did not trust the army to uphold exemplary behaviour. The houses were, of course, full of goods that could be stolen and sold. It appears that Broghill had been charged with preparing the town to be repopulated and it was incumbent on him to keep the infrastructure safe from harm. A second proclamation on that Thursday morning warned:

> Whereas the gardens in and near this town and liberties, are in great hope to be a good help to the inhabitants if care be taken that the roots and fruit be preserved, from the violence of soldiers.[161]

The proclamations are very revealing and suggest that there may have been some resentment building up against wealthy merchant Catholics living along the main thoroughfare of King's Street. Many of the merchants had gardens wherein they may have jealousy guarded and probably sold fruit and vegetables. If O'Brien's and previously Boyle's letters are to be believed then the army was close to starvation, and with social order now being replaced by military government, soldiers may have felt entitled to act as they pleased. Broghill though, had pointed out that 'other inhabitants' had also 'wrongfully entered' gardens in town, in the abbeys and in the suburbs, and destroyed them. Protection of the gardens, as a source of food, was crucial without any guarantees of continuing support from England. But there was more for Broghill to do and the final proclamation of that day anticipated a Catholic backlash once those in the Confederate strongholds encountered the exiles walking the roads and countryside. They were sure to be angered by what they would see and hear and Broghill prepared those now left inhabiting Youghal:

> These are to give warning that all residents within the town and the Suburbs, who are above the age of seventeen and under the age of seventy-five be forthwith after this proclamation, standing at their doors furnished with such arms as they have or can procure, and be ready to pursue further directions.[162]

In this state of emergency, constables were appointed to survey the suburbs and abbeys to make sure the proclamation was followed, with a list of names of those residents who remained unarmed to be handed into Broghill at one o'clock. No such Catholic revenge mission would immediately take place but Broghill and O'Brien were not about to allow themselves lapse into self-congratulatory over-confidence. Youghal was effectively being turned into a military base and the plans had been in place probably since the onset of the ceasefire and certainly after Richard Boyle's death. Evidence that plans had been drawn up is manifest in the speed of the Catholic expulsion, the arming of the remaining citizens and the announcement of yet another order made a few weeks later when Broghill demanded, 'all aged men unfit for HM Service, and are at the public charge, as also all Women and children, fail not forthwith to prepare themselves by England the next shipping — daily expected — to embark for England, where they are better able to afford them relief than this'.

Being 'unfit for service' was obviously a reference to fighting, and the removal of all women and children points to an expectation of war. Also, that ships from England were 'daily expected' means Broghill and O'Brien had already organised the transportation of Protestants unable to fight a war weeks beforehand. The ships that carried out the deportations were almost certainly parliamentarian.

Youghal was no longer a centre of social interaction between
people of differing religions, culture, race or ethnicity that had
been expanding since the days of the first Norman families. Indeed,
socially, politically and commercially the town was contracting. When
Broghill ordered 'all women and children' he only meant those not
strong enough to take up arms. Some women and children remained
in the town, particularly those employed in trade and keeping house
as well as children in apprenticeship to master tradesmen. Broghill
however, warned against any attempts to hide persons reluctant to
leave and by this we should assume many families feared they would
not see each other again: 'I shall not fail to have them put out of the
Town, and punish the inhabitants who shall afford relief to such
as disobey my command.' The New English who had arrived under
Boyle's stewardship could not have foreseen the scenario of returning

to England, leaving their fathers, brothers and husbands behind in a world turned upside down. Those left behind had to adapt quickly. Many of them were, overnight, turning their attentions from trade skills to thoughts of siege and war, taking on a new career as auxiliaries. Indeed, everyone was now expected to turn his or her hand toward the inevitability of conflict in an increasingly volatile atmosphere. Anyone not in the army, including 'women, boys or maids ... above the age of thirteen and under three score ...' were ordered to be ready with 'spades, pickaxes, wheelbarrows and all other needful instruments'.[163] Broghill then set about letting out properties previously 'inhabited by Irish and English papists' to the remaining residents for a moderate weekly rent. What type of building and how many rooms was dependent on rank and the number of children in an officer's family. He was, however, furious to discover that many of the citizens had been guilty of breaking into the empty houses, shops and businesses to extract furniture for burning and had also taken door and window frames, ceilings and structural frameworks. The same destruction was being perpetrated in Cork with a reported 3,000 empty houses being ransacked 'and as many in Youghal'.[164]

While Broghill's militarising of Youghal continued apace, Ormond maintained royal diplomacy with the Confederates and successfully negotiated another ceasefire to be called on 10 September 1644. A stand-off between the Confederate forces of James Touchet and General Monro at Fort Charelemont in Ulster threatened to destabilise peace but nothing came of it. Broghill, while happy to announce the coming winter truce, was determined to keep the residents on their toes, ordering that the town's fortifications be revamped with work to begin at seven in the morning until four in the afternoon with an hour break for dinner. Perhaps with less focus on the possibility of attack, the governor turned his attention to the spiritual wellbeing of his soldiers. He told them there was no better way to thank God for their fortunes in war than to prostrate themselves before the alter every Sabbath and feast day. He ordered the army to present themselves on Bow Street (present-day Parnell Place) before the gates of the church in full uniform with arms 'prepared and fixed' where they would follow Broghill into service. Those who failed to attend were fined a week's wage.

With winter coming, news had reached Youghal that their Protestant peers in Amsterdam had collected charity money for the 'poor distressed Protestants' in Cork and Youghal. The supplies were to be distributed amongst the population of the towns irrespective of whether the recipients were soldiers or regular citizens. The money was used by the 'Committee for the Affairs of Ireland' in London to finance the seafaring mission of mercy to Ireland. Skipper Jacob Low in his ship the *Castel de Mina* was consigned to dock at Youghal. The cargo consisted of beans, white peas, salt and oatmeal. While Broghill expressed great appreciation for the cargo, he said the joy was offset by the town's 'miseries'. His humour was lifted however by the fact that the 'Hollanders' were so willing to relieve them and would upset Irish rebels: 'besides the satisfaction of having another nation, so sensible of our wrongs and miseries, as to send us their relief, it has so much perplexed and dis-animated the Irish Rebels, that the greatness of their discontentment is little inferior to our joy'.[165] On 20 November, another ship from London, *The Blessing* under Captain Thomas Winall, brought into Youghal 500 barrels of oats, 74 bags of biscuits and 200 cheeses. The year ended though with the customary worries over Catholic movements and impending doom.

Broghill departed for London to give a firsthand account of Munster's travails. He left the control of Youghal in the hands of William Fenton. Before leaving, he wrote to Richard Osborne, an old ally of Broghill's father, Richard Boyle. Osborne was a neighbour of the Boyle's, residing at Castle Knockmoan in County Waterford. In his letter, Broghill threatened to declare Osborne a traitor and taking the side of the Irish if Osborne did not make clear his intention to 'take the oath'. This was certainly the Solemn League and Covenant Oath. Broghill said he would be 'heartily sorry' to see an old family friend being disassociated and urged Osborne to contact Fenton immediately to clear any ambiguity attached to his reputation. Broghill had also demanded that the soldiers in Youghal publicly raise their hands and verbally swear to the oath. Broghill's apparent impatience with Osborne and his insistence on a show of loyalty, from a previously trusted aide, betrayed Broghill's uneasiness at a time of ceasefire. His urgency may have been based on intelligence regarding rebel movement around

Youghal in which, perhaps, Osborne was being associated. Meanwhile, Murrough O'Brien wrote to Captain Winall of *The Blessing*, still docked in Youghal, advising him to stay in the harbour. O'Brien said he had gathered information that the enemy had 'suddenly intended' to approach Youghal. He added that there was no other ship of sufficient strength to repel an attack and made it incumbent on *The Blessing* to protect the town. This intelligence regarding a possible assault may not have been related to Osborne or Broghill's suspicions of him but it was in fact sound. Within months, all apparent fears and predictions of a siege scenario would be realised with war coming to Youghal's doorstep.

9

Blood on the Blackwater

The 1645 Siege of Youghal

The New Year of 1645 saw Youghal residents hold on grimly to the conviction that they were about to be attacked by the Catholic Confederate armies. A letter signed by a number of officials including Lord Broghill, William Supple, William Fenton Godfrey Green, Percy Smyth and a host of others was sent to Murrough O'Brien asking him to travel to London and convince parliament of the depth of Youghal's problems. Broghill had already been to England to urge parliament to support the Munster war effort. The London government, however, had financial problems of its own with the civil war raging on. The cloud of fatalism settling on the Youghal council was evident in the closing message of its letter to O'Brien: 'For your safe voyage the prayers of all distressed Protestants in this province will be fervent.'

By March, sickness descended on Youghal. The town could not afford to be struck down with illness as men, women and children were expected to take up arms. Any compromise of their full health was seen as an opportunity for preying rebels. Broghill blamed the spread of disease on the 'distemperature of the air, proceeding from noisome (foul) dunghills.' The practice of human and animal waste being left in piles at the backs of houses, at doors and on the street was still very common. Broghill also ordered that horses be given preference over cattle for grazing prime grasses in the suburbs of the town. The move was to ensure that horses be fit for military action. Bringing horses outside the North and South Gates to graze could be a perilous exercise. Certainly, horse minders, grooms or soldiers would be required to bring weapons to defend themselves against rebel snipers.

Those living in the suburbs and exposed to the danger of attack would have cast an envious eye toward the walls and gates, particularly at night when the gates of the town were locked.

A more potent ill wind than that emanating from dunghills on the Youghal streets began to drift toward the town by the beginning of April. The Confederate commander, James Touchet, who many thought had missed an opportunity to advance the Catholic cause in the stand-off at Fort Charlemont in Ulster, had turned around and headed south, toward Munster. While the ceasefire was still official it meant nothing to men such as Touchet. The southern campaign was underway. Touchet led a two-pronged attack on Munster with Thomas Preston besieging and taking the Duncannon Fort in Wexford earlier in the year. An attempt by Touchet to gather crucial supplies left for him at Imokilly was scuppered by O'Brien whose forces came out of Cork to intercept the Confederates. O'Brien, as was his wont, set the provisions on fire and with the help of a company from Youghal continued to burn the land to slow Touchet's progress. This did not prevent the rebel commander from appearing before Youghal on 16 April with an audacious demand that Catholic mass should be said in St Mary's within six days. Broghill responded by reporting to the Confederates that Protestant service had been celebrated regularly for the past six months. Touchet's demand for mass to be celebrated in Youghal may have been more about military reconnaissance than religion, as he made no attempt to remain in the area or engage in any hostile action. Later, after O'Brien again engaged Touchet in a skirmish in the countryside between Castlelyons and Fermoy, he questioned captured Confederate prisoners about their commander's intentions. They confessed that Touchet had designs for an attack on Youghal, believing that it would not hold out for long. It was clear that the Confederate commander had a strategy for the taking of Youghal and was waiting for the right time to move.

O'Brien's injured were taken to Cork and Youghal where they were treated by local surgeons. Meanwhile, the Protestant forces captured a member of the notorious Condon family during the engagement with the rebels. The captors declared the prisoner had cut out the tongues and chopped off the noses of enemy horses.

Touchet, whose army managed to outride the flaming wildfires of O'Brien's burning fields, was now camped at Cappoquin Castle. Here, he demanded the surrender of the governor of the castle and his troops. Touchet displayed some flair for humour in his letter writing. Having told the governor at Cappoquin to pull in his flag and surrender, he promised he would allow the soldiers free passage from the area and would order his own armies to stand aside. Those inside the castle were entitled to feel some scepticism though, as Touchet added, 'if any misfortune happens to you, you are not to blame me, either in this world or the next, having given you this timely notice.' The inhabitants were given half an hour to surrender, which they did. Touchet then marched on to Conna Castle where he admitted to 'putting some to the sword and hanging the rest'.

Touchet's rampage through the Blackwater valley brought him to Mogeely Castle the following day. He stated in his letter to the Mogeely governor that he 'seldom' gave quarter when he found resistance. He informed the occupants of the castle that he was before them because of the trouble they had brought to the country. Intriguingly, Touchet's letter reveals how the enemy, adrift from the safety of both Cork and Youghal, were trying to negotiate their way out of their predicament. Touchet said he was growing tired of their 'day to day' promises to surrender the castle and 'become yourself of our party', suggesting the enemy would rather join the ranks of the Catholic Confederacy than die. The following day he lost patience and submitted another notice: 'You will be infallibly hanged ... or put the sword.' He then sent in terms for their surrender. He told them the governor, the ward and the women would be allowed to make 'safe convoy to Youghal'. The soldiers would also be guaranteed free passage to Youghal on giving up all their provisions and arms. If they refused he threatened to 'pull them out by the ears'. According to the records the inhabitants surrendered. However, they were stripped of their clothes and marched barefoot along the 15 kilometres to Lismore Castle. Those inside Lismore Castle were encouraged to look upon their naked and humiliated peers in the hope that their debasement would induce an immediate surrender. Touchet was not present at the siege, expressing his unwillingness to see the destruction of a house where he had been welcomed and entertained prior to the war. He sent Major-General Purcell to take the castle. Purcell had failed to take Lismore when Broghill defended it three years earlier. This time it took five to six days to secure control of it. The forlorn Lismore prisoners were eventually released and told to walk to Youghal, arriving there late at night.

On 28 June, having rejoined his Confederate army, Touchet camped on the grounds of Temple Michael, a few hundred metres from Molana Abbey. As was customary, Touchet offered quarter to the occupants. The governor refused. The following day Touchet submitted a letter:

> If I be not short of memory, you may remember that when yesterday I sent for you, you did not only refuse to come, but in my defiance flourished a sword on top of that Castle I tell you Sir, for this, I will shoot you out of the cannon's mouth, and give my soldiers the massacring of all under your warders.[166]

Touchet followed this up with another notice, this time using words such as 'terror' and 'destruction'. When this failed, he offered yet another option to those inside. He told the governor of the castle he would guarantee them safe passage to Youghal 'provided you march out instantly'. Though these were favourable terms to the besieged enemy, what happened next reveals much about the condition of Touchet's army and his leadership qualities, and how both may have had consequences for later events at Youghal. The commander states in his memoirs that an 'accident' occurred while he engaged in some relaxation by heading across the Temple Michael lands to hunt. Having secured the castle he handed responsibility over to a Colonel Hennessey. However, with Touchet out of sight, Hennessey was forced to enter Temple Michael castle to protect those inside from his own men. Touchet heard gunshots in the distance and returned immediately to find his soldiers running into the woods. Hennessey reported their mutinous behaviour and after a prolonged chase, with beating drums and trumpet blowing, Touchet rounded up his company. The commander spoke to all those involved and then offered them a chance to draw lots. Two from each battalion, the unlucky lot winners would be shot. However, Touchet thought the numbers for execution were 'too great'. A second drawing of lots was held for 'two only, which suffered'.[167]

Touchet's problems at Temple Michael reveal the indiscipline officers were faced with amongst the ranks. If in saying two of his company 'suffered' he meant they were executed, then he had the ability to rein in such indiscipline. However, he doesn't make it explicitly clear if he did shoot the two soldiers. The reports that inevitably came back to Youghal from those who were freed from Temple Michael and the other castles along the Blackwater valley belt would have given Broghill some confidence that the Catholic Confederates were undisciplined and unfocused. While Broghill would not refuse Protestant refugees fleeing to Youghal he could ill-afford to feed and house them. However, the intelligence they had to offer regarding Touchet's company, such as numbers, weapons, horses and general state of the Confederates was invaluable to the port garrison leaders, who by now were preparing for an assault on the town.

The Siege of Youghal

Aware of the Confederates approaching Youghal, help was immediately sought by Broghill and O'Brien, who had since been appointed by parliament as President of Munster. On receipt of intelligence regarding Confederate movements, parliament sent assistance to Munster. On 5 July, William Penn, Admiral of the Irish Seas, discussed the Youghal situation with O'Brien and several commanders over dinner aboard his ship in Cork harbour. Youghal's possible destruction was digested along with the best of meat and fine wine. It was agreed amongst the officers that O'Brien would send soldiers from Cork and Kinsale to Youghal. The man-of-war frigate *Duncannon* was dispatched by Penn under Captain Samuel Howett to Kinsale to transport 100 soldiers for the protection of Youghal. At Cork harbour, the *Mayflower* was docked and taking on as many men as it could hold. Meanwhile, in Youghal, preparations were also afoot for the evacuation of women and children, but only those related to the elite of the town. According to Penn, Captain Claxon arrived at Cork harbour coming from Youghal with Lady Broghill and other 'women of quality' as well as many children for their safety.

The following day Penn received intelligence that a battalion from the Youghal garrison had travelled out to attack the Confederates who were approaching, killing 300 of them. He reported that the rebels had set down about 3 miles from Youghal. Penn set sail from Cork harbour and arrived at Youghal at five in the afternoon on 8 July. The *Mayflower* and another frigate, the *Nicholas*, were already sitting in the bay having carried out a reconnaissance mission. The next morning Penn went ashore in a small boat and dined with Youghal governor Sir Percy Smith. At this meeting, most likely taking place in the war rooms of Boyle's former residence, strategies to negate a Confederate siege were discussed over dinner. Smith insisted that both the northern and southern areas of the town needed protection. Despite some reluctance from Penn to expose his ships to possible cannon fire, he agreed to place a ship at either end of the town. The *Duncannon* was placed at the north end (present-day Green's Quay) while the *Nicholas* surveyed the south end at the mouth of the bay. Following a second meeting, this time on Penn's ship, Smith gave him a letter from O'Brien requesting ammunition be brought into the town. Penn called a council of war with his officers from all the ships and they agreed to share with the town what arms they could. Broghill then took one of Penn's ships to Cork harbour. There he met with O'Brien to discuss the state of affairs in Youghal.

Meanwhile, Touchet, in his own words, 'camped loosely' outside Youghal on the north side in order to 'distress the place'.[168] Major-General Purcell, who led 1,500 men, accompanied Touchet. Purcell and his company were sent with two cannons to the entrance of Youghal harbour at the south side of the town (present-day Lighthouse hill). The plan was to prevent provisions and weapons coming into the town by sea. Purcell's two cannons would have to be pulled, probably by ox, uphill and around the back of the town in order to reach the other side. The Cork Hill route would have been too dangerous, being so close to the fortified towers of the town walls, meaning the march would have been an arduous drag across the fields. It is likely that Purcell took his force and cannons up a narrow passage from the Quarry Road and across the western hills through Springfield. From here, he may have followed a dried-out path that used to carry water from Springfield toward the south hill of the town overlooking the bay. Purcell would have found the top of Poison Bush Hill following this path. With the south entrance to Yougal blocked by Purcell's artillery, Touchet left a number of Confederate soldiers at the north end of the river by Youghal and returned to Temple Michael. There, under the cover of darkness, he slipped his own company and cannons across the river during the night. He wrote in his memoirs, 'and before day had my two guns planted at the ferry-point, over against Youghal'.[169] The Confederates worked through the night and constructed a 20-foot ditch in rectangular shape with two 12-foot ramparts (platforms) to mount their cannons.

Youghal was now under close siege. Touchet's forces would be joined by Thomas Preston, who had successfully taken the fort of Duncannon in Wexford. To counteract Confederate movements, parliament sent another ship with 300–400 men from Naseby, England. They had originally been part of King Charles's royalist force but were defeated and captured by Cromwell at Naseby. Parliament thought the prisoners an ideal addition for Penn. However, they had no stomach for battle and, having landed at Youghal, absconded to the Confederate forces. Parliament called them 'brutes, void of reason or understanding' that had run to the 'unclean beasts' of the Catholic Confederacy.[170] Touchet and Preston would have welcomed the addition of 300 to 400 men to their ranks.

The scene was set and on Sunday 13 July, over the calm waters of Youghal Bay, the first shots of the siege were fired. Penn reported the close sighting of Confederates on the hill to the east of the harbour. The horsemen were preparing ground for the erection of another cannon on the Waterford headland of Passage Point. This meant that Youghal was effectively squared off by two points on the Waterford side of the river – Passage Point and Ferry Point and by two points on the Youghal side – north and south of the town. Both the *Duncannon* and the *Nicholas* fired at the horsemen on Passage Point, without success.

Penn then ordered that 100 men were to be sent ashore to help the town as had been agreed with Sir Percy Smith. They also brought with them the agreed amounts of ammunition.

Three days after the opening of hostilities, the *Nicholas* fired on Confederate guns at Poison Bush on the south side. Penn took a small boat from his own ship and boarded the *Nicholas* to inquire about the incident. Through a spyglass, Penn and Captain Bray witnessed a number of the Confederates at the top of the hill in the area of Poison Bush digging earth to build a platform for their cannons. Penn was satisfied that the firing range of the guns could not damage the parliament ships from that distance. That evening the blast of cannons could be heard breaking the summer air over Youghal. Shots were fired from the town fort on the quayside across the river to where the Confederates were now placing a cannon on the hill of Passage Point. The following morning hostilities intensified when Touchet's cannons on the ferry point blasted at the *Duncannon* as she surveyed the river waters. The ship returned fire before a sudden explosion ripped through her decks. In flames, she slowly began to sink, remaining semi-submerged having settled in the shallow water north of the ferry point. The Youghal council of war later recorded that it was an 'unfortunate accident by some fire in the gunroom' with Penn making the same claim in his journal. O'Brien would later say that a Confederate cannon ball took the head off a woman holding a candle in the gunpowder room of the ship, with obvious consequences. Admiral Penn counted ten dead but notes that Captain Howett, the master and other crew survived.

The sinking of the *Duncannon* was a major boost to the Confederates and a shocking blow to someone of the stature of Penn. Onlookers in Youghal would have been enveloped by a sense of dread as they watched the *Duncannon*'s masts burn to a cinder. Admiral Penn was furious and, as much as he pressed, he could not convince his men to go back out to the stranded man-of-war to retrieve weapons, guns and provisions.

Later that day the Confederates turned their guns and pointed them at the walls of the town. It was a day when Penn and Sir Percy Smith would narrowly avoid death. Two Confederate boats that had come downriver to supply Touchet and Thomas Preston were intercepted by one of Penn's barges. As Penn, Smith, officers and

town officials observed the situation from the fort on the quay, Confederate guns from the ferry point opened fire on the town. Penn described the walls as flying 'thick about our ears'.[171] Two lieutenants and two soldiers were killed and five others injured. A distressed Penn returned to his ship in the bay where the surviving injured from the *Duncannon* were on board, still refusing to agree to a salvage mission. The next morning saw hostilities resume when the *Nicholas* was hit several times by the cannon on the hill of Passage Point, killing two crew-members and repelling the ship from entering the harbour. Despite the presence of big guns on both sides of the river, relative freedom of traffic further out in the bay afforded ships from Cork to keep supplying Penn with goods and weapons, most of which were taken perilously into the quayside. A supply ship also arrived from Milford Haven offering relief to the parliament seamen.

Communication continued between the parliament ships in the bay and town officials by letter. A fire was lit on the tower of South Abbey to inform the ships in the bay when it was safe to come ashore. Support from O'Brien and Vice-Admiral John Crowther continued with efforts to get food and supplies into Youghal.

With the siege dragging on into the end of July, both sides exchanged fire without causing serious damage. Penn recounts that skirmishes took place off the strand of Youghal between parliament and Confederate boats. Confederate musketeers also lined the strand, cliffs and rocks, firing at will at boats seeking safe passage to the town. At ten in the evening on 30 July, Touchet began a relentless bombardment of the quay walls with cannon balls hurtling across the river. The barrage continued all night and for the following four or five days. Penn's patience was stretched to the limit when a Captain Thomas Dorwich refused to enter Youghal harbour. Dorwich was escorting two small fishing boats laden with provisions, but having seen the Confederate guns he would not budge, even though his own wife and children were trapped in the town. Penn threatened to tie him to the mast and send in the ship. Dorwich eventually agreed to assist the boats.

There is little evidence to describe conditions within Youghal at this point of the siege. Sorties from the garrison did take place infrequently and the cannon at Poison Bush was later attacked and dismounted. Penn reported that some residents who had left the town to cut grass in the suburbs in order to feed cattle and horses were shot and killed while the parliament record states:

> The town is very much straightened for provisions, for although they have not passing 1,400 fighting men, yet they have at least 6,000 women and poor children, so that 100 barrels of wheat is but a pound of bread for a soul considering how it may shrink in the baking and distributing.[172]

By 9 August intelligence was trickling through to Penn that Touchet and Preston had started to retreat from the environs of Youghal. A week later, the Confederates were reported to be 6 miles from the town. The two-month siege was all but over. Touchet wrote in his memoirs that the arrival of more ships from Cork convinced him that continuing the siege was pointless. He simply remarked that he 'marched off' and spent the rest of the campaign ruining the harvests. Meanwhile Admiral Penn gathered all his company on the deck of his ship on 18 August in Cork, announced he was relinquishing leadership and handed command to Vice-Admiral John Crowther. They then sailed to Youghal. Penn stayed a number of days, taking in a service for his soldiers at St Mary's Collegiate Church by his minister, presumably in celebration of their defence of Youghal. He then left for Milford Haven. Though Touchet and Preston departed, it did not end the hostilities around Youghal. Attacks on the town continued well into the end of the year. However, the concerted effort of the Confederate commanders to seize the crucial strategic port from the hands of parliament and drive a wedge between it and the port of Cork had failed.

Touchet and Preston's failure has been cited as a turning point in the war in Munster. Parliament believed that had Youghal collapsed then the rest of Munster would follow. Reasons for the Confederates' collapse at the siege are varied. It is thought that Preston had little respect for Touchet, thereby negating a combined effort and undermining the campaign.[173] Infighting and indecision amongst the Confederate leaders may have been a debilitating factor.[174] There is also a theory that the lord deputy and ally to O'Brien, the Earl of Ormond, had pressured the Supreme Confederate Council during its ongoing talks to send word to Touchet not to take Youghal, although using Youghal as a bargaining chip may have been an advantage to both the Confederacy and Ormond throughout the negotiations for different reasons. Touchet is somewhat flippant in his memoirs about the outcome, expressing no regret, as if it mattered little to him that the town was not taken. However, the inability to achieve what would have been major progress in the war for the Confederates might be more tactical and straightforward rather than the result of conspiracy theories, weak leadership and political bartering.

Touchet's campaign along the Blackwater valley met with little resistance. This may have created an unqualified confidence in the Confederates' minds. The campaign appears successful. Touchet took the castles without spilling much blood, if any. However, the castles were more or less hopelessly exposed in rural vicinities already surrounded by Confederate strongholds. Youghal, on the other hand, while suffering to a degree, was a tougher nut to crack. Strategically, it was considered a high priority to parliament, whose control of the Irish Sea played a huge role in supplying the town with provisions and weapons. The geographical nature of Youghal is also an important factor not considered by historians. The Confederates knew that penetration by sea, as evidenced in the accounts, was extremely difficult, if not impossible. An attack from the hills on the well-fortified walls to the west along Raheen Road appears to be an option not taken by the Confederates, who opted instead to strangle supply routes by river and sea. The walls on the hill behind the town are remarkably well preserved. It may be that camping in the open area before the walls on Raheen Road would have left the Confederates exposed to attack from behind on the open plains by O'Brien's Cork troops, which was the case with the cannons at Poison Bush. The only other option was to barge their way through the narrow entrances at the South and North Gates. Storming the town would have resulted in huge casualties. The only viable option, the one taken, was to shoot from a distance and hope the town would surrender or starve. However, the Confederates themselves struggled with a lack of food supplies and weapons. Judging by Touchet's tone, it became obvious to them that the waiting game in the open environment was affecting their efforts and patience more than it was those within the relative comfort of the town walls. Neither Touchet nor Preston could have predicted how long they would have to persist with a siege. Every parliament ship that entered Youghal waters with supplies, weapons and soldiers drained the confidence from the Confederates already exhausted from the campaign across the summer months. It is far from certain that had Youghal fallen to the Confederates the rest of Munster would have followed, as the parliamentarians professed. With Waterford and Wexford under control of the Confederates the loss of Youghal would, however, have created a south-eastern belt of resistance against Protestant interests. The fact that such a strong line of anti-government ports did not transpire would be significant in the coming years, not just for Youghal or Munster but for the whole nation of Ireland as it faced its greatest challenge since Henry VIII declared sovereignty over the country in 1542.

10

Death or Hell

Oliver Cromwell and
the Military Coups of 1649

Those sitting in the gallery of the Youghal court in October 1646 may have sniggered or even booed at the misfortune that had befallen Elizabeth Silvester. Elizabeth was found guilty for being a 'scold, a thief and an incontinent woman'. She was joined in the dock by the Widow Coney for 'having a bastard'.[175] Widow Sheffield was also being shamed for blocking a gutter at Tynte's Castle to the extent that a very large pool made it impossible for people to pass. Others, such as Major Gifford, were being charged for dumping their dung into their neighbour's garden. The guilty, with the exception of Major Gifford, could expect to find themselves in the stocks along King's Street or to be standing in the pillory cage, their public humiliation complete. It had been almost a year since Youghal was gripped by fear of death and starvation in the two-month siege by the Confederates. The courts, council meetings, markets and fairs were reopened and fully operational. Relative normality was returning despite the war raging on across the country.

On 12 July Bunratty Castle in Limerick fell to the Confederates. The castle had been occupied by the somewhat ineffectual and negligent Barnabas O'Brien, who had honeymooned in Youghal during Boyle's golden years. Admiral Penn was present at the siege of Bunratty but lacked the good fortune he had experienced in Youghal. Two weeks later, the seemingly inexhaustible Earl of Ormond had secured another peace treaty with the Confederacy, at least on paper. Matters had become increasingly complicated amongst the various stakeholders.

The Holy See of Rome, much to the surprise of the Irish, appointed and sent Monsignor Gianbattista Rinuccini as Papal Nuncio, to parley with the Confederate Catholics of Ireland. It was an insertion of a great external and largely uninvited authority into the complexity of the conflict. Unfortunately for the Supreme Council of the Catholic Confederacy, it had already agreed to terms with Ormond and King Charles, whose position in England was growing weaker by the day. Many of the original demands the Ulster insurgents had hoped to achieve in 1641 were met in the treaty. Among these were concessions made to Catholics for the holding of offices, landownership confirmation, amnesty from acts of war and changes to a number of plantation schemes, such as the one in Connacht. The Supreme Council of the Catholic Confederacy had fought hard and, to a degree, won some political ground in the Ormond Peace Treaty. The problem with Rinuccini, at least where the Irish Confederacy was concerned, is that he believed the treaty had fallen short on the protection of the Catholic faith. The Church was focused on ecclesiastical rather than political or social designs. Rinuccini denounced the treaty, hence throwing confusion into the political, social and religious reality of life in war-torn Ireland. The Papal Nuncio went further still, ordering excommunication to all that supported the Ormond peace treaty. The Vatican however, did not welcome or approve of Rinuccini's punitive declaration. By September 1646, Rinuccini joined the Irish clergy in creating the 'New Supreme Council' in Kilkenny, thereby creating division in the Confederacy and stagnating the progress of their political agenda.[176] In truth, the Irish nation had become scaffolding without braces, built around a fractured ideology that was neither wholly political nor religious. There was no foundation to build on because there was no central theme to the war since its outbreak in 1641 and now, five years later, there was no central body on which the different factions could rely on for guidance. Added to this malaise in confidence and purpose was the less-than-helpful allegiance of royalist Catholics to a king whose utmost concern was the preservation of his monarchy. His reliance on Irish Catholics to support him against the increasingly hardline parliament and Puritan power of Cromwell in England was paramount in the success of the treaty. Charles gave concessions to the Irish Catholics because they represented the least of three evils: parliament, death or Catholic support. In all, Ireland was a desperate landscape populated by desperate men.

During this period, tensions grew between Murrough O'Brien and Lord Broghill (Roger Boyle). The Boyles were never particularly taken with the President of Munster, especially after he claimed credit for the victory at Liscarrol where four of Richard Boyle's sons had fought, with one of them being mortally wounded on the battlefield. The men had co-operated throughout the siege of Youghal to protect Protestant interests. Though they were both descendants of Irish aristocracy and long-serving agents of the Crown in Ireland they also recognised the power of parliament. However, Broghill remained suspicious of O'Brien. He resented O'Brien's reticence in wholly accepting the full terms of the Solemn League and Covenant Oath.[177] Broghill was entrenched in the Elizabethan traditions of his father and the adventurer policies of Raleigh. He believed Ireland would have to succumb eventually to English culture and religion. He had grown up in Youghal where those policies appeared to be a success. Now resident in London, Broghill began to challenge O'Brien by undermining him in a whispering campaign at Westminster. He was effectively looking to re-inherit the control of Munster that his father had once enjoyed.

Throughout 1647, in spite of the fragile Ormond peace treaty, violence continued to burst out like a persistent rash across the provinces. Lines of loyalty and division were been drawn amongst the various factions. Ormond lost control of Dublin, handing it over to the parliamentarian forces of Michael Jones, before relinquishing his seat as Lord Lieutenant of Ireland. With Youghal secure for now, Murrough O'Brien was relatively free to continue his crusade against the Confederates on behalf of parliament across Munster. In September he decorated the pantheon of his notoriety at Cashel. With hundreds of men, women and children trapped in the castle, O'Brien offered them quarter if they could pay £3,000 and a month's pay to his army. The besieged refused. O'Brien, with over 2,000 soldiers carrying swords and pistols, stormed the castle at three in the afternoon. What transpired has become a debate for historians. A wholesale massacre is probably wide of the mark but so too is the contention that civilians were killed, including women and children, only because they had picked up arms.[178] Whatever the exact truth, there is little to argue that the madness of the war, with incomprehensible acts of violence and cruelty, common and regular throughout these years, still managed to create a legend out of Cashel. The event cemented the reputation of O'Brien as Catholic enemy number one. Having taken the castle, O'Brien's forces set the town of Cashel alight for the inability of its residents to forward money to their aggressors.

The following year, in April 1648, O'Brien took an extraordinary step that was certain to surprise all parties, not least parliament and Cromwell in London; he re-declared his loyalty to King Charles in opposition to the parliamentarians. The king had been arrested and, much to O'Brien's dismay, held captive in England. Like many others, O'Brien had advocated for the reduction of the Crown's absolute powers, but he was against a total removal of the king. As much as O'Brien had shown resilience and fortitude on the side of parliament, the base treatment of the king was foreign to his thinking and alien to the ancient structure of government for a nation. O'Brien made his officers and soldiers swear allegiance to the Crown, threatening to kill anyone who refused. It was, particularly after Cashel, a stunning reverse. For the Protestants of Youghal the sudden defection of their leader to the cause of King Charles would have created a great sense of unease and no little amount of confusion, though there would be plenty of sympathy for his reasoning. Since the outbreak of the war, parliament and O'Brien had been active, militarily and financially, in securing the town's safety. The garrison there had taken the Solemn League and Covenant Oath as a sign of their commitment to parliament. Now, those same people were expected to forsake very recent events, ignore the oath and concentrate all their efforts on defending the interests of the imprisoned and forlorn king. The emphasis of the war had shifted away from the social, political and religious rights of Catholics to a straight fight between those loyal to the king and those sympathetic to the rising Protestant/Puritan parliamentarians of England who were looking to overthrow the monarchy. Youghal's destiny and that of its people, as a consequence, lay between O'Brien, Ormond and the Catholic Confederates on one hand and Broghill, Cromwell and the parliament in England on the other.

O'Brien's reversal had effectively shifted him into unknown territory. He would now be negotiating with the very people he had set out to destroy – the Confederacy. Indeed, by May 1648, only a month after his change of heart, he secured a truce with the Catholics. Rinuccini was outraged that Catholics would bed in with the desecrator of Cashel. Again, he threatened excommunication for anyone who signed up to the clauses of the O'Brien truce. By October, Ormond was being encouraged to align O'Brien's army with Confederate forces. In London, watching events unfold, Broghill had a decision to make about where his allegiance should lie. O'Brien's surprise defection to the king offered Broghill an opportunity to regain control over his family's town of Youghal and ascend to the title held by his father as Earl of Cork.

Cromwell Looks to Ireland

The year 1649 began dramatically with the trial of Charles I. By the end of January the king was beheaded. Parliament had gone where many thought they could not and would not venture: the overthrow of the monarchy. England was now a republic. The way was clear for Cromwell and parliament to run England as a purely constitutionalist state. The event created shock waves across Europe where monarchies were the mainstay of government. In both Ireland and Scotland faint hopes were still held that Charles II could be restored to the vacant throne. Royalist Protestants and Catholics as well as a faction of the Confederates in Ireland created a new alliance, sealed by Ormond, in the hope of reinstating the Crown. Murrough O'Brien, now an unlikely ally of the royalist forces, was effectively fighting side by side with his old enemy, James Touchet. Touchet and others, such as Ormond, had shifted their concerns to a straight fight between parliament and reclaiming the Crown for Charles II. Meanwhile, many of the Catholic Confederates, disillusioned by the new coalition, held grimly to the belief that the war was still about the Catholic cause, backed by the support of the Papal Nuncio, Rinuccini. However,

Rinuccini was so dismayed by the Royalist–Confederate coalition that he gave up the Irish ghost and left the country.

For O'Brien and Ormond, descendants of the Old English and steeped in the history of the Norman family dynasties, a world that had no king could not be countenanced or even imagined. For them, the dissolution of the three kingdoms was an absurdity. The world of seventeenth-century Ireland and Britain had been turned upside down before, but this was a world turned inside out, a sort of parallel universe. God, and God only, had the right to appoint or remove a king, as had always been determined by divine providence. For the constitutionalists in England there was logic in the belief that the beheading of a fuddled king was the purification of both Church and State. As God-fearing as Cromwell was, he could not accept what he saw as a corrupt regime, lapsed Protestantism and an absolutist king who behaved more like a demigod, abusing the gift of divine providence, rather than using it wisely to lead his people. Charles I represented a cancer that needed to be removed before it spread across three nations.

Meanwhile, officials in Youghal, still in constant communication with O'Brien, played an astute and obedient waiting game. Over the four years since the siege, O'Brien's communications with the town council were concerned with the financing of his Munster army and the garrison in Youghal. He recommended that the council appoint Adam Warring as mayor in the summer of 1647. The council, of course, agreed. Warring was a close associate of O'Brien and could therefore act as his ears and mouth while he continued his campaigns abroad the countryside. O'Brien struggled throughout the years 1647–49 to secure direct support from England and placed a heavy burden on the corporation. His decision to declare for the beleaguered Charles following the king's arrest in 1648 had a knock-on effect in Youghal. Outside of the confusion it caused amongst officials about how they should subsequently behave, it opened the gates of the town to returning Catholics.

It is more than probable that Catholics had been trickling back into Youghal and Cork in any regard. However, with O'Brien now a royalist and Broghill in London, there was nothing, other than the suspicions of the town's Protestant population, preventing Catholics from 'going home'. It is extremely difficult to know how many of the formerly expelled Catholics regained ownership of their properties and businesses, but the commercial viability of the town demanded that Catholic professionals, their expertise and contacts, at least be reintegrated into the social fabric for commercial purposes alone. Youghal, almost by default, settled back into relative normality. On 2 May 1649, the Earl of Ormond sent a letter from Kilkenny Castle to the Youghal Council expressing the 'absolute necessity of having a certain quantity of biscuit forthwith provided, for the use of His Majesty's army'.[179] Ormond was in fact looking for four thousand-weight of biscuit to be made in the town bakery. The biscuits were to be shipped to New Ross and were to be well packed and delivered no later than the end of the month. Clearly, locals were still under order from the Royalist camp of O'Brien and Ormond, though they heard little now from O'Brien who was fighting a successful campaign in Drogheda and Dundalk. Youghal was in a very difficult position. Its political, religious and social future depended on whether they would stick with O'Brien or twist to Broghill and Cromwell. In June the heat was being turned up when parliament formally appointed Oliver Cromwell Governor-General of Ireland and Commander-in-Chief of the Army. They then sanctioned Cromwell to take his New Model Army into Ireland to finally cure its ills.

Whether information about Cromwell's appointment reached Youghal by the time they were up to their elbows in biscuits for O'Brien's and Ormond's army is unknown. It is also impossible to know if Youghal soldiers, residents and officials had, at this stage, faith in the royalist cause, though they were bound to have been aware of O'Brien's successes against parliament forces in Drogheda and Dundalk. Cromwell's arrival was still weeks away. Wexford, Waterford, Cork and Kilkenny remained firmly on the side of Ormond and O'Brien so it is reasonable to assume that Youghal felt secure as part of the urban centre chain. As a reminder by officials as to where Youghal should be standing in such uncertain times, Youghal fishermen Andrew Whittingstall, Hugh Richards, William Walker and Thomas Roe were warned not to board any type or size of parliament ship or boat. This was no small matter. With parliament ships virtually ruling the Irish Sea, Youghal could quickly become isolated from life-saving supplies, not to mention the sufferance brought on by the blockading of trade. There is no evidence to suggest at this stage of the war, prior to Cromwell's arrival, that thoughts of mutiny existed in the minds of Youghal inhabitants. O'Brien was sure to remain confident that a town which had such a long history of being fiercely royalist, in both Catholic and Protestant quarters, would share his outrage at the death of the king. Town leaders may well have been out in sympathy with the President of Munster. However, they could just as easily have mused, in equal measure, whether the town could withstand an onslaught by Cromwell's forces.

Before departing for Ireland, Cromwell held discussions in London with Lord Broghill, clearly outlining his plans for Ireland and for Munster. Broghill, who also found the idea of an English republic difficult, would require some persuading by Cromwell to renege on his loyalty to the Crown. Broghill initially supported a restoration, with the exiled Charles II waiting in the wings. However, there was too much for Broghill to gain in considering Cromwell's proposals for Ireland, not least the possible riddance of O'Brien. Such a move would clear the path for his ambitions for Munster. He chose his side wisely. The winds of providence were at Cromwell's back and Broghill knew that if the General of the New Model Army was to go to Ireland, given its chaotic state and divisions, then he had reasons to be optimistic that Cromwell could finally bring Ireland under control. Dublin was already in parliament hands and if Cromwell could secure the major ports in Munster – Cork, Kinsale and Youghal – then he could control the province. Broghill was in a good position to bargain. If he could sway allegiance from the three ports toward Cromwell, then he would be owed a favour in return. For Youghal, a dilemma had arisen that the town's residents and army could not have expected. Forced by O'Brien to obey his declaration, first to the imprisoned and then deceased King Charles, they were crushed by the weight of dilemma on which side they should place their futures. The choice was straightforward: O'Brien, who had military control of their town and of Munster, or Cromwell, who had military control of England and would soon be at their doorsteps.

The Military Coups of 1649

Cited, perhaps, as the greatest English writer and author of *Paradise Lost*, John Milton was a Puritan and a republican. He believed in Cromwell. He wrote, 'God is decreeing some new and great period. What does He then but reveal himself ... as his manner is, first to his Englishmen?' The Puritan fanaticism afforded Cromwell and Milton the luxury, without embarrassment, of claiming God was manifest through the virtues of Englishness. Such a righteous and awe-inspiring syndicate between the sword and the cross was not new, of course; it had driven warriors forth since Emperor Constantine, who, visualising the cross of Jesus in the sky, entered Rome to decree a new Holy Roman Christian Empire in 312. On 15 August 1649, Oliver Cromwell was repeating history, albeit the same God behind him. The new decree was to cleanse Christianity of the Catholic heresy. He arrived with his New Model Army in Dublin believing his mission, to suppress Irish barbarism, was wholly sanctioned and supported by God's good works. He had sailed from Milford Haven with over thirty ships and 4,000 men. A second squadron departed the following day. Close to eighty ships were bound for the Munster ports. Depending on the success of the sailings, and presumably, on which would be the more welcoming, Youghal and Kinsale were nominated as possible ports for the landing. Fortunately for Youghal, rough seas and high winds diverted the ships north to Dublin.[180] On 10 September Cromwell stood before Drogheda and demanded a surrender of the town. The forces at Drogheda refused. What transpired is well documented. Drogheda's inhabitants were slaughtered. Somewhere between 2,000 and 3,000 were massacred, clergy and civilians amongst them. Cromwell put the day's work down to the 'spirit of God', adding:

> It hath pleased God to bless our endeavors in Drogheda ... The enemy were about 3,000 strong in the town ... I do not think 30 of the whole number escaped with their lives. Those that did are in safe custody for the Barbados ... I wish that all honest hearts may give the glory of this to God alone, to whom indeed the praise of this mercy belongs.

For Cromwell, justice had been meted out to those who had perpetrated the sins of 1641. He also saw the event as a deterrent to future Catholic actions: 'this is a righteous judgment of God upon these barbarous wretches ... it will tend to prevent the effusion of blood for the future, which are satisfactory grounds to such actions.'[181]

The reverberations of the legend of Cromwell are still felt today but it is difficult to judge their measure contemporaneously. O'Brien's own massacre at Cashel was quickly forgotten by the Catholics now fighting by his side and atrocities on both sides had been plentiful across the country for eight years. Reports of the massacre would have reached Youghal but how it was accepted is impossible to determine. If Cromwell's intent was to terrorise through excessive violence it may well have worked. However, officials in Youghal might still have thought the war a dangling sword that might fall either way. Uneasiness turned to tension when Cromwell's army marched ominously south toward Wexford. When Cromwell's second-in-command, Michael Jones, approached the Rosslare Fort, the defenders scarpered.[182] A second massacre of thousands would send further shock waves, this time rattling the gates of Youghal, Cork and Kinsale. The pressure began to tell on the Munster ports.

During October 1649 a significant shift in power took place when officers Townsend, Warden and Gifford revolted in a coup against the Governor of Cork City, Robert Starling. Overnight, the city had declared for Cromwell's Puritanical policies and parliament. That Starling was so easily overrun and so quickly displaced shows the depth in the lack of confidence the army felt in Murrough O'Brien, whose grip on Munster was loosening. While the city of Cork was preparing to open its gates to parliament, Cromwell's forces took New Ross on 19 October. O'Brien, no doubt aware that Cromwell was advancing along the south-eastern coast and angered by the loss of Cork, made plans to arrest this development by seizing Youghal. Travelling south, he could not gauge the mood in the town, and after the collapse of Drogheda and Wexford and the defection of the military in Cork he could not afford to await the outcome. The level of pressure on Youghal officials, officers and soldiers accelerated, now that the town was sandwiched between Cork and the approaching New Model Army.

By mid-October it was clear, to the military at least, that a change was coming. Secret discussions began in Youghal between a group of captains and lieutenants. Heading the agenda was the carrying out of a possible coup against local agents of O'Brien and Ormond to secure the town for Cromwell. Tentative opinions about possible outcomes were expressed privately amongst military personal. A calculated judgement was required to ascertain the chances of success should a coup be attempted. Names of possible resistors would be counted, as would the numbers of soldiers that could be depended on to carry out an insurgency. The insurrection began when Lieutenant-Colonel John Windham approached Captain Vere Hunt, still sleeping in his bed. Windham swore Hunt to secrecy and informed him that he intended to make a number of arrests of those he knew were still loyal to O'Brien and the Governor of Youghal, Sir Percy Smyth. Windham asked Hunt for his assistance. Hunt obliged.

Meanwhile, Sir Percy Smyth had received intelligence that a group had formed and were plotting to wrestle control of the town from him. He admitted to a Captain Graham that he knew a plot was in place and, according to Graham, was supportive of the coup but for reasons best known to him alone, could not take part in it. While Smyth dithered, the coup leaders made their way along King's Street to the house of Jonas Cloves to conduct a meeting. Lieutenant Windham and captains Richard Dashwood and Thomas Smith joined Cloves and the town mayor, John Smith, to discuss strategies and expectations. In the meantime, a number of the Cork coup leaders had taken to the road to travel to Youghal in an effort to convince the garrison to follow their lead and declare for Cromwell. They never made it to the port town, having been intercepted by O'Brien's men at Tallow.

Unaware of the situation and perhaps even expecting support from Cork, the Youghal group decided to commence a seizure of the town from Sir Percy Smyth. The coup was carried out with little fuss and Smyth, though treated respectfully, was displaced from official influence over the town. However, the timing of the takeover was ill advised. Cromwell was still some distance away and O'Brien and his army, determined not to see the defection of Youghal, reached the town the very next day. Camped outside the walls, an irate O'Brien delivered a sobering message in which he threatened to hang the mayor and the leaders of the uprising. Lieutenant Windham, standing on the town walls to communicate, came to an agreement with O'Brien that the coup leaders would step down and Sir Percy Smyth would be reinstated as governor. In return, he wanted assurances from O'Brien that he would not enter the town, thereby ending the twenty-four-hour takeover. O'Brien agreed to the terms and reversed his forces toward Cork where his own residence was in danger. The first attempted coup of Youghal had failed but a number of factors would lead to a second attempt two weeks later on 3 November 1649. In the first attempt, Windham had moved too early. Cromwell was still bogged down in New Ross and had yet to encounter a very stubborn Waterford city, defended by the one and only James Touchet. With O'Brien's army at the gates of Youghal, it was wise of Windham to deliver the town back to Sir Percy Smyth, thereby saving lives and almost certainly his own. Windham and the Youghal group may have lost confidence in their ability to resist an O'Brien offensive, particularly as they had also received intelligence that O'Brien had arrested some of the original Cork defectors at Tallow.

The second attempted coup in Youghal took place after O'Brien failed in his attempt to retake Cork. In a volatile environment in Youghal, where clear lines of loyalty had now been drawn, not to mention the approach of Cromwell and news of O'Brien's failure, the Youghal group were again encouraged to seek assistance from Cork. On 3 November, Cork captains Warden and Gifford rode to Youghal to secure the town for Cromwell. News of their arrival reached Youghal officers Nicholas Munckton, Richard Dashwood and Thomas Smith while they were drinking pints of wine in the White Hart alehouse between seven and eight o' clock in the evening. A 'small boy or maid' burst into the alehouse to announce that Warden and Gifford were at the south entrance of Base Town, the South Gate. The three officers immediately ran to the scene only to find Sir Percy Smyth drawing the gate chain across it to prevent its opening. Smyth's attempt to hold out until some conditions were agreed with the Cork captains came to a swift end. Lieutenant Windham and others arrived on horseback riding up Common Street, brandishing their swords at the defiant governor. Smyth was advised to return to his house for his own safety. The gates were opened and the Cork captains and their company entered Youghal. Meanwhile, a Captain Liones and a company of soldiers approached the North Gate, also claiming the town for Cromwell. Smyth, still fraught from his encounter with Windham, sought the help of a Major Supple to prevent the opening of the North Gate. Standing on a platform with their swords drawn, Smyth and Supple attempted to repel the advances of Liones. The gates were opened eventually but no information is available as to what happened to Smyth and Supple. In any event, the second coup was a success and Youghal, declaring for parliament, was now free for Cromwell to enter.

It is probable that had the coup failed and O'Brien had been able to take control of the town, another siege would have followed. With Cork gone to parliament and Cromwell approaching, Youghal would

have been hopelessly exposed. Given the amount and size of armoury that Cromwell used to batter Drogheda, a siege would have been short lived and devastating in terms of infrastructure and, of course, lives. With winter setting in and an arduous and bloody campaign behind him, Cromwell would not have welcomed nor appreciated a siege of Youghal. No doubt such possible outcomes had been discussed amongst the coup leaders in Jonas Cloves' house prior to the successful November coup. With no appetite for destruction Youghal had once again survived, firstly in the 1645 siege by holding up their arms and secondly in 1649 by holding up their hands.

It was two weeks later when Cromwell received the news that Cork had taken up his cause and that Youghal had also joined the parliament ranks. Cromwell was struggling to take the besieged city of Waterford. Meanwhile, Cork coup leader Colonel Townsend left the city on the ship *Nonsuch*. He was carrying a letter from officials with their submissions regarding the future of themselves and the city for Cromwell to study. Townsend was joined aboard the *Nonsuch* by a number of other officers, including captains Gifford and Warden, so instrumental in assisting the November coup at Youghal. On their way to meet Cromwell they entered Youghal harbour and met a parliament ship called *The Garland* coming in from Dungarvan. Cromwell had loaded *The Garland* with 500 soldiers and £1,500 for Cork. On board was Lord Broghill, once a royalist from a great family of royalists, his colours now firmly fixed to the Cromwellian mast on his triumphant return to Youghal. New Mayor of Youghal, Thomas Warren boarded *The Garland* and met with Broghill. Like the defectors of Cork, the mayor had listed a number of propositions, drawn up by officers and town officials for Cromwell to consider, but Broghill warned him that 'it would be more for their honour to desire no conditions.'[183] No argument was put against Broghill's advice and Youghal officially submitted to Cromwell. The council members had signed a letter, which asked Cromwell to be favourable to their positions. Before religion or allegiance to parliament or the overthrowing of the monarchy, uppermost in their minds was to display their complete subservience and to hold on to their properties and titles. It read:

> May it please your Excellency we have been a long time humble
> suitors to Almighty God, for that happy success to your endeavours,
> which the success of Lo. Broghill and part of your forces here
> hath at last presented unto us. With what thankfulness to God and
> comfort to ourselves, we have received them we have to others to
> testify. Our humble suite unto your Excellency, is, that seeing by
> the divine power your actions have hitherto progressed, we may
> by the result of them posses your honours, favour, and protection,
> in our charter, privileges, lives and estates which we most humbly
> submit to your Excellency.[184]

It is highly likely that the council had prayed hard for whomever was
closest to Youghal and who had the greater chance of success so its
decision on which side to declare for could be made all the easier.

The language and tone of the letter would have pleased Cromwell
greatly. The council was quick to point out the glory of the 'divine
power' that had brought Cromwell to Ireland and in touching
distance of Youghal. For all that, it also begged for the status quo to be
maintained and it is telling that they included their lives in the list of
their future hopes. Cromwell replied that:

> by any power committed unto me, by the Parliament, you shall
> find me willing to answer your expectations, and wherein I may
> prefer any thing unto the Parliament in England for your further
> advantage, I shall be ready to do it, when I receive particulars from
> you. In the mean time I rest, your very loving friend. O. Cromwell.
> Ross, 14 Nov. 1649.[185]

Cromwell's line, 'when I receive particulars from you', was bound to
unsettle those who feared him. He would bring their case to parliament
but only after he carried out his own investigation into their affairs.
Those who had sworn to follow O'Brien and his switch to the king
eighteen months earlier were bound to be preparing their stories and
excuses. A long line of colonels and captains, previously heads of the
garrisons at Cork and Youghal before turning them over to Cromwell,
also signed a submission of obedience including a grovelling apology:

They submit themselves to the power of their own nation in the
Parliament of England, and to his Excellency, Lord Lieutenant,
Cromwell, and hope they will be forgiven their former submission
to Ormond, as they were seduced by the subtlety and power of their
late commanders.[186]

Most crucially, the officers also asked for 'indemnity' for past actions.
Many of them had taken up arms with O'Brien against Cromwell's
parliament throughout the previous year. Cromwell was, of course,
both pleased and relieved, with the onset of winter, that so many of
the garrison leaders of Cork and Youghal would ease his progress in
Munster. It was also in his best interests to have them ready for war in
the New Year. He promised not to cause any 'hurt' to the soldiers and
inhabitants of Cork and Youghal who had declared for parliament
and encouraged them to bring into the fold others of a like mind
'in the Protestant interest in this nation'. Cromwell added a weighted
caveat; he would only consider those who were declaring allegiance
out of honesty and not 'policy or necessity'. This apparent openness
was an act of diplomacy at a time when Cromwell was struggling
to seize Waterford City. Cromwell knew well that, almost to a
man, all the submissions he received from Cork and Youghal were
dishonest and totally driven by policy and necessity. That particular
inconvenience to truth mattered little for now, at least until the war
for Munster was won.

The Youghal officers suggested to Cromwell that he might appoint
Broghill as the commander of Munster. At best, it was a politically
astute move. At worst, they were simply mouthing the words of a pre-
arrangement over which they had no influence. Either way, they got
their wish and indemnity was also granted them. Broghill had long
envisaged such an appointment since his discussions with Cromwell
in London. The domino effect of towns and villages collapsing in
subordination to Cromwell and Broghill was the clicking into place of
his most imagined design: regaining the control of Munster. Bandon,
Mallow, Cappoquin, Dromana, Dungarvan and others followed the
principal port towns of Youghal, Cork and Kinsale in opening their
doors to Cromwell and his New Model Army.

Cromwell Marches on Youghal

On 2 December 1649 Oliver Cromwell and the New Model Army abandoned the siege of Waterford City and marched on toward Youghal. His army, as successful as they had been to this point, needed rest, feeding and rejuvenation. Three days later he entered the town of Youghal. It is likely he crossed at the Ferry Point, passing the charred and semi-submerged ruin of the *Duncannon* on his way. For Youghal Protestants, particularly those in favour of parliament, the pageantry of the New Model Army approaching across the river, ablaze with flags and armoury, may have been a comforting sight. For any remaining Catholics, the sombre beat of the drum echoed the marching feet of the 1645 expulsion. Cromwell was the manifestation of Hell's fury. With the return of Broghill and the arrival of Cromwell there would be no toleration of Catholics. Neither would there be any ambiguity or flipping of loyalty as witnessed when O'Brien offered an unexpected opportunity to Catholics to return to Youghal in 1648. Cromwell's war had a singular vision for Ireland: a Protestant nation under the rule of parliament and the Commonwealth. Protestant royalists had reason to be fearful too, but none would fear Cromwell as much as the Anglo-Irish Catholic Gentry and, of course the Gaelic Irish. If there were any Catholics lingering in Youghal, as Cromwell crossed the river, they would not be there for much longer. Docking at the quay, Cromwell was welcomed with fresh supplies from England.

While he spent some time at Boyle's college house, Cromwell sought a private residence and viewed the house of a Mr Simme on the main street. Whether this was the same three-story building known as the 'magazine', now gone, adjoining St John's Priory is unknown.[187] Broghill meanwhile had taken the house of the now disaffected O'Briens in Cork. Displaced governor, Sir Percy Smyth, who made poor judgments during the October and November coups in Youghal, was imprisoned. During his stay in Youghal Cromwell lost an important military leader in Michael Jones who fell ill and died. Jones had been a significant campaigner for parliament, taking Dublin from Ormond and played a central role in the assaults on Drogheda and Wexford. Cromwell gave a moving funeral oration at St Mary's Church. It is thought that during the winter break Cromwell carried out regular inspections of his men, lining them up along King's Street. It was likely to have been a quiet, reserved and sober Christmas in the town. Cromwell spent much of the time in contemplation and consideration of the coming spring campaign.

The Irish clergy shattered Cromwell's peace in Youghal by publishing a statement against him. At a table, in Mr Simme's rooms, he composed a damning reply against the Catholic bishops of Ireland. Perhaps dismayed by the evolving nature and focus of the war, away from Catholic rights to royalty versus parliament, the Irish clergy, at the Convention of Clonmacnoise, called on Catholics all over Ireland to unite and go to war for their faith against a common enemy. Cromwell was given a printed version of the bishops' statement. He titled his response 'A Declaration of the Lord-Lieutenant of Ireland for the undeceiving of deluded and seduced people … in answer to certain late declarations and acts framed by the Irish Popish Prelates and Clergy in a conventicle at Clonmacnoise'. In typical forthright language, he began by attacking the Catholic Church for keeping the people suppressed for the sake of 'filthy lucre' so that they could 'bridle, saddle and ride them at your pleasure'. He told the bishops that their 'covenant' was with 'Death or Hell'. The next passage in his speech demonstrates perhaps, better than any passage written from Cromwell's irritated quill, how he viewed the problems that had overwhelmed Ireland. His words propagated the ancient belief that the power of superior races was not the creation of man but the deliberate design of God. His inability to grasp criticism of England and Englishness by the bishops betrayed an Anglo-eccentric complex manifest in his apparent bewilderment at such criticism. For Cromwell, Ireland had spoiled the union of the two nations with the 1641 uprising and had bitten the hand that fed it. Ireland had disrespected the natural order of things, namely, the rightful subordination of its people to a superior race that had settled the country through legal transactions:

Remember, ye hypocrites, Ireland was once united to England. That was the original 'union.' Englishmen had good inheritances, which many of them purchased with their money; they and their ancestors, from you and your ancestors. They had good Leases from

Irishmen, for long times to come; great stocks thereupon; houses and plantations erected at their own cost and charge. They lived peaceably and honestly amongst you. You had generally equal benefit of the protection of England with them; and equal justice from the Laws … You broke this 'union'! You, unprovoked, put the English to the most unheard-of and most barbarous Massacre (without respect of sex or age) that ever the Sun beheld. And at a time when Ireland was in perfect Peace … And yet then, I say, was this unheard-of villainy perpetrated, – by your instigation, who boast of 'peace-making' and 'union against this common enemy.' What think you: by this time, is not my assertion true, is God, will God be, with you? I am confident He will not![188]

Not that it would bring any relief or comfort to the Catholics now beyond the safety of Youghal, but Cromwell, to his credit, was at length to distinguish between the lay people of Ireland and the offices of the Catholic Church. He accused the bishops and priests of seducing and fooling the common people. He would, he contested, bring no harm to those who had been honestly tricked by the educated in the Church:

As for the People, what thoughts they have in matters of Religion in their own breasts I cannot reach; but shall think it my duty, if they walk honestly and peaceably, Not to cause them in the least to suffer for the same. And shall endeavour to walk patiently and in love towards them, to see if at any time it shall please God to give them another or a better mind.[189]

As ever, despite the courtly manners, as was the discourse of the day, he concluded with a chilling warning:

… if this People shall headily run on after the counsels of their Prelates and Clergy and other Leaders, I hope to be free from the misery and desolation, blood and ruin, that shall befall them; and shall rejoice to exercise utmost severity against them.[190]

Cromwell signed off on the speech 'Given at Youghal', dated January 1649. Where, and if, he read it in Youghal is not known. All proclamations were read at the centre of the town at the Market Cross. If he wanted to make a speech to the general public, almost certainly exclusively Protestant, then Market Cross was the place to do it. Here also, he had room to gather his forces and town dignitaries. If there were any Catholics left in the town, or standing in the street, the speech would have cut colder than the January air. Catholics in Youghal had come to understand ambiguity rather than tolerance. In times of peace they took opportunities to meet and obviously to pray. During the war years they were first expelled before returning to the fold under the uneasy alliance of their military leader, Murrough O'Brien, to the king. They had come to understand the vagaries of political life and the unpredictability of their own, being so determined by outside forces, such as the social, political and religious change in England. When something fell in England, it was heard in Youghal. If any of them read or heard Cromwell's speech they would have become familiar with something new: the right to exist in silence, as shadows, functioning as a harmless and equally useless element of Youghal's social ecology, but not as an effective component to its survival. They also knew that should they mutate into something more active they would be cut from the chain. Never before, and never again in Ireland, was or could a speech of its kind be made.

By the end of the month, with his troops refreshed, Cromwell departed Youghal and marched to the Limerick border. The increasingly confident Broghill was also operating in the area. Having lost Cork and then Youghal, O'Brien's army pushed westward and was held up in the borders of the Limerick and Kerry counties. Cromwell's tour of duty took in Callan, Fethard and Cashel. Youghal acted as a vital supply line to his mission during the Munster winter campaign of 1650; 'guns, ammunition, or other things from Youghal' were shipped up the river Blackwater. By March, the men who had stoically defended Youghal throughout the 1645 siege clashed in conflict when Broghill intercepted O'Brien on his way to Mallow and defeated him. O'Brien retreated to Connacht. Meanwhile, the parliamentarian forces marched on to Kilkenny to take the castle after a short siege. After making a vain attempt to halt English progress at Carlow, Confederate commander

James Touchet succumbed to the power of the New Model Army and also fled to Connacht. Cromwell then secured a treaty with the royalist Protestants to give up their arms. The last of the Catholic forces still fighting were now isolated with the royalist coalition smashed. Clonmel was next taken though at a cost of over 2,000 of Cromwell's men.

Cromwell's stay in Ireland was coming to a close. The Lord-Lieutenant had received news from England that Scottish royalists, keen for a restoration of the monarchy, had intentions to invade England. Though not thoroughly satisfied that Ireland was under parliament's control, he quickly returned to Youghal. On 29 May 1650 Cromwell transferred his command to his son-in-law Henry Ireton. After nine months in Ireland he walked down Quay Lane in Base Town, Youghal, on the south side of Trinity Castle and boarded the *President*. He sailed for Bristol and would not return. Ireton continued the Irish campaign, driving the remaining Catholic forces toward the west. Ormond, having surrendered at Kilkenny, also crossed the River Shannon into Connacht. The increasingly desperate Catholic clergy rejected Ormond and by the end of 1650 he left Ireland. Thomas Preston, who had tried to take Youghal in the 1645 siege, left Ireland for the Continent, dying in Paris in 1655. Preston's military colleague at the Youghal siege, James Touchet, persisted a little longer but as the war wore on he was finally defeated along the river Shannon by Ireton. He fled Ireland in 1651, taking up military service in France. Murrough 'the burner' O'Brien had become a victim of his own ability to drop a cause as quickly as he picked one up. Neither trusted by parliament nor the Catholic Confederates, he was forced to abandon Ireland, also for France, in December 1650. Lord Broghill would finally win the title President of Munster, but not until 1660 when the restoration of the Crown in England was complete, ironically having gained favour with Charles II.

Cromwell had toppled a monarchy, an unimaginable act in the times, yet he was comfortable with being referred to as His Highness, even in the earliest days of his ascent to power. During his time as Lord Protector of the Commonwealth he bestowed knighthoods and took on the trappings of royalty. He died of illness in 1658, a constitu-tionalist but a king in all but name. It is impossible to know how those in Youghal, who accompanied Oliver Cromwell through the streets and to the Quay Gate, felt as he boarded a small boat to take him to his ship. Some would have feared his departure while others would have felt relief. As a town, Youghal had done exactly as Cromwell professed in his speech about the relationship between Ireland and England: 'You had generally equal benefit of the protection of England', but only because it bent with its every fluctuating political and religious wind. From Richard Boyle's cosmopolitan trade centre to a garrison town, Youghal was profoundly changed by the events of 1641–50. Political and religious tensions would fester in the coming years. These tensions, coupled with great uncertainty and the influence of new arrivals and ministers, who held high suspicions of the dark arts, would create an environment at the beginning of the 1660s that allowed the town to be plunged into an unparalleled state of hysteria and trauma.

11

Social, Political and Religious Paranoia

The Florence Newton Witch Trial

With the timing of a killer instinct, *pestis bacilli*, better known as the bubonic plague, returned to Europe in the mid-1640s. Its deadly contagion meandered like a ghost across the war-torn and weary landscapes. Ireland, already leper-like from a decade of sieges, starvation, killings and burning of harvests, could ill-afford to host the most ancient of enemies. By September 1651 it visited a depressed post-Cromwell Youghal. The title of a letter written by town officials to the Revenue Commissioners of County Cork summed up the mood perfectly. 'The Humble Petition of the Mayor and Council of the Poor Town of Youghal' may not have brought a tear to a revenue commissioner's eye, but it certainly revealed the economic decline brought on by the aftermath of national chaos and destruction. Added to this newfound humility was the woebegone realisation that the plague was one fight that could not be won. It simply ignored all titles, positions and religions. Indeed, one might say that its unilateral lack of prejudice in choosing victims was a welcome change from the man-made madness of the preceding years. The letter from the Youghal council began less than cheerfully:

> Showing to your honours the sad and deplorable condition of this
> Incorporation by diverse emergencies that hath fallen upon us, as by

the late great judgment of God upon us, in the sickness which long
continued to the wasting of many families and impoverishing of the
inhabitants ...[191]

Just as it had done in 1348–49, the plague ripped through the fabric
of society and wiped out entire families. The mass movement
and close living quarters of soldiers in the field was a perfect
environment for breeding the infection. Cramped urban centres
like Youghal were also very welcoming to the spectre of death and
its swift movement.

Youghal's environmental conditions had not advanced greatly
throughout the 1600s. The practice of butchers slaughtering cattle
outside their shops continued into the middle of the century. Cattle
often escaped the clutches of butchers, their throats half cut to charge
down the street, blood effusing from their opened veins. Public
outcry reached fever pitch when the ranging beasts killed children,
stampeding about the street without sense or direction. These were
the conditions of a town that virtually encouraged the visitation of
the epidemic, carried on the back of the brown rat. A death toll is not
recorded for the plague that lasted between two and three years but it is
thought that up to a tenth of the population perished.[192]

In such circumstance the Youghal Council pleaded that it could
not afford to pay its contributions to the revenue. A request was made
to remove a £20 a month rate charged to the liberties of the town.
The commissioners were also asked to reduce another charge of £40
a month. The office of the revenue, to its credit, removed the tax on
the liberties and reduced the £40 charge. The post-Cromwell years
would prove to be some of the most difficult for Youghal. One of the
first tasks of the council was to concern itself with identifying land
and property ownership. Dwellers and claimants were told to present
their titles and deeds before the council. Following the occupancy of
properties and land after the two expulsions of Catholics in 1645 and
1649, confusion surrounded a number of claims and counter-claims
that were forwarded and debated.

Across the country, a land rush was taking place following the Act
of Settlement of Ireland in 1653 under Cromwell's new government.

The reconquest of Ireland was not as straightforward as parliament would have hoped. Youghal already had a high proportion of New English settlers prior to 1641 so resettlement was limited, though the population inevitably dropped. War veterans and widows of those killed in action, fighting for Cromwell's cause, were given former Catholic properties in the liberties of Youghal. Though Cromwell has been credited with the legendary statement 'To Hell or to Connacht', it was people such as Broghill who had a heavy-handed influence in transplantation, overseeing placements and settlements for his associates and favourites in Munster. He faced difficulties from demanding adventurers who had set prices for land adjacent to Youghal as early as the Catholic expulsions of 1645. While Broghill was looking to exact the best price, the depressed economy dictated low fees and limited rent revenues from new settlers and landowners. Confiscation of land from those who had taken up arms against parliament was being ironed out amongst London adventurers, investors and officers. Soldiers of Cromwell who were seeking recompense for pay arrears were also being rewarded with parcels of land and property.

Meanwhile, deportations of Irish men, women and children continued apace in the transplantation programme. Many of the Irish were sent to Jamaica, Barbados and Virginia to be sold as slaves. Over half the population of Montserrat was to come from Ireland. A rounding up of Catholics living 20 miles within Youghal, Cork and Kinsale was ordered; 300 men aged between 12 and 50 years and 250 women aged between 12 and 45 years would be shipped to New England in America to work on the English plantations there. Many of these prisoners were the expelled Catholics who once knew and enjoyed life in Youghal under the administration of Broghill's father, Richard Boyle. Broghill suggested that many of that number could be found wandering the land as vagrants. Having been 'arrested', the people were sent to Kinsale and shipped out.[193] The transplantation of the Irish would take several years without ever being total or complete. Meanwhile, Irish soldiers fled to Catholic nations as close as Spain and as far away as Poland. A number of Catholic soldiers, now living in the Mediterranean, had adopted a piratical life and returned to Irish waters as early as 1652, sailing from Sicily to pillage ships off Youghal. The transplantation programme split Irish families, spreading them to opposite ends of the world. Irish landowners that could not convince newly appointed courts that they had remained constantly loyal and had not taken up arms against parliament were removed west of the Shannon.

A New Religious and Political Paradigm

Two extremely strong elements of change in the development of Youghal emerged in the aftermath of the Cromwellian war. Firstly, the religious landscape had been radicalised by the need for one religion (Protestantism) to supersede another (Catholicism). This period of religious readjustment did not affect the machinery of officialdom in Youghal to any great extent but the religious and social climate had changed dramatically since 1640. A Puritan influence, brought by Cromwell's army, had settled in the town. Many Puritans believed toleration to be a sin, namely toleration of the Kingdom of the Anti-Christ (Catholicism).[194] Ministers in Youghal spent most of their services in St Mary's preaching to Cromwell's ex-officers, officials and soldiers. The Puritan influence on the council was gradual as was its growing impact in the offices of magistrates, constables and bailiffs.

Protestant ministers were being dispatched into Ireland as Cromwell tried to mould the new government. Seven of these ministers met in Dublin in 1652 to discuss the best possible way of teaching the gospels. The exercise proved more difficult in practice with ministers in England reluctant to come to Ireland. In 1653 Cromwell wrote to the American colonies requesting preachers and settlers return to preach in Ireland. The setting up of ministries in places like Cork and Youghal was often a prolonged and laborious process of vetting the candidates and viewing recommendations. It did not help the committees' cause that Protestantism was an umbrella belief-system under which several satellite sects were operating in the community; Presbyterians, Episcopalians, Anglicans as well as the Anabaptists and the Independents, who argued fiercely over issues such as the baptism of infants, fought for followers. These sects often existed in the same towns within shouting distance of one another. The chosen minister's character had to be conducive to the general beliefs or needs of the congregation. Where this did not happen, it created tensions. In 1655 a group of eight ministers formed a subcommission in County Cork to identify a list of preachers who could be found, placed and paid, for their ministry in the county. Preachers had to be 'Godly, able to preach, not scandalous and faithful to the Commonwealth'.[195] James Wood was identified as one such candidate and was appointed preacher for Youghal on a handsome salary of £120 per year in 1652. It would be wrong to suggest that Wood had entered a town rife with multiple sects or organisations. However, there was enough religious divergence to allow a colourful collage of methodologies to advertise themselves to lost souls.

At the time that Wood held office in Youghal, Quakeresses Elizabeth Fletcher and Elizabeth Smith preached in the major towns of Munster with some success. Such visits often led to mob resistance and heated exchanges. Wood and the Quakers shared a mutual and irreversible animosity. Dissenters often applied terms such as 'vipers' and 'serpents', with the obvious connotations, to Quakers. However, they had at least received a warmer reception than the outright 'anti-Christian' Catholics. Despite the antagonism, Quakers continued to preach in towns such as Youghal, entering meeting places or giving private prayer sessions. Colonel Phaire, who had been an important figure in Cromwell's New Model Army and was present when Youghal submitted to parliament, entertained Quakerism. This reveals the open and often adventurous nature of the religious society of the day, particularly with military personnel resisting conventional thinking. Another, less known group, the Ranters, like the Quakers, embraced the idea of the spirit dwelling within the person. They believed that by having this sort of communication directly to God, the preacher bestowed with such a gift was not bound by the rules of conventional society. Preachers could therefore often make outlandish claims about the perceived powers of good and evil and behave erratically with legitimate cause as they saw it. Self-made reasoning around the mysteries of spirituality, the unpredictable behaviour of nature and the failing of the human body often gave rise to mystics, prophets and self-styled preachers. Such company was present in Youghal throughout the 1650s.

In a world full of unexpected events, people consulted with those who claimed to have special abilities or powers. They sought guidance, solace and comfort about unsettling occurrences that could not be understood or explained. They sought cures and treatments for illnesses. What appears logical and even pedestrian today was full of dread and wonder for them. It was an age when magic and science, God and the Devil were all operating as active agents in the same arena. From infant mortality to the sudden death of livestock to hailstorms and skin rashes, from impotency to heart attacks and strokes, an explanation was required for each. In the absence of literacy, science and education, at least among the common classes, superstition afforded as much comfort as it did fear in the bewilderment of uncertainty. The credible and accepted practice of magic was also part of the discourse in surviving and understanding the mysteries of life.

Furthermore, the political paradigm had shifted. For many, during the years of the Commonwealth, readjusting to the Brave New World of Oliver Cromwell as the Lord Protector, with King Charles II in exile, was a chasm that could not be crossed or closed. It seemed to them that the world itself had lost its head along with Charles I in 1649. Perhaps this inability to grasp the concept of a constitutionalist parliament without a divinely appointed figurehead of royal lineage was the force that caused Cromwell to default to a king-like role. By 1658 confidence in the Protectorate was waning and England began to consider a return to more familiar form of governance. Support grew for the return of the monarchy. In September of that year, Cromwell died of illness and was succeeded by his son, Richard. However, by 1660 the Crown was restored to England and Charles II brought the balance of tradition back to the kingdoms, although official religion was still lost in limbo.[196]

Catholics in Ireland were right to believe that their efforts in the latter days of the 1640s would be rewarded with tolerance of their faith. Many had fought for the Crown as royalists against Cromwell's parliament. A revision of the 1653 Act of Settlement, by which so many of them had been displaced, was the least that they sought. In the early days of the restoration Charles II gave a rather loose, premature and broadly liberal impression of tolerance to all religions under the assurance that they would not damage the welfare of the kingdoms. This allowed Catholics to speak up for their claims to property and religious rights. Charles II would go on to revise the land settlements of 1653, giving further hope to the disenfranchised Catholics. Both Protestant and Catholic royalists expected to be treated favourably under new legislation. An Irish sea-captain by the name of George Codd turned up in Youghal in 1660 declaring he would exact revenge on the English for dispossessing him. The scene caused consternation in the town because Codd's apparent boldness was perceived by Protestants to be a sign of the shifting political sands. The town mayor, Richard Myres, was so concerned about the incident he reported it to the Dublin government.[197] The reaction by officials to Codd's claims was a mark of the insecurity felt in the highest offices of the town. The restoration of the Crown had undermined those Protestants who had gained land and positions of influence from the Act of Settlement in 1653 and throughout the years of Cromwell's Protectorate. They were acutely aware of the manner of their successes, achieved by them with the beheading of the king's father a decade earlier. The whirlwind that had lifted them up was now blowing in their faces. The ultimate explosive scenario for the Youghal parliamentarians, like a leaked gas, was an emboldened Catholic community, buoyed by the return of the monarchy, seeping back into the social dynamic. Cromwell's Puritan settlers and sympathisers in Youghal became increasingly agitated about the uncertainty of their futures.

These two primary elements of change since Cromwell's conquest now dominated thinking and action in Youghal. Therefore, the mindset of the political and religious scene in the town by 1660 was tormented by a lethal and contradictory cocktail of paranoia on one hand and self-grandiosity on the other. This strained, volatile and economically impoverished community, still traumatised by the recent war and plague, required a unifying element onto which officials, Church and people could focus their attention. They required a common cause to cement the divergent doctrines together: a body politic, a communal spirit from which direction could be taken and in which the people could place their trust. In the absence of such a dynamic, fear filled the void. The people of Youghal would indeed be united; their common enemy would be the supernatural. For the greater part of a year, Youghal was obsessed by the presence of evil, the workings of witchcraft and the possibility that Satan had sabotaged their world.

Mary Longdon and Florence Newton

During Christmas 1660 a young maid by the name of Mary Longdon was sweeping the porch of the house of her master, John Pyne, in Youghal. Florence Newton, an elderly widow, asked the girl for a piece of beef from Pyne's powdering keg but she refused. Newton allegedly scolded the girl, saying 'Thou had'st as good give it me.' Two weeks after Newton had grumbled at the girl she intercepted the maid on her way to the town well. Newton was clearly agitated as she knocked the water pail from Longdon's head. She kissed the young girl and pleaded for any animosity between the pair to be resolved: 'I pray thee let thee and I be friends; for I bear thee no ill will, and I pray thee do thou bear me none.'[198] These were the words supposedly expressed by Newton. There is only one legitimate reason why the old widow would urgently plead with Mary Longdon to be friends only two weeks after she initially asked for the beef; rumour must have reached Newton that the young girl had begun to express fears about being scolded and that she was interpreting it as a bewitching. As an elderly, illiterate and impoverished widow, Newton was aware that her public profile made her susceptible to accusations of casting an embittered curse. It would, after all, be her only means of revenge against a cruel and uncaring youth. The irrational fear in Longdon would have received a sympathetic hearing from plenty of peers and elders alike. It is right to assume also that Mary Longdon had knowledge of what a witch's curse could do and how to point to a scolding as evidence of witchcraft.

Newton was right to fear the worst. Within days of Newton kissing Longdon 'violently', the maid claimed she woke up in her bed late at night to find two figures standing over her. One was a 'little old man in silk clothes' and the other a woman with a veil over her face. In Longdon's story, the little old man removed the veil from the woman's face to reveal that it was Florence Newton. The man then allegedly told Longdon that should she follow his advice she would have all that her heart desired. The maid, of course, told the man that her heart belonged to Jesus. That Mary Longdon included a 'little old man in silk clothes' in her story raises the very real possibility that literature of devil worship or witchcraft was present in Youghal. It was almost certainly not printed there in either book or pamphlet form but given the religious dynamism of the day and the vested interests in spirituality and demonology it is very likely that Longdon had access to, or was exposed verbally, to matters of the occult. The 'little old man' that Longdon refused to bargain with for her soul was of course Satan, or an agent of Satan. The implication of guilt for Newton was obvious.

According to Longdon's account, Newton had the ability to appear suddenly at her bedside in the company of a demon and the ability to fly, and had already given her soul to the dark arts. There is no evidence to suggest that a book such as the *Malleus Maleficarum* (The Book of Witches) was available to read to Longdon or that Youghal was a wholly or exceptionally misogynist society or indeed that it disregarded elderly women, especially widows. However, there is little doubt that women were expected to uphold a moral life. Youghal authorities had introduced a cage and a cucking stool into the town as early as 1654.[199] The cage resembled a human-sized birdcage that held one person at a time for public humiliation, typically as a consequence for petty crimes. The cucking stool was used as a deterrent against women for scolding, adultery, prostitution and a plethora of petty crimes. The victim was tied into a stool at the end of a long beam attached to a base, often on wheels. The stool was sometimes dipped into water. Such an apparatus for the punishment of women shows that the public psyche in Youghal was well tuned into the possibility of a demonic possession of Florence Newton. The town was simply falling in line with a phenomenon sweeping across the Continent.

At this time, Europe was at the height of what has been termed the 'Witch Craze'. In a period of intense persecutions, lasting well over 200 years, it is estimated that somewhere between 200,000 and 300,000 people were killed, the vast majority of them women, including children. Countless other women were tortured, mutilated, sexually abused and outcast from society. It has been argued that the witch craze was in fact a gendercide in which a largely misogynistic and patriarchal society pinned all of the world's ills on women as convenient scapegoats. The scope of the argument is extremely broad but there is overwhelming evidence, not least in the death toll of women executed, but also in the spurious nature of their 'crimes' to suggest that gendercide is indeed the appropriate term.[200] Women, often working in midwifery, were suspected of being responsible for the death of children. Some who were herbalists and others who were pharmacists were accused of creating harmful medicines that exacerbated human illness and killed livestock. Women, especially spinsters and widows without male protection or defence were often the innocent victims of personal vendettas. Charges of witchcraft were also perpetrated against women who owned property and land desired by powerful and influential men. Witch trials were mostly concentrated in rural areas and held in small courts. Ministers often acted as judges and jurors. They were all too ready to accept bizarre and incredible accounts as evidence of witchcraft for fear that their reluctance to do so was a sign of heresy. Confessions were extracted by torture, and execution methods varied from beheadings to drownings, hangings to burnings. Witch trials were not common in Ireland, though a number of cases around possessions had been heard in the previous decades to 1661. However, neighbouring Scotland had a high number of trials and executions, certainly much higher than in England. The majority of witch trials and executions throughout Europe took place in Germany, though few countries on the Continent could claim to be 'witch-trial free'.

The Puritan influence in Youghal at the time of the Florence Newton case has been cited as the cause of the suspicion that the Devil was present in the town.[201] Certainly the Puritans had a keen interest in stemming witchcraft but Mary Longdon's ability to mimic the symptoms of being bewitched reveals a wider knowledge of demonology and its effects across the community. It is unlikely that her hysteria was a performance coached by senior figures that had an agenda against an old widow. Longdon may have had her own motives such as a youthful desire for attention and fame, guilt for her own possible indiscretions or simple spite. Longdon knew Florence Newton for three to four years prior to the accusation of witchcraft. Whatever her reasons, Newton was a clichéd stereotype of a witch who fell foul of a hysterical community well versed in the art of catching, identifying and torturing witches.

Witch Testing and Demonology

Florence Newton was damned whether she could or could not prove her innocence. Long before she was taken to the court in Cork she had been tried and convicted by so-called experts: men who desired to be at the centre of a national controversy as a means to boost their importance and influence. Following Newton's 'visit' to Longdon at her bedside with the Devil, the maid said that she felt stones rain down on her. She claimed they turned invisible upon hitting the floor and that they followed her wherever she went. Added to this, Longdon stated that she fell into violent fits, vomiting out straw, nails and wool. She screamed out Newton's name as her tormentor. Such stories were given credibility with confirmation from her master, John Pyne, who attested to strange happenings in his house. He willingly described the Bible suddenly jumping from Mary's hands to the floor and how the maid 'in the twinkling of an eye' could be moved from one room to the next while she slept. On 26 March, almost three months after the initial incident, Youghal mayor, Richard Myres, in consultation with Longdon's family and neighbours, who swore that the girl's stories were true, summoned Newton to his house. The old widow denied the accusation of bewitching. Perhaps in panic or perhaps even out of spite, Newton then told the mayor that there were others in Youghal who could do far worse than her. She gave him the names of two other widows: Goody Halfpenny and Goody Dodd. Myres' reaction also reveals that belief in the dark arts and knowledge of traditional ways to deal with them was prevalent in Youghal.

The mayor ordered a boat so he could carry out a witch experiment in the harbour. Myres did not use the cucking stool to dip the suspected witches into the water. His preferred method was more direct, known as 'swimming the witch'. The three suspects would have their hands tied to their feet and be lowered into the water, with obvious consequences. In the impossible event that they would float, thereby rejecting the baptismal waters, they would be found guilty of witchcraft. On hearing the mayor's intentions, Newton confessed to 'overlooking' and said she was very sorry for her actions. It is interesting that the beleaguered widow would know the difference between bewitching and overlooking, which simply meant casting an 'evil eye' without real malice. In any event, both Halfpenny and Dodd were called. They denied the charge and stated they would be happy to go to trial. Myres then consulted with Mary Longdon who cited Newton as the one and only source of her demonic pains. Both Myres and the appointed preacher, James Wood, then sought evidence of Newton's ability to cause physical harm by bringing her to the close proximity of Longdon without the maid knowing she was present. They were satisfied that Longdon's sudden fits were attributable to the presence of the witch, held in another room of the house.[202] Newton was subsequently imprisoned at the South Gate jail. Here, in cold, filthy and cramped conditions, she would be subjected to inhumane questioning and torture.

Having a witch jailed in Youghal created both fascination and terror. Newton's reputation grew by the day. Only two days after her imprisonment a group of men, Nicholas Pyne, Roger Hawkins, Joseph Thompson and others, visited the South Gate jail. In what must have been a crushingly intimidating atmosphere for the widow, they told her it was the general opinion of the town that she was guilty of bewitching Mary Longdon. Newton collapsed to her knees, reiterating her belief that she simply overlooked the maid and kissed her because she knew she could not do her any harm. Again, she cited Goody Dodd and Goody Halfpenny as the source of Longdon's torment. Stories spread amongst the community that the witch was visited within the prison by a demon. The demon was said to have made rattling noises and when pressed about it the next day, Newton admitted it was her familiar, in the shape of a greyhound. It is significant that the community were even aware of what a familiar represented: a demon or the Devil in the shape of an animal. Such claims were very rare in Ireland at the time.

A further example of a type of expertise in demonology was evidenced when the men carried out a witch-test. Taking a tile from the prison wall, they rubbed it on the ground where Newton slept. They brought the tile to Mary Longdon's home and placed it in the fire until it was red-hot. Longdon's urine was then poured onto the hot tile. News spread quickly across the town that as the urine steamed from the tile the witch convulsed in pain on the prison floor. Given that the community of Youghal was well versed in the behaviours of a witch and the rumours that others such as Halfpenny and Dodd were involved in the dark arts, it is certain that Youghal people felt extremely uneasy in their beds at night. More pertinently, those who had direct contact with Newton were bound to be reflecting on any mishaps or misfortunes in their lives.

Some of the legends of witchcraft, included the burning of babies to use the oil from the carcasses to smear their own bodies for the Devil's pleasure, dismembering males by magic and collecting the organs for placing in birds nests, turning cow's milk into blood and creating hailstorms. Not everyone believed in such absurdities and books like the *Malleus Maleficarum*, which outlined in great detail the complete guide to witches and even proposed evidence-based research and testimony as proof of their existence, were often dismissed as total nonsense. Mary Longdon's accusations were fantastical, the embodiment of hysteria but they allowed a deeper, more sinister reasoning for tragedy within the town. Myres' determination to carry out a water experiment was a reaction to the belief that Newton was responsible for the deaths of three children belonging to Aldermen in the town. Myres lost a child of his own during the period of the case when his daughter Grace died. Convinced the death was due to demonology, he ordered an autopsy. The results showed no obvious signs of mistreatment. However, he remained convinced that witchcraft had taken the three young lives, as well as his daughter's. It was said in court that the 'witch' had fatally kissed them; that was enough. It would not be the last death attributed to the suspected sorcerer.

By April, the only talk in Youghal was of Florence Newton. Jailer David Jones and his colleague Francis Besely engaged in some high spirits at the expense of Newton. The two men fuelled each other's excitement by talking about her powers and the creatures that slipped in and out of her cell. They paid a late-night visit to the jail. Jones and Besely taunted Newton through the small grate on the prison door asking her to say the Lord's Prayer. Memory failed her. Jones and Besely spent the night, no doubt hoping to witness something supernatural. When day broke, as Besely later testified, Newton kissed Jones on the hand through the grate of the prison door. Two weeks later Jones was dead, having complained to his wife Eleanor and his friend Besely that Newton was at his bedside 'pulling at his arm' and that he was in great pain.[203]

Other curious onlookers throughout the summer months of 1661 tormented Newton. That particular indignity, however, would be insignificant in comparison to the witch-finding tests carried out by self-proclaimed experts and those who claimed to know how to discover a witch. One man who claimed to have researched the subject was Valentine Greatrakes. Greatrakes was a native of Affane, County Waterford, though he was familiar with and to Youghal. His father had won the tender to supply the town with limestone during the building boom financed by Richard Boyle. His family had been close associates of the Boyles and Greatrakes himself was a friend of Roger Boyle (Lord Broghill) and his brother Robert Boyle, who was forging a reputation in England for his skills in chemistry. Greatrakes' brother-in-law John Nettles had been Mayor of Youghal in 1657. Nettles had acted as an agent for London investors throughout the Act of Settlement period and transplantation. Greatrakes had left the country at the beginning of the 1641 war when his family fell on hard times; his father, too had been murdered. While living in England he acquired an interest in iatrochemistry: the use of chemistry for the curing of diseases.[204] He returned to Ireland as a soldier under Oliver Cromwell, becoming a close associate of Colonel Phaire. The two gentlemen shared an interest in Quakerism and no doubt discussed its virtues on its arrival in Youghal.

Greatrakes had a particular interest in the aforementioned belief systems of both the Quakers and the Ranters. He was drawn to the idea that both good and evil spirits possessed the body and that the body could be used as a conduit for good or evil purposes. For now, Greatrakes' spiritual sensibilities had not yet reached their peak, certainly not in terms of publicly proclaiming any special gifts he had; that would come later. However, his association with a number of influential men like Nettles, Phaire, Broghill, Stout, Wood and others afforded him the opportunity to express his belief to them that he could either discover what demon possessed Newton or that he could heal her. Whatever his motive, Greatrakes had an interest in diseases and, as illness was often seen as demonic in origin, he might well have offered his 'expertise' in the hope of applying it in the case of the local witch. There would be no court application to vet his knowledge or credibility. If Greatrakes had expressed his desire to experiment on Newton to his friends then there was nothing other than their refusal to prevent him carrying it out. His credentials were built around intuition and the claim that he had researched the methods on how to discover a witch. Witchcraft literature was probably available to him while in England. If he had such a book in his possession in Youghal he would surely have produced its contents against Newton as irrefutable evidence. Greatrakes' method for discovering the nature of Newton's demonic possession was typically barbaric.

Before investigating Florence Newton, Greatrakes went to see Mary Longdon in the company of Edward Perry and Thomas Blackwell, a local surgeon. He told the maid he intended to carry out an experiment to verify both her accusations and their suspicions. They then sent for Newton. It is unknown in whose house the experiment took place but it is very probable it was either the home of one of the inquisitors or in the home of Longdon's master, John Pyne. A shoemaker had also been summoned to the house. The following story was later recounted as evidence in court. The widow was sat on a stool. While the others held Newton to the stool the shoemaker hammered an awl (long, thick nail) through her leg in an effort to make the awl stick to the stool. The shoemaker had to perform the task three times before the awl finally lodged in the seat. Newton was then ordered by the men to get off the stool. The widow complained that she could not move and was 'very weary'. She was pulled off the stool with the awl firmly fixed to the seat of it, ripping Newton's flesh. The shoemaker went to remove the awl and it fell into his hand. Much to the astonishment of the men, half an inch of the awl had broken off. The wonders of the experiment did not end there as they searched in vain to find any mark on the stool where the awl had been driven in. One of the inquisitors then took a second awl from the shoemaker placing it in Mary Longdon's hand. While two of the men held Newton's arm another clasped Longdon's hand with the awl in his. They 'ran violently at the witch's hand'.[205] The awl was again damaged as they failed to pierce the flesh. Blackwell, being a surgeon and thinking one of his implements might come in handy, produced a lance, or surgical knife. He cut Newton's hand open by one and a half inches but it did not bleed. He proceeded to cut the other hand and then both bled.

It is right to presume that, in the minds of the inquisitors, the 'damaged' awls were the result of some demonic possession that was displaying its supernatural strength and power. The bleeding of both hands,

as opposed to one, was most likely interpreted as a sign of God's works mimicking as they did the bleeding hands of Jesus on the cross. There is no reference to the testing as a method for extracting a confession. There was a total conviction amongst the community that Florence Newton was a witch and so a confession to a treaty with the Devil was not required. Torture for this purpose was widely used across Europe. Confessions were often made following excruciatingly cruel acts of violence such as pouring boiling water down a twisted cloth that was shoved into the victim's throat before being jerked out suddenly, causing organs to be drawn up. Other methods included the mangling of women's breasts with hot irons and the insertion of hot irons into the private area. Suspected witches were often shaved of all bodily hair because they were thought to hide charms and amulets in unexposed parts of their bodies. Hot pins were inserted into fingers having had the nails pulled off and thumbscrews crushed the fingers until blood spurted out.[206] Newton may have been subjected to a body shaving or a body search but it was not recorded at the trial. She was spared the techniques mentioned above, but hardly treated humanely, probably because Greatrakes viewed the process as a matter of science rather than torture. For the excited Greatrakes and his colleagues the wonders performed had little to do with Newton as a person. To their minds, the torture inflicted on her was justifiable as a means to draw out the conflicting spirits of good and evil. Newton was but a physical conduit for matters way beyond the comprehension of mere mortals. Greatrakes and his colleagues were carrying out their duty. This was science as designed by God. The inquisitors performed their task as both physical and spiritual surgeons on a hapless subject, as if curiously dissecting a dead animal for the purpose of advancing critical investigations. The experiment served a dual purpose; it would rationalise the fears of Youghal society and it would prove without doubt that Florence Newton was an agent of the Devil. In this context, Greatrakes was both social healer and witch-finder.

The Witch Trial

The extraordinary events of 1661 offered an opportunity to a number of important people in Youghal who would benefit greatly from the Florence Newton witch trial held at a Cork court in September of that year. From the moment Mary Longdon threw her first fit in January 1661 it became clear to a good deal of influential men that the case would draw attention from far and wide, not least the ears of Westminster and Dublin. Characters on the list of witnesses against Florence Newton were men of high importance in Youghal. Not only were most of the witnesses vulnerable to the political and religious changes taking place under the Restoration, as mentioned earlier, they also feared losing their livelihoods with the proposed changes to land ownership. Many of the witnesses against Florence Newton had been active participants for parliament in the war against the Crown and perhaps saw the trial and the crisis as an opportunity to solidify good reputations. If they could take a positive role in finding evil and ridding one of the most important towns in the kingdom of it, then they might find themselves indispensable and due some reward for their service.

Nicholas Pyne, a relation to Mary Longdon's master, John, was a close associate of Greatrakes and had already been immersed in land disputes throughout the previous decade. Pyne would be a key witness in Newton's trial. Nicholas Stout, another trial witness, had fallen foul of Lord Broghill, who had accused Stout of refusing to provide support to the Youghal garrison during the war and for calling his father, Richard Boyle, 'a fool and an ass'. He was in financial dire straits by the time the Newton case was in the full attention of the nation. The trial judge, Mr William Aston, also knew Greatrakes well. Aston had previously ruled at a court sitting to decide a land dispute between Greatrakes and the Prendergast family. He had found in favour of Greatrakes. The weight of evidence against Florence Newton meant the trial on 11 September in Cork was nothing more than a show of the government's determination to cleanse Youghal of evil. The fact that the trial was moved to Cork shows the importance of the event. It was probably thought that the court in Youghal was too small to house a trial of such magnitude.

Florence Newton had no defence and after months of incessant humiliation and both physical and mental torture she was in no position to present a persuasive argument against the outlandish and hysterical claims levelled against her. Newton must have endured morbid fascination, excited terror and some customary abuse when she was taken by cart through the streets of Youghal for the arduous journey to Cork. When she got to the court she found Mary Longdon repeating her feverish fit, writhing on the floor, wide eyed and tight jawed, begging to be released from her bewitching tormentor. Gazing incredulously from the bench, Newton may even have wondered if she actually possessed such power. Making sense of the depth of hate, bile, vitriol, spite and violence she was subjected to would have been beyond any innocent's comprehension, even if Newton knew that she carried all the trappings of a stereotypical witch. Many women pleaded guilty to witchcraft just to make the madness stop. They confessed to sorcery in lieu of other 'crimes' such as sexual deviancy, adultery or prostitution. Whatever her thinking on entering the court, Newton would have known her fate was sealed before the doors were even opened.

The widow was clasped in bolts and chains as a precaution against the hurt she was perceived to be causing the young maid. Newton was often removed from the court altogether while evidence was given against her. All of the stories related above were submitted as a case for the prosecution. In one chastening instance Newton was called upon to say the Lord's Prayer. Nicholas Stout testified that he had tried to get Newton to say it on several occasions in the Youghal prison but she failed to do so. She made four attempts at the prayer in court but could not remember the line 'And forgive us our trespasses'. When a clerk in the court was ordered to assist her, she simply repeated, 'Ay, Ay trespasses, that's the word.'[207] Exhausted, Newton could offer no other reason for her lapse in religious obedience other than a loss of memory. Meanwhile, the awestruck galleries, if not already entertained enough, were treated to exhibited evidence of wool, crooked pins and straw. The items were covered in white foamy spittle. They were brought to the courtroom having been expelled from the throat of Mary Longdon following a prolonged fit in a house nearby. Nicholas Stout, John Pyne, Nicholas Pyne, Valentine Greatrakes, Richard Myres and other important men completed their testimonies. The last recorded witnesses were David Jones' wife Eleanor and his former colleague Francis Besely, who testifed how David Jones had died.

The collection of conflated eyewitness accounts, witch-testing results and exhibits, not to mention displays of witchcraft at work in the court, created a show trial of insurmountable proportion for the languorous Newton. Though her sentencing by the court is missing from the record, her crimes were befitting of a burning. Newton was charged with the murder of David Jones and the torment of Mary Longdon by means of witchcraft. Most likely added to these charges were the murders by witchcraft of three young children. The court heard that she had a familiar and that she had been in the company of the Devil at the bedside of the young maid, having got there by means of magic. The convicted witch was not seen as a sorcerer alone, a dabbler in medicine, a mischievous midwife or an abuser of a gift but one that had bargained with the Devil. She had sold her soul in exchange for power. The distinction was crucial when it came to sentencing. The extent of Newton's perceived powers was not just based on simple black magic or bad medicine but the power to kill by touch and, even more telling, having demons in her company. This evidence was paramount in the view of court officials that Youghal was in danger of being lost completely to an uncontrollable outbreak of demonology. It was a view shared by figures of influence in Youghal and

Dublin. Another reason to suspect Florence Newton was burned was the absolute fear of burying a body that was proven in court to have supernatural powers. Further to this was the problem of where to bury her. There is no record either of where her execution was carried out, but the Youghal officials, so central to her trial, would have desired a public banishing of sorcery and the exorcism of evil from the town. An execution in Youghal would serve as a denouement to the trauma of 1661. It would also stand as a purging of the carnage and paranoia evidenced in the previous two decades. The execution of Florence Newton was a panacea for Youghal's ills, a catharsis, a moment to fan the flames of fear and then watch it turn to smoke and ash. Whether she was burned or hung, Florence Newton was only guilty of lacking felicity, money and the company of influence. Her forbearance in the face of a prolonged and cruel lie, based entirely on fantasy and fuelled with ignorance, had stolen her soul in a way that Satan never could, long before it destroyed her body.

Power from the Darkness

Those who took part in the testing and questioning of a convicted witch could rightly expect to receive favour and fame for their exploits. For some, it was enough to be associated with the notorious event. Mary Longdon, a hysteric, hell-bent on being the centre of attention, knew that her fame was secured and her part in the story would demand eternal queries of fascination and sympathy. Other figures central to the events of 1661 would also benefit. Trial witnesses John Pyne and Edward Perry were appointed bailiffs in 1664. Perry would become Mayor of Youghal ten years later, and Nicholas Stout replaced Richard Myres as mayor in the year of the trial. Preacher James Wood had a more controversial outcome to his career. Though he immediately had his annual pay increased, Wood was then described as a hypocrite by the Quaker community in Youghal. His demise culminated in being jailed for two years in 1663 for holding an illegal and secretive religious meeting in Youghal. Following his release he continued to preach but was widely derided as a religious vagrant.[208]

The man to gain most from the Florence Newton saga was Valentine Greatrakes. His imagination was fired by his encounter with Florence

Newton. While working as a Clerk of the Peace for Cork he was first struck with the belief that God had given him a gift:

> About four years since I had an impulse which frequently suggested
> to me that there was bestowed on me the gift of curing the king's
> evil, which for the extraordinariness thereof, I thought fit to conceal
> for some time; but, at length, I told my wife; for whether sleeping
> or waking, I had this impulse; but her reply was, 'that it was an
> idle imagination.' But, to prove the contrary, one William Maher,
> of the parish of Lismore, brought his son to my wife — who used
> to distribute medicines in charity to the neighbours — and my
> wife came and told me that I had now an opportunity of trying my
> impulse, for there was one at hand that had the evil grievously in the
> eyes, throat, and cheeks; whereupon I laid my hands on the places
> affected, and prayed to God, for Jesus' sake, to heal him. In a few
> days afterwards the father brought his son so changed that the eye
> was almost quite whole; and to be brief (to God's glory I speak it),
> within a month he was perfectly healed — and so continues.[209]

The story of the healing hands of Greatrakes spread throughout the neighbouring counties. It was claimed by an associate of Greatrakes that he had become so popular that he could no longer work his wonders from his home at Affane and set up a surgery in Youghal. He counselled hundreds of people who came to Youghal in the boatloads throughout the early part of the 1660s. To cure the public's ills Greatrakes simply laid his hands on the 'sufferer' and prayed. He had powerful allies who were willing to accept his gift as reality. People such as Lord Broghill (now the Earl of Orrery) allowed him to perform at his house in Charleville. The fame of his powers attracted attention in England where he received an invitation from a Lord Conway who hoped Greatrakes, now generally referred to as 'The Stroker', could cure his wife of persistent headache. His time in England was clouded in controversy with argument for and against his claims over whether God had anointed him with a gift or whether God was present in his body and acting through him. In any instance, he failed to cure Lady Conway. By 1666 he performed without great effect before Charles II. Hailed as a faith healer by some, derided as a charlatan by others, Greatrakes, disillusioned by the controversy his gift created, returned to Affane to farm until his death in 1683.

The witch craze that afflicted Youghal in 1661 was the eruption of conflated crises in the social, political and religious orders of the town. The chronic lack of purpose and leadership at local, national and kingdom level contributed to an outburst of neurosis revealing a hollow and sobering truth about the chaos of early modern Youghal; it was a confused town in constant flux and friction. The records from the *Corporation Book of Youghal* for a period before, during and after the Florence Newton affair are missing. Perhaps it is simply a coincidence. However, there is good reason for it to have been deliberately destroyed. With improvements in science and medicine the very concept of witch-induced magic was eventually dismissed. The craze had begun to touch the lives of women associated with the higher echelons of society, such as ministers' wives. Such men of influence simply could not entertain the thought that their class could be so afflicted and threatened. For Youghal, having Satan in their midst would have been enormously damaging for trade and commerce. The fear amongst the people of the day of being threatened by the presence of evil should not be underestimated. However irrational it appears, it would have been enough to negate trade and therefore had a direct and negative effect on the town's economy. It would have benefitted the town's coffers to forget Florence Newton as quickly as she had been elevated to perverse stature as the Devil's bride. In the later developing societies of logic, pragmatism, education and science, the stories of Newton, Longdon and Greatrakes would become amusing but also embarrassing for a town of such importance and tradition to the Crown. What happened in Youghal throughout 1661 should not be read simply or singularly as an absurdity perpetrated by a self-centred girl and a group of ambitious men in the maelstrom of a neurotic post-war society. Though the characters involved were ready to make the most of the situation to advance varied securities for their careers, livelihoods and properties, their utter belief in the supernatural should also be accepted as a crucial factor in creating hysteria amongst an ailing society disabled by a political, spiritual and religious malaise.

Epilogue

In 1679, only one hundred years after the Earl of Desmond, Gerald Fitzgerald, stood before the gates of Youghal, torch in hand, a ship called the *Encrease* was docked at the town quay. It was taking on board the Irish who, dispossessed of land and property, were being shipped off to the far reaches of the British Empire in America.

Overlooking his decks, a very busy Captain Phillip Poplestone counted his commodities as they boarded his ship, leaving behind their homes and families never to return. Twenty Catholic slaves were bound for the tobacco plantations in Maryland, America. Thomas Hennessey would have been thinking of his wife, Catherine, who would follow him nine days later on a second ship called *The Globe*, carrying a further forty-five Irish slaves. Captain Poplestone, having paid his £100 to Talbot County landowner and American plantation magnate Lord Baltimore, was looking to receive 1,000 acres of untouched American soil in payment for his Irish slaves. The 1679 sailings from Youghal reveal the workings in the expansion of the British Empire and how it had engulfed the town on its way west to the New World ever since the plantation programme was drawn up in the 1550s. The expansion programme, if it can be called that, had profoundly affected the creation of early modern Youghal in terms of infrastructure, culture, religion, administration and political thinking, as well as action, with Henry VIII's declaration of sovereignty over the Kingdom of Ireland in 1542. The Irish slaves may well have hoped for a better life, though it was a case of meeting the new boss, same as the old boss. However, one could hardly fault them if they lacked sentimentality for the scarred and brutal history they were leaving behind. That the Irish, at least those without education, trade or skills and those dispossessed of them, were still being rounded up and shipped out thirty years on from Cromwell's arrival shows the plight of the Gaelic Irish in the continuing crisis of the seventeenth century. They had long found Youghal a staunch defender of the Crown, then of Cromwell and then of the Crown again. They also found it a centre for Protestant interests with little or no sympathy to Catholic concerns. For all that, not all Catholics in Munster or the Youghal area emigrated and gradually they repopulated trades, businesses and the force of the labouring underclass in the town.

For all the Protestant fears of losing property, status and their careers at the beginning of the Restoration in 1659, the New English elite in Youghal continued to hold sway for the remainder of the century and beyond. This was mostly due to the continuing and powerful influence of Broghill. He would never reach the levels of commercial success enjoyed by his father but his antagonism toward Catholics fuelled a determination to protect the 'true religion' in Youghal. Throughout the tumultuous political period of his lifespan, whether it was for Crown, parliament or Restoration, his social and political motives were copper-fastened to that commitment. Broghill was proactive in trying to suppress the kind of multi-disciplined sects and their doctrines that emerged in the 1650s as well as banning Catholic meetings within Youghal, though Catholics were virtually free to meet in rural settings. The town gates were locked on Sundays during services and sermons in both the morning and afternoon. Broghill's policies were not exactly welcomed by the Kingship of Charles II and he was both vexed and angered by the removal of the Presidency of Munster office in 1672. Such a move was alarming to his Protestant allies in Youghal.

The vision for and perception of Youghal as a well-run Protestant civic centre under the moral guidance of a single Church was a false one. For all the efforts of Raleigh, Boyle, Cromwell and Broghill, the Old Catholic families, long steeped in the mercantile traditions of the seaport, remained. They had one useful commodity above the vagaries of religious tolerance and intolerance: the ability to be indispensable to the commercial fortunes of the New English investors and adventurers. In short, they were needed, even in and in spite of the semi-paralysed and anaemic economy of the late 1600s. Ascension to positions of power and influence, however, was virtually impossible for them. Rural Catholics too found employment with many of the post-Cromwell landowners. Many of these ex-military, who gained property in lieu of payment, knew little or nothing about farming.

In Youghal, the Protestant elite would occupy the best stone houses in the town with the majority of the expanding Catholic population taking up residence in the cramped, wooden cabins of the liberties north and south of the town gates, and though the public and official conversations would continue to be based on a policy of subordination, private thinking allowed for an unwritten contract of communal and mutually beneficial civility between Youghal Catholics and Protestants. The distance between Broghill's thinking and that of London was wide enough to create the same inconsistency in governance as had existed at the onset of the plantations. There would be one remarkable difference as the seventeenth century came to a close: the suppression of the Gaelic-Irish voice in policy and decision-making. However, for Youghal, not much had changed in close to a millennium. The town was tied to the royal umbilical cord, as it had always desired to be.

Administrative concerns in the Youghal Corporation continued to be occupied with the setting of rents and rates. With no apparent reason to believe the town was susceptible to attack, the militia companies returned to regular training such as expeditions to Claycastle where they camped overnight. The soldiers were given a barrel of beer and small pay for their efforts. Crime continued to be a problem throughout the closing decades of the century. Materials were ordered and tradesmen paid by the council to refurbish the town gates, the pillory cage, the prison and stocks for holding criminals. A finger stocks was also ordered as punishment for those damaging the town walls and town properties. The social welfare/charity system found orphans being housed with widows and families who, for their efforts, received payment from the council. The 'Exchange' was built on the north side of the Quay Gate for housing trade goods, and the postmaster of Youghal was paid to print the *Youghal News Book*. These books preceded newspapers and were about sixteen pages in length, approximately 5 by 6 inches in size and carried both local and national news as well as information about events in England and Scotland.

Youghal would continue to be a garrison town of importance, opening its gates to the French Protestant refugees who fled Catholic persecution in France in the 1680s. During the Williamite war the town succumbed to the Orange brigade of Captain Thomas Pownall in August 1690. Pownall was advancing from Waterford on his way to Mallow and was travelling with fifty dragoons (mounted infantry) when he arrived at the North Gate of Youghal on 2 August. Pownall sent a message to the mayor, Robert Ball, warning him that if the town tried to hold out against his forces he would bring it to ruin. He demanded a surrender and to be allowed entry to the town. Ball discussed the matter with the council and officers of the town's militia throughout the day and into the evening. Eventually, at ten o'clock that night, Ball rode out of the North Gate with three companies of foot soldiers and surrendered Youghal to the Orangemen.

The demise of Youghal at the close of the century is evidenced by what Pownall found inside its walls. Though there were fourteen cannons mounted at various points for its protection, the guns were in fact nothing more than decorations as there was 'neither powder nor ball'.[210]

It would be over a century before Youghal would recover an economy to match that of Richard Boyle's period. The 1761 revenue returns highlighted not only the town's survival but also its rejuvenation. Similar to the first half of the 1600s, the peace of early to mid decades of the 1700s allowed for a growth in trade as Youghal regularly imported and exported from an array of European ports. The types of imports prove more than anything the cosmopolitan nature of Youghal. They also offer a great insight to the town's society, how people lived and the extent of wealth in both its social and commercial circles.

From Bristol, merchants imported medicines, dyes, seeds, sugars, currants, cheese, sugar candy and treacle, as well as glass for windows, mirrors, ready-made coach doors for carriages, coffin handles, nut crackers, needles, smoothing irons, hand bells and snuff boxes. Other imports included children's shoes, hair powder, thread, silk, silk ribbons, sleeve buttons, spectacles and spectacle cases, thrash bags, tobacco pipes, petticoats and leather belts. From ports such as Chester came white salt, from Liverpool, cheese, cups, plates and saucers, from Minehead, barley, beer, cider and candlewick, from Swansea, ox-bones and wheat. Beyond Britain, lemons, liquorice, oranges, raisins, almonds, figs, grapes, olives, linseed oil, wine, vinegar, copy paper and cork came in from Bordeaux, Le Harve, Nantes, Rochelle, Bilbao, Cadiz and Lisbon. Goods such as pottery, iron, timber, whalebone, iron pots and pans were unloaded on the quayside from Holland, New Zealand, Belgium, Germany and Norway. Youghal harbour was thick with ships such as the *Lisbon Merchant*, the *Britannia*, the *Mary Ann*, the *George Christ*, the *Exchange*, the *Elizabeth* and many, many others. Import and export commerce would lead to a second building boom. The Trinity Castle was torn down and, using some of the old stone, the current Clock Gate was built in its place in 1777. Other buildings of note were the Red House, the Mall House and St Mary's parish church. Piece by piece the quay walls disappeared. Youghal's suburbs expanded north along the river and south along the bay. On the hill to the west, the magnificent walls of the 1200s would remain.

The town of Youghal would still face many challenges – the 1798 rebellion and the great famine to touch on just two, but never in its history had two generations witnessed such a fascinating and equally terrifying period as that of its early modern formation. Youghal was either central to or directly affected by two rebellions, a sacking, a civil war, a siege, plantations, an economic boom, famines, plagues, and a witch trial, all in the duration of one lifespan: eighty years. The micro-history of Youghal, particularly from the latter 1500s to the latter 1600s, is also the macro-history of Britain and Ireland and vice versa. The histories of both are intrinsically linked by the melding together of cultures through assimilation, colonisation and conquest, creating an early modern social, political and religious pulse that beat incessantly through Youghal's Irish heart and its English blood.

A map of Youghal drawn around the 1590s by William Jones. (Courtesy of Trinity College Dublin)

Notes

1. Richard Caulfield, *The Council Book of the Corporation of Youghal* (Guildford, 1878), p.viii.
2. Samuel Hayman, 'The Ecclesiastical Antiquities of Youghal – No.II', *Proceedings and Transactions of the Kilkenny and South-East of Ireland Archaeological Society*, vol.3 (1855), p.328.
3. The National Archives of England, 'Irish Material in the Class of Ancient Petitions (SC 8) in the Public Record Office', Reference: SC 8/283/14111, 92.
4. Caulfield, *The Council Book of Youghal*, p.xxvi.
5. Henry Allen Jeffries, *Cork: Historical Perspective* (Dublin, 2004), p.84.
6. Some confusion exists about the name 'Water Gate' which is believed by locals to be placed at the end of Quay Lane. This is due to inaccurate information given with the Pacata Hibernia map used on the cover of this book. The original Water Gate was placed at the north end of the town at the end of O'Neill/Crowley Street as seen on the William Jones map. The Quay Gate, not the Water Gate, was situated at the end of Quay Lane.
7. Anthony M. McCormack, *The Earldom of Desmond 1463–1583: The Decline and Crisis of a Feudal Lordship* (Dublin, 2005), p.92.
8. Samuel Hayman, *The New Hand-book for Youghal, Fourth Series* (Lindsay, 1858) p.10.
9. Ciaran Brady, 'Faction and the Origins of the Desmond Rebellion of 1579', *Irish Historical Studies*, vol.22, no.88 (Sept. 1981), pp.289–312.
10. McCormack, *The Earldom of Desmond 1463–1583*, p.92.
11. Colm Lennon, *Sixteenth-century Ireland: The Incomplete Conquest* (Dublin, 2005), p.212.
12. Henry Sidney, 'Sidney's Memoir of His Government of Ireland 1583', *Ulster Journal of Archaeology*, first series, vol. 3 (1855), pp.33–52, 85–109, 336–57.

13. Ibid., p.43.

14. Ibid., p.50.

15. Brady, 'Faction and the Origins of the Desmond Rebellion of 1579', pp.289–312.

16. McCormack, *The Earldom of Desmond 1463–1583*, p.113.

17. Peter Piveronus, 'Sir Warham St Leger, Organizer-in-Chief of the Munster Plantation Scheme of 1568–69, Evidence from the Hand-Writing Analysis of Selected Documents in the PRO, London', *The Canadian Journal of Irish Studies*, vol.6, no.1 ('Literature, Language and Politics in Ireland', June 1980), pp.79–89.

18. McCormack, *The Earldom of Desmond 1463–1583*, p.113.

19. Brady, 'Faction and the Origins of the Desmond Rebellion of 1579', pp.289–312.

20. Thomas Churchyard, *A General Rehearsel of Warres: Called Churchyardes Coise*, Edward White (London, 1579).

21. Caulfield, *The Council Book of Youghal*, p.xliii.

22. Richard Caulfield, *The Council Book of the Corporation of Cork City* (Guildford, 1876), p.xvi.

23. Brady, 'Faction and the Origins of the Desmond Rebellion of 1579', pp.289–312.

24. Lennon, *Sixteenth-century Ireland*, p.226.

25. Brady, 'Faction and the Origins of the Desmond Rebellion of 1579', pp.289–312.

26. Caulfield, *The Council Book of Youghal*, p.xliii.

27. Lennon, *Sixteenth-century Ireland*, p.212.

28. Hayman, *The New Hand-book for Youghal*, p.21.

29. *Calendar of State Papers Ireland*, vol. 78, 45.1.

30. John Curry and Charles O'Connor, *An historical and critical review of the civil wars in Ireland, from the reign of Queen Elizabeth, to the settlement under King William. With the state of the Irish Catholics, from that settlement to the relaxation of the popery laws, in the year 1778. Extracted from parliamentary records, state acts, and other authentic materials* (Dublin, 1810), p.26.

31. John Pope Hennessey, *Raleigh in Ireland* (London, 2011), p.27.

32. Caulfield, *The Council Book of Youghal*, p.xlvi.

33. Paul E.J. Hammer, *Elizabeth's Wars: War, Government and Society in Tudor England, 1544–1604* (Hampshire, 2003), p.80.

34. Ibid.

35. Ibid., p.109.

36. Hennessey, *Raleigh in Ireland*, p.17.

37. Alfred O'Rahilly, 'The Massacre at Smerwick (1580)', *An Irish Quarterly Review*, vol.27, no.108 (Dec. 1938), pp.690–92.

38. Ibid., pp.5–6.

39. David Dean, 'Elizabethan Government and Politics', in Robert Titler and Norman Jones (eds), *A Companion to Tudor Britain* (Oxford, 2009), p.52.

40. Hennessey, *Raleigh in Ireland*, p.36.

41. Hiram Morgan, 'Never Any Realm Worse Governed: Queen Elizabeth and Ireland', *Transactions of the Royal Historical Society*, sixth series, vol.14 (2004), pp.295–308.

42. Edmund Spenser, *A View of the Present State of Ireland*, edited by Alexander B. Grosart, first edition (London, 1894).

43. Raymond Jenkins, 'Spenser with Lord Grey in Ireland', *PMLA*, vol.52, no.2 (June 1937), pp.338–53.

44. Hennessey, *Raleigh in Ireland*, p.22.

45. Lennon, *Sixteenth-century Ireland*, p.229.

46. Anthony M. McCormack, 'The Social and Economic Consequences of the Desmond Rebellion 1779–83', *Irish Historical Studies*, no.34 (May 2004), pp.1–15.

47. Spenser, *A View of the Present State of Ireland*.

48. McCormack, 'The Social and Economic Consequences of the Desmond Rebellion 1779–83', p.230.

49. Ibid., p.230.

50. Ibid., p.234.

51. Nicholas Canny, *Making Ireland British 1580–1650* (Oxford, 2001), p.149.

52. Caulfield, *The Council Book of Youghal*, pp.xxix–xxx.

53. Ibid., p.xxx.

54. Ibid., p.xliv.

55. Ibid., p.xllv.

56. Ibid.

57. Ibid. p.xiv.

58. Hennessey, *Raleigh in Ireland*, p.32.

59. Ibid., p.56.

60. Ibid., p.57.

61. Susan Flavin, 'Consumption and Material Culture in Sixteenth-century Ireland', *Economic History Review*, vol.64, no.4 (Nov. 2011), pp.1144–74.

62. Edward Edwards, *The Life of Sir Walter Raleigh* (London, 1868), p.97.

63. Hennessey, *Raleigh in Ireland*, p.57.

64. Pauline Croft, 'Trading with the Enemy 1585–1604', *The Historical Journal*, vol.32, no.2 (June 1989), pp.281–302.

65. Edwards, *The Life of Sir Walter Raleigh*, p.102.

66. Ibid.

67. Hennessey, *Raleigh in Ireland*, p.77.

68. Dean, 'Elizabethan Government and Politics', p.52.

69. Raymond Jenkins, 'Spenser: The Uncertain Years 1584–89', *PMLA*, vol.53, no.2 (June 1938), pp.350–62.

70. For further reading see Ray Heffner, 'Edmund Spenser's Family', *Huntington Library Quarterly*, vol.2, no.1 (Oct. 1938), pp.79–84.70.

71. Edmund Spenser, *A View of the Present State of Ireland*, Alexander B. Grosart (ed.), first edition (London, 1894)

72. Ibid.

73. Lennon, *Sixteenth-century Ireland*, pp.295–96.

74. Thomas Morrissey. 'Among the Irish Martyrs: Dominic Collins, SJ, in His Times (1566–1602)', *An Irish Quarterly Review*, vol.81, no.323 (Autumn 1992), pp.313–25.

75. Lennon, *Sixteenth-century Ireland*, p.294.

76. Ibid., p.295.

77. Ibid., p.298.

78. Ibid., p.299.

79. Caulfield, *The Council Book of Youghal*, p.xlvi.

80. Morrissey, *Among the Irish Martyrs*, pp.313–25.
81. Ibid., p.321.
82. Ibid., p.322.
83. Lismore Castle Papers, National Library of Ireland, Collection List No.129, p.27.
84. Haries to Archer, Lisbon, 19 January 1603; Roman A.S.J.; Mss.Castil.33, f.94; Latin trans., q. Finnegan pp.409–10 in Morrissey, *Among the Irish Martyrs*, pp.313–25.
85. Hayman, *The New Hand-book for Youghal*, p.36.
86. J.G. Hawkes and J. Francisco-Ortega, 'The Potato in Spain during the Late 16th Century', *Economic Botany*, vol.46, no.1 (Jan.–Mar. 1992), pp.86–97; Patricia J. O'Brien, 'The Sweet Potato: Its Origin and Dispersal', *American Anthropologist*, new series, vol.74, no.3 (June 1972), pp.342–65; William H. McNeill, 'The Introduction of the Potato into Ireland', *The Journal of Modern History*, vol.21, no.3 (Sept. 1949), pp.218–22.
87. Hennessey, *Raleigh in Ireland*, p.66.
88. For an exploration of Boyle's tombs see Clodagh Tait, 'Colonising Memory: Manipulations of Death, Burial and Commemoration in the Career of Richard Boyle, First Earl of Cork (1566–1643)', *Proceedings of the Royal Irish Academy. Section C: Archaeology, Celtic Studies, History, Linguistics, Literature*, vol.101C, no.4 (2001), pp.107–34.
89. Terence O. Ranger, 'Richard Boyle and the Making of an Irish Fortune, 1588–1614', *Irish Historical Studies*, vol.10, no.39 (Mar. 1957), pp.257–97.
90. Lismore Castle Papers, National Library of Ireland, Collection List No.129, p.27.
91. Cal. SP. Ire., 1600–01, p.94. Quoted in T.W. Moody (et al.), *A New History of Ireland, Volume III: Early Modern Ireland, 1534–1691.*
92. Caulfield, *The Council Book of Youghal*, p.xlvi.
93. Ibid., pp.41–42.
94. Ibid., p.45.
95. Ibid., p.59.
96. Ibid., pp.5–6.
97. Ibid., p.5.
98. Ibid., p.7.
99. Ibid., p.53.
100. Ibid., p.137.
101. J.C. Appleby, 'Settlers and Pirates in Early Seventeenth-century Ireland: A Profile of Sir William Hill', *Studia Hibernica*, no.25 (1990), pp.76–104.
102. Caulfield, *The Council Book of Youghal*, p.137.
103. Ibid., pp.xlviii–l. Baker attested he heard Nutt say he had twenty-five men and that thirty-eight had left him at Long Island. The pirate's plan was to 'lye off and on betwixt Ireland and the port of Torbay, near Dartmouth, for a fortnight yet to come'. He had sent an envoy to Apsham, near Exeter where, according to Baker's account, Nutt had a wife and three children to 'solicit the obtaining of his pardon'. Nutt planned to sail to Torbay and wait for the envoy to return. Nutt and the envoy had agreed upon a signal for the envoy to come aboard: 'The Capt. will remove his flag out of the main-top into the fore-top, and thereupon his man is to come aboard him, and certainly he will go ashore at Torbay by night and put his goods.' Should the envoy fail to turn up then Nutt had a back-up plan. A pardon was already in place for him and his crew from the 'Prince of Orange' (Maurice of Nassau,

in the Netherlands) and a ship called the *John* was heading to Newfoundland
for them. However, Nutt and his company trusted the Dutch even less than
they trusted the English Crown and Nutt obviously was tiring of the hunt.
Nutt did seek a pardon and that Eliot afforded him one but, once ashore,
he was arrested and tried. Nutt was about to be hanged when Sir George
Calvert,intervened on his behalf. It was Calvert that Nutt had worked for
three years previously in Newfoundland.

104. Caulfield, *The Council Book of Youghal*, p.103.
105. Raymond Gillespie. *Seventeenth-century Ireland* (Dublin, 2006), p.6.
106. Jane Ohlmeyer, '"Making Ireland English": The Early Seventeenth-century
     Peerage', in Brian Mac Cuarta SJ (ed.), *Reshaping Ireland 1550–1700:
     Colonization and Its Consequences* (essays presented to Nicholas Canny)
     (Dublin, 2011), p.143.
107. Canny, *Making Ireland British 1580–1630*, pp.308–21.
108. Samuel Hayman, 'Youghal Money of Necessity', *The Journal of the Royal
     Historical and Archaeological Association of Ireland*, fourth series, vol.5,
     no.37 (Jan. 1879), pp.35–37.
109. Caulfield, *The Council Book of Youghal*, p.108.
110. Ibid.
111. W.H. Grattan Flood, 'Fennor and Daborne at Youghal in 1618',
     The Modern Language Review, vol.20, no.3 (July 1925), pp.321–22.
112. Caulfield, *The Council Book of Youghal*, p.64.
113. Ibid., p.69.
114. Ibid., pp.55–56.
115. Ibid., pp.100–102.
116. Ibid., pp.124–25.
117. Lismore Castle Papers, National Library of Ireland, Collection List No.129,
     p.105.
118. Robert Boyle was only 8 when he entered Eton College in 1635. At 14 he
     was taken to Geneva to complete his education. After five years he returned
     to the war-torn British Isles in 1644. He created a chemistry laboratory a
     year later. He spent two years in Ireland between 1652 and 1654 during the
     Cromwellian land settlements to attend to his Irish estates. On returning
     to England he began working earnestly in science. Two years later an
     experiment with air, compressed gas and pressure led to his discovery of
     Boyle's Law. Boyle had many interests other than chemistry. He delved in
     theology, biology and maths; a man of his age. Boyle died in 1691.
119. Caulfield, *The Council Book of Youghal*, pp.58–59.
120. Ibid., pp.147–48.
121. Ranger, 'Richard Boyle and the Making of an Irish Fortune, 1588–1614'.
122. Ohlmeyer, 'Making Ireland English', p.140.
123. Nicholas Canny, *The Upstart Earl: A Study of the Social and Mental World
     of Richard Boyle First Earl of Cork 1566–1643* (London, 1982), p.10.
124. Ibid., p.11.
125. Ibid., p.16.
126. Ibid., p.19.
127. Sheffield City Library, WWM Str P 6/38, Strafford Papers. Quoted in Tait,
     'Colonising Memory'.
128. For further reading see Patrick Little, 'The Earl of Cork and the Fall of the

Earl of Strafford, 1638–41', *The Historical Journal*, vol.39, no.3 (Sept. 1996), pp.619–35.

129. From this point on, and especially after Boyle's death, Our Lady's College, which was situated where an orchard adjoining the gardens stands today, fell into disrepair. Boyle's college house, known locally today as the 'French Convent', took prominence. It was a more modern, accommodating and comfortable building than the old college. The house faces Boyle's gardens and is referred to incorrectly as 'St Mary's College'. Coupled with this was the preference for Lismore Castle as the family seat by his sons. Roger Boyle preferred not to take up his father's residence in Youghal, who always referred to the town as 'home'. For all its historical significance and the controversy it caused Boyle, its ruination and disappearance receives little recording.

130. Little, 'The Earl of Cork and the Fall of the Earl of Strafford, 1638–41', pp.619–35

131. Caulfield, *The Council Book of Youghal*, p.l.

132. ibid, p.212.

133. For further reading on this debate see 'What Really Happened in 1641' in Jane Ohlmeyer (ed.), *Ireland from Independence to Occupation, 1641–1660* (Cambridge, 1995), pp.24–42.

134. Raymond Gillespie, *Sixteenth-century Ireland: Making Modern Ireland* (Dublin, 2006), pp.123–52.

135. Caulfield, *The Council Book of Youghal*, p.211.

136. Historical Manuscripts Commission, Omnondne., s., ii (London, 1908), p.12. Quoted in Joseph Cope, 'The Experience of Survival during the 1641 Irish Rebellion', *The Historical Journal*, vol.46, no.2 (June 2003), pp.295–316.

137. Ibid., p.l.

138. 'Waterford during the Civil War 1641–1653: Traits and Stories from T.C.D. Depositions', edited by Thomas Fitzpatrick, *Journal of the Waterford and South-East of Ireland Archaeological Society*, vol.XIV (1911).

130. Dorothea Townshend, *The Life and Letters of the Great Earl of Cork* (California, 1904), p.392.

140. Caulfield, *The Council Book of Youghal*, p.229.

141. David Edwards and Thomas Powell, 'The Ship's Journal of Captain Thomas Powell, 1642', *Analecta Hibernica*, no.37 (1998), pp.251, 253–84.

142. Townshend, *The Life and Letters of the Great Earl of Cork*, p.415.

143. Ibid., p.423.

144. David Dickson, *Old World Colony: Cork and South Munster 1630–1830* (Cork, 2005), p.32.144.

145. 'Waterford during the Civil War 1641–1653: Traits and Stories from the T.C.D. Depositions'.

146. Edwards and Powell, 'The Ship's Journal of Captain Thomas Powell, 1642'.

147. Caulfield, *The Council Book of Youghal*, p.223.

148. Ibid., p.436.

149. Ibid., p.240.

150. Gillespie, *Sixteenth-century Ireland*, p.161.

151. Townshend, *The Life and Letters of the Great Earl of Cork*, p.438.

152. Caulfield, *The Council Book of Youghal*, pp.234–35.

153. Gillespie, *Sixteenth-century Ireland*, p.166.

154. Caulfield, *The Council Book of Youghal*, pp.247–48.
155. Ibid., p.545.
156. Ibid., p.546.
157. The expulsion order stated that if residents refused to leave they were to be punished 'on pain of death'. Ibid.
158. John Prendegast, *The Cromwellian Settlement of Ireland* (London, 1870), p.83.
159. Caulfield, *The Council Book of Youghal*, p.li.
160. Ibid., p.545.
161. Ibid., p.546.
162. Ibid.
163. Ibid.
164. John Cunningham, 'Oliver Cromwell and the Cromwellian Settlement of Ireland', The Historical Journal, vol.53, no.4 (Dec. 2010), pp.919–37.
165. Caulfield, *The Council Book of Youghal*, p.549.
166. Caulfield, *The Council Book of Youghal*, p.553.
167. James Touchet, *The Earl of Castlehaven's Memoirs: or his Review of the Civil Wars in Ireland 1642–1651* (London, 1681), pp.86–87.
168. Ibid.
169. Ibid., pp.87–89.
170. Caulfield, *The Council Book of Youghal*, pp.lii–liii.
171. Granville Penn, *Memorials of the Professional Life and Times of Sir William Penn. vol. 1* (London, 1833), p.123.
172. Caulfield, *The Council Book of Youghal*, pp.lii–liii.
173. For a comprehensive look at the importance of the maritime conflict and the role it played in the siege of Youghal see Elaine Murphy, *Ireland and the War at Sea, 1641–1653* (Suffolk, 2012), pp.46–47.
174. Thomas L. Coonan, *The Irish Catholic Confederacy and the Puritan Revolution* (Dublin, 1954), p.198.
175. Caulfield, *The Council Book of Youghal*, p.259.
176. Tadhg Ó hAnnracháin, 'Vatican Diplomacy and the Mission of Rinuccini to Ireland', Archivium Hibernicum, vol.47 (1993), pp.78–88.
177. Patrick Little, *Lord Broghill and the Cromwellian Union with Ireland and Scotland* (Suffolk, 2004), p.34.
178. For further reading on this perspective see St John D. Seymour, 'The Storming of the Rock of Cashel by Lord Inchiquin in 1647', The English Historical Review, vol.32, no.127 (July 1917), pp.373–78.
179. Caulfield, *The Council Book of Youghal*, p.280.
180. Murphy, *Ireland and the War at Sea, 1641–1653*, pp.46–47.
181. Antonia Fraser, *Cromwell: Our Chief of Men* (Phoenix, 2002), p.423.
182. James Scott Wheeler, *Cromwell in Ireland* (Dublin, 1999), p.96
183. Caulfield, *The Council Book of Youghal*, p.liv.
184. Ibid., p.lvi.
185. Ibid., p.557.
186. Ibid.
187. Samuel Hayman, 'The Ecclesiastical Antiquities of Youghal – No.III', The Journal of the Kilkenny and South-East of Ireland Archaeological Society, new series, vol.1, no.1 (1856), pp.14–28.
188. Thomas Carlyle (ed.), *Oliver Cromwell's Letters and Speeches II: Letters From Ireland, 1649 and 1650* (London, 1897).

189. Ibid.
190. Ibid.
191. Caulfield, *The Council Book of Yougal*, p.289.
192. Dickson, *Old World Colony: Cork and South Munster 1630–1830*, p.40.
193. Prendegast, *The Cromwellian Settlement of Ireland* (London, 1870), pp.90–91.
194. Great Britain Parliament, *Cromwellian Settlement of Ireland, 1641–1650: Four Rare Puritan Tracts Concerning the Affairs of Ireland* (London, 1641).
195. John D. Seymour *The Puritans in Ireland, 1647–1661: Volume XII* (Oxford, 1921), p.104.
196. Jacqueline Rose, 'John Locke, "Matters Indifferent", and the Restoration of the Church of England', *The Historical Journal*, vol.48, no.3 (Sept. 2005), pp.601–21.
197. Peter Elmer, *The Miraculous Conformist: Valentine Greatrakes, the Body Politic, and the Politics of Healing in Restoration Britain* (Oxford, 2013), p.132.
198. Glanvill, *Sadducismus Triumphatus: or, A Full and Plain Evidence Concerning Witches and Apparitions. Fourth Edition* (London), p.313.
199. Caulfield, *The Council Book of Yougal*, p.299.
200. For a detailed exploration of the gendercide argument see the excellent Anne Llewellyn Barstow, *Witchcraze: A New European History of the Witch Hunts* (London, 1994).
201. Glanvill, *Sadducismus Triumphatus*, p.322.
202. Ibid.
203. Ibid.
204. Roger French and Andrew Wear (eds), *The Medical Revolution of the Seventeenth Century* (Cambridge, 1989), p.42.
205. Glanvill, *Sadducismus Triumphatus*, p.119.
206. Barstow, *Witchcraze*.
207. Glanvill, *Sadducismus Triumphatus*, p.317.
208. Elmer, *The Miraculous Conformist*, p.131.
209. Valentine Greatrakes, *A Brief Account of Mr. Valentine Greatrakes and Divers of the Strange Cures by him Lately Performed* (London, 1666), p.211.
210. Caulfield, *The Council Book of Youghal*, p.lviii

Bibliography

Appleby, J.C., 'Settlers and Pirates in Early Seventeenth-century Ireland: A
  Profile of Sir William Hill', *Studia Hibernica*, no. 25 (1990), pp. 76–104
Armstrong, Robert, *Protestant War: The 'British' of Ireland and the Wars of the*
  Three Kingdoms (Manchester University Press, 2005)
Barnard, T.C., *Cromwellian Ireland: English Government and Reform in Ireland*
  1649–1660: English Government and Reform in Ireland, 1649–60 (Oxford
  University Press, new edition, 2000)
Beigun Kaplan, Barbara, 'Greatrakes the Stroker: The Interpretations of His
  Contemporaries', *Isis*, vol. 73, no. 2 (1982), pp. 178–85
Bowen, Desmond, *History and the Shaping of Irish Protestantism* (Peter Lang, 1995)
Brady, Ciaran. 'Faction and the Origins of the Desmond Rebellion of 1579',
  Irish Historical Studies, vol. 22, no. 88 (1981), pp. 289–312
Bruce, John, Douglas, William and Lomas, S.C. *Calendar of State Papers,*
  Domestic Series, of the Reign of Charles I (Longman, 1858–97)
Calendar of State Papers, Ireland, vol. 78, 45.1
Canny, Nicholas, *Making Ireland British 1580–1650* (Oxford, 2001)
Canny, Nicholas, *The Upstart Earl: A Study of the Social and Mental World of*
  Richard Boyle First Earl of Cork 1566–1643 (1982)
Carlyle, Thomas (ed.), *Oliver Cromwell's Letters and Speeches II: Letters From*
  Ireland, 1649 and 1650 (London, 1897)
Caulfield, Richard, *The Council Book of the Corporation of Youghal* (Guildford, 1878)
Caulfield, Richard, *The Council Book of the Corporation of Cork City*
  (Guildford, 1876)
Churchyard, Thomas, *A General Rehearsel of Warres: Called Churchyardes Coise*
  (Edward White, 1579)
Conyngham, D.P., *Lives of the Irish Martyrs* (Fredonia Books, 2001)

Coonan, Thomas L., 'The Irish Catholic Confederacy and the Puritan Revolution', *The Irish Ecclesiastical Record: A Monthly Journal Under Episcopal Sanction*, ser. 5, vol. LXXXIV (1954), pp. 287–88

Cope, Joseph. 'The Experience of Survival during the 1641 Irish Rebellion', *The Historical Journal*, vol. 46, no. 2 (2003), pp. 295–316

Croft, Pauline. 'Trading with the Enemy 1585–1604', *The Historical Journal*, vol. 32, no. 2 (1989), pp. 281–302

Cunningham, John. 'Oliver Cromwell and the Cromwellian Settlement of Ireland', *The Historical Journal*, vol. 53, no. 4 (2010), pp. 919–37

Curry, John and O'Connor, Charles, An historical and critical review of the civil wars in Ireland, from the reign of Queen Elizabeth, to the settlement under King William. With the state of the Irish Catholics, from that settlement to the relaxation of the popery laws, in the year 1778. Extracted from parliamentary records, state acts, and other authentic materials, Dublin, 1810

Daems, James William. Edmund Spenser's *A View of the Present State of Ireland: Sovereignty, Surveillance, and Colonialism* (Thesis, BA, University-College of the Fraser Valley, 1997), pp.1–78

Darcy, Eamon, *The Irish Rebellion of 1641 and the Wars of the Three Kingdoms* (Royal Historical Society, 2013)

Delamer, Ida, 'Freedom Boxes', *Dublin Historical Record*, vol. 32, no. 1 (1978), pp. 2–14

Dickson, David, *Old World Colony: Cork and South Munster 1630–1830* (Cork University Press, 2005)

Douglas, Ken, *The Downfall of the Spanish Armada in Ireland* (Gill and Mcmillan, 2009)

Edwards, David and Powell, Thomas, 'The Ship's Journal of Captain Thomas Powell, 1642', *Analecta Hibernica*, no. 37 (1998), pp. 251, 253–84

Edwards, Edward, *The Life of Sir Walter Raleigh* (London, 1868)

Elmer, Peter, *The Miraculous Conformist: Valentine Greatrakes, The Body Politic and the Politics of Healing in Restoration Britain* (Oxford, 2013)

Fitzpatrick, Thomas (ed.), 'Waterford during the Civil War 1641–1653: Traits and Stories from T.C.D. Depositions', *Journal of the Waterford and South-East of Ireland Archaeological Society*, vol. XIV (1911)

Flavin, Susan, 'Consumption and material culture in sixteenth-century Ireland', *Economic History Review*, 64, 4 (2011), pp. 1144–1174

Fraser, Antonia, *Cromwell: Our Chief of Men* (Phoenix, 2002)

Gaughan, Jessie A., 'Ireland Blockaded (1644–1657)', *The Irish Monthly*, vol. 45, no. 530 (1917), pp. 502–6

Gentles, Ian, *The English Revolution and the Wars in the Three Kingdoms, 1638–1652* (Longman, 2007)

Gillespie, Raymond, 'The Circulation of Print in Seventeenth-century Ireland', *Studia Hibernica*, no. 29, 1995–1997, pp. 31–58

Gillespie, Raymond, *Sixteenth Century Ireland: Making Modern Ireland* (Gill and Mcmillan, 2006)

Glanvill, Joeseph, *Sadducismus Triumphatus: or, A Full and Plain Evidence Concerning Witches and Apparitions* (Fourth Edition, London, 1701)

Grattan Flood, W.H., 'Fennor and Daborne at Youghal in 1618', *The Modern Language Review*, vol. 20, no. 3 (1925), pp. 321–22

Great Britain Parliament, *Cromwellian Settlement of Ireland, 1641–1650: Four Rare Puritan Tracts Concerning the Affairs of Ireland* (London, 1641)

Greatrakes, Valentine, *A Brief Account of Mr. Valentine Greatrakes and Divers of the Strange Cures by him Lately Performed* (London, 1666)

Hammer, Paul E.J., *Elizabeth's Wars: War, Government and Society in Tudor England, 1544–1604* (Palgrave Macmillan, 2003)

Harris, Tim and Taylor, Stephen (eds), *The Final Crisis of the Stuart Monarchy: The Revolutions of 1688–91 in their British, Atlantic and European Contexts* (Boydell Press, 2013)

Hawkes, J.G. and Francisco-Ortega, J., 'The Potato in Spain during the Late 16th Century', *Economic Botany*, vol. 46, no. 1 (1992), pp. 86–97

Hayman, Samuel, 'The Ecclesiastical Antiquities of Youghal', *Royal Society of Antiquities of Ireland*, vol. 3, no. 2 (1855), pp. 326–36

Hayman, Samuel, 'The Ecclesiastical Antiquities of Youghal. no. III.', *The Journal of the Kilkenny and South-East of Ireland Archaeological Society*, New Series, vol. 1, no. 1, (1856), pp. 14–28

Hayman, Samuel, 'Youghal Money of Necessity', *The Journal of the Royal Historical and Archaeological Association of Ireland*, Fourth Series, vol. 5, no. 37 (1879), pp. 35–37

Hayman, Samuel, *The New Hand-book for Youghal* (Fourth Series, Lindsay, 1858)

Hayman, Samuel, 'The French Settlers in Ireland: no. 4. The Settlement at Youghal, County Cork', *Ulster Journal of Archaeology*, First Series, vol. 2 (1854), pp. 223–29

Heffner, Ray, 'Edmund Spenser's Family', *Huntington Library Quarterly*, vol. 2, no. 1 (1938), pp. 79–84

Hennessey, J.P., *Raleigh in Ireland* (K. Paul, Trench & Co., 1883)

Horsley, Ritta Jo and Horsley Richard A., 'On the Trail of the "Witches": Wise Women, Midwives and the European Witch Hunts', *Women in German Yearbook*, vol. 3 (1987), pp. 1–28

Jeffries, H.A., *Cork: Historical Perspective* (Four Courts Press, 2004)

Jenkins, Raymond, 'Spenser with Lord Grey in Ireland' *PMLA*, vol. 52, no. 2 (1937), pp. 338–353

Jenkins, Raymond, 'Spenser: The Uncertain Years 1584–89', *PMLA* vol. 53, no. 2 (1938), pp. 350–362

Kelly, Maria, *A History of the Black Death in Ireland* (The History Press, 2004)

Kramer Heinrich and Sprenger, James, *The Malleus Maleficarum*, Cosimo, Inc. (2007)

Lawless Lee, Grace, *The Huguenot Settlements in Ireland* (Heritage Books, 2008)

Lenihan, Pádraig, *Confederate Catholics at War 1641–1649* (Cork University Press, 2001)

Lennon, Colm, *Sixteenth Century Ireland: The Incomplete Conquest* (Gill and Macillan, 2005)

Linge, John, 'The Royal Navy and the Irish Civil War', *Irish Historical Studies*, vol. 31, no. 121 (1998), pp. 60–71

Lismore Castle Papers, Collection List no. 129, National Library of Ireland, p. 27

Little, Patrick, 'The Earl of Cork and the Fall of the Earl of Strafford, 1638–41', *The Historical Journal*, vol. 39, no. 3 (1996), pp. 619–35

Little, Patrick, *Lord Broghill and the Cromwellian Union with Ireland and Scotland* (Boydell Press, 2004)

Llewellyn Barstow, Anne, Witchcaraze: A New European History of the Witch Hunts (Pandora, 1994)

Lowe, John, 'Charles I and the Confederation of Kilkenny, 1643–9',

Irish Historical Studies, vol. 14, no. 53 (1964), pp. 1–19

Mac Cuarta, Brian S.J. (ed.), *Reshaping Ireland 1550–1700: Colonization and its Consequences*, Essays Presented to Nicholas Canny (Four Courts Press, 2011)

McCaffery, Wallace T., *Elizabeth I War and Politics 1588–1603* (Princeton University Press, 1992)

McCormack, Anthony M., *The Earldom of Desmond 1463–1583: The Decline and Crisis of a Feudal Lordship* (Four Courts Press, 2005)

McCormack, Anthony M., 'The Social and Economic Consequences of the Desmond Rebellion 1779–83', *Irish Historical Studies*, 34 (2004), pp. 1–15

McCracken, Eileen. 'The Woodlands of Ireland Circa 1600', *Irish Historical Studies*, vol. 11, no. 44 (1959), pp. 271–96

McGurk, John, *The Elizabethan Conquest of Ireland: The 1590s Crisis* (Manchester University Press, 1997)

McNeill, William H., 'The Introduction of the Potato into Ireland', *The Journal of Modern History*, vol. 21, no. 3 (1949), pp. 218–22

Moody, T.W., Martin, F.X. and Byrne, F.J. (eds), *A New History of Ireland, Volume III Early Modern Ireland, 1534–1691* (Oxford, 1993)

Morgan, Hiram, 'Never Any Realm Worse Governed: Queen Elizabeth and Ireland', *Transactions of the Royal Historical Society*, Sixth Series, vol. 14 (2004), pp. 295–308

Morrissey, Thomas, 'Among The Irish Martyrs: Dominic Collins, S.J., in His Times (1566–1602)', *An Irish Quarterly Review*, vol. 81, no. 323 (1992), pp. 313–25

Murphy, Elaine, *Ireland and the War at Sea. 1641–1653* (Royal Historical Society, 2012)

O'Brien, Patricia J., 'The Sweet Potato: Its Origin and Dispersal', *American Anthropologist*, New Series, vol. 74, no. 3 (1972), pp. 342–65

Ó hAnnracháin, Tadhg, 'Vatican Diplomacy and the Mission of Rinuccini to Ireland', *Archivium Hibernicum*, vol. 47 (1993), pp. 78–88

Ohlmeyer, Jane (ed.), *Ireland from Independence to Occupation, 1641–1660* (Cambridge, 1995)

Ohlmeyer, Jane, 'A Failed Revolution? The Irish Confederate War in its European Context', *History Ireland*, vol. 3 (1995), pp. 24–28

O'Rahilly, Alfred, 'The Massacre at Smerwick (1580)', *An Irish Quarterly Review*, vol. 27, no. 108 (1938), pp. 690–92

Orpen, Goddard H. and Charles I., 'An unpublished letter from Charles I to the Marquis of Ormonde', *The English Historical Review*, vol. 36, no. 142 (1921), pp. 229–34

Orpen, Goddard H., *Ireland Under the Normans*, vol. 4 (Oxford and Clarendon Press, 2010)

Ó Siochrú Mícháel, *God's Executioner: Oliver Cromwell and the Conquest of Ireland* (Faber and Faber, 2009)

Palmer, William, *The Problem of Ireland in Tudor Foreign Policy: 1485–1603* (Boydell Press, 1995)

Penn, Granville, *Memorials of the Professional life and Times of Sir William Penn. Vol 1* (London, 1833)

Percavel-Maxwell, M., *The Outbreak of the Irish Rebellion of 1641* (McGill-Queen's University Press, 1994)

Piveronus, Peter, 'Sir Warham St. Leger: 'Organizer-in-Chief of the Munster Plantation Scheme of 1568–69', Evidence from the Hand-Writing Analysis of Selected Documents in the PRO, London, *The Canadian Journal of Irish Studies*, vol. 6, no. 1 (1980), pp. 79–89.

Prendegast, John, *The Cromwellian Settlement of Ireland* (London, 1870)

Ranger, Terence O., 'Richard Boyle and the Making of an Irish Fortune, 1588–1614', *Irish Historical Studies*, vol. 10, no. 39 (1957), pp. 257–97

Rose, Jacqueline, 'John Locke, 'Matters Indifferent', and the Restoration of the Church of England', *The Historical Journal*, vol. 48, no. 3 (2005), pp. 601–21

Seymour, St John D., *The Puritans in Ireland 1647–1661*, vol. XII (Oxford, 1921)

Seymour, St John D., 'The Storming of the Rock of Cashel by Lord Inchiquin in 1647', *The English Historical Review*, vol. 32, no. 127 (1917), pp. 373–80

Shrewsbury, J.F.D., *A History of Bubonic Plague in the British Isles* (Cambridge University Press, 2005)

Sidney, Henry, 'Sidney's Memoir of His Government of Ireland 1583', *Ulster Journal of Archaeology*, First Series, vol. 3 (1855), pp. 33–52, 85–109, 336–357

Spenser, Edmund, *A View of the Present State of Ireland* (Alexander B. Grosart, ed.) (First Edition, London, 1894)

Steneck, Nicholas H., 'Greatrakes the Stroker: The Interpretations of Historians', *The History of Science Society*, vol. 73, no. 2 (1982), pp. 160–77

Tait, Clodagh, 'Colonising Memory: Manipulations of Death, Burial and Commemoration in the Career of Richard Boyle, First Earl of Cork (1566–1643)', *Proceedings of the Royal Irish Academy. Section C: Archaeology, Celtic Studies, History, Linguistics, Literature*, vol. 101C, no. 4 (2001), pp. 107–34

The National Archives of England, 'Irish Material in the Class of Ancient Petitions (SC 8) in the Public Record Office', Reference: SC 8/283/14111, 92.

Titler, Robert and Jones, Norman (eds), *A Companion to Tudor Britain* (Oxford, 2009)

Townshend, Dorothea, *The Life and Letters of the Great Earl of Cork* (California, 1904)

Touchet, James, *The Earl of Castlehaven's Memoirs: or his Review of the Civil Wars in Ireland 1642–1651* (London, 1681), pp. 86–87

Tylenda, S.J. Joeseph, N., *Saints and Feasts of the Liturgical Year* (Georgetown University Press, 2003)

Wheeler, James Scott, *Cromwell in Ireland* (St Martin's Press, 1999)

Williams, Sheila, 'The Pope-Burning Processions of 1679, 1680 and 1681', *Journal of the Warburg and Courtauld Institutes*, vol. 21, no. 0.5 (1958), pp. 104–18

Woodward, Donald, 'The Anglo-Irish Livestock Trade of the Seventeenth Century', *Irish Historical Studies*, vol. 18, no. 72 (1973), pp. 489–523

Index